Teen Health Series

Drug Information For Teens,
Fourth Edition

Drug Information For Teens, Fourth Edition

Health Tips About The Physical And Mental Effects Of Substance Abuse

Including Information About Alcohol, Tobacco, Marijuana, E-Cigarettes, Cocaine, Prescription And Over-The-Counter Drugs, Club Drugs, Hallucinogens, Heroin, Stimulants, Opiates, Steroids, And More

OMNIGRAPHICS
155 W. Congress, Suite 200
Detroit, MI 48226

Bibliographic Note
Because this page cannot legibly accommodate all the copyright notices, the Bibliographic Note portion of the Preface constitutes an extension of the copyright notice.

* * *

Omnigraphics, Inc.
Editorial Services provided by Omnigraphics, Inc.,
a division of Relevant Information, Inc.
Keith Jones, *Managing Editor*

* * *

Library of Congress Cataloging-in-Publication Data

Names: Omnigraphics, Inc., issuing body.

Title: Drug information for teens : health tips about the physical and mental effects of substance abuse : including information about alcohol, tobacco, marijuana, prescription and over-the-counter drugs, club drugs, hallucinogens, stimulants, opiates, steroids, and more.

Description: Fourth edition. | Detroit, MI : Omnigraphics, Inc, [2016] | Series: Teen health reference series | Includes bibliographical references and index.

Identifiers: LCCN 2015038887| ISBN 9780780813588 (hardcover : alk. paper) | ISBN 9780780814028 (ebook)

Subjects: LCSH: Teenagers--Drug use--United States. | Teenagers--Alcohol use--United States. | Teenagers--Health and hygiene--United States. | Drugs--Physiological effect. | Drug abuse--United States--Prevention. | Alcoholism--United States--Prevention.

Classification: LCC HV5824.Y68 D774 2016 | DDC 613.8--dc23

LC record available at http://lccn.loc.gov/2015038887

Table of Contents

Part Three: Tobacco, Nicotine, And E-Cigarettes

Part Four: Marijuana

Part Five: Abuse Of Legally Available Substances

Part Six: Abuse Of Illegal Substances

Part Seven: Other Drug-Related Health Concerns

Part Eight: Treatment For Addiction

Part Nine: If You Need More Information

Preface

About This Book

Recent scientific research shows that teenagers' brains are wired in a way that makes them prone to take risks. Because the part of the brain that is responsible for weighing consequences (the prefrontal cortex) is still developing, teenagers sometimes make choices based on their emotions or whims rather than the possible outcome of a situation. This is one reason why some teens experiment with drugs and alcohol. Many factors can influence this impulsive decision: the desire to look cool or have fun, the desire to fit in with a particular group of people, or the desire to escape life's stressors.

Recent studies show while overall teenage substance use is steadily declining, many teenagers still make the choice to use drugs and alcohol. A recent survey reports that in 2014, 37.4% of 12th graders admitted drinking an alcoholic beverage, and 21.2% of 12th graders reported marijuana use. It also revealed that about 4.8% of teenagers used prescription drugs for non-medical reasons. Frequent drug use by teenagers can often lead to addiction, a chronic condition caused by changes in brain chemistry. This condition can lead to health problems during adulthood, including infectious diseases, organ damage, and cancer.

Drug Information For Teens, Fourth Edition provides updated facts about drug use, abuse, and addiction. It describes the physical and psychological effects of alcohol, tobacco, marijuana, e-cigarettes, cocaine, prescription and over-the-counter (OTC) drugs, club drugs, hallucinogens, heroin, stimulants, opiates, steroids, and many other drugs and chemicals that are commonly abused. It includes information about drug-related health concerns, such as HIV infection, drug-facilitated rape, mental illness, violence, and suicide risks. A section on substance abuse treatment describes care options and provides resources for helping yourself, a family member, or a friend recover from addiction. Resource directories provide contact information for national organizations, hotlines and helplines, and other sources of support.

How To Use This Book

This book is divided into parts and chapters. Parts focus on broad areas of interest; chapters are devoted to single topics within a part.

Part One: General Information About Addiction And Substance Abuse defines substance abuse and addiction, explains why people get addicted and how drugs affect brain chemistry. It provides information on preventing drug abuse, as well as the social and legal aspects of drugs, including peer pressure, statistics on teen drug use, and the Drug Enforcement Administration's Controlled Substances Act which categorizes drugs according to their legal status, medicinal qualities, and harmful effects.

Part Two: Alcohol presents facts about the use and abuse of alcohol, and addiction in teens and their family members. It also discusses alcohol poisoning, statistics on alcohol consumption, and related health concerns.

Part Three: Tobacco, Nicotine, And E-Cigarettes presents facts on several forms of tobacco use, including cigarettes, smokeless tobacco, and secondhand smoke. The latest information on e-cigarettes is also provided. Various health risks associated with smoking are discussed in detail. Information on the benefits of quitting—and how to quit—is also provided.

Part Four: Marijuana includes facts about marijuana, marijuana abuse among teens, and associated health effects of marijuana including mental illness, and changes in brain chemistry. Information about medical marijuana and the related federal and state laws is also included.

Part Five: Abuse Of Legally Available Substances includes facts about the abuse of prescription and over-the-counter medications, including commonly abused pain relievers, depressants, stimulants, and cold and cough medicines. Information about other legally available substances—such as inhalants, steroids and sports supplements, and caffeine—is also included.

Part Six: Abuse Of Illegal Substances offers basic information about some of the most commonly abused illegal substances, including ecstasy, ketamine, and other club drugs; LSD, PCP, and other hallucinogens; methamphetamine, cocaine, and other stimulants; heroin and other opiates.

Part Seven: Other Drug-Related Health Concerns covers some important topics that are associated with drug use but not necessarily related to the direct effects of the substances themselves. These include mental illness and suicide risks associated with drugs, risky sexual behavior, the spread of infectious diseases via drug paraphernalia, violence due to drug abuse, and drugged driving.

Part Eight: Treatment For Addiction discusses how to deal with addiction, the principles of treatment, the various types of treatment, and the process of recovery. It offers encouragement for those teens who need to seek help themselves and provides tips for helping friends and loved ones who may have a substance abuse problem.

Part Nine: If You Need More Information includes a directory of national organizations that provide drug-related information and a directory of places providing support services, including hotline and helpline phone numbers. A state-by-state list of referral services will help readers find local information.

Bibliographic Note

This volume contains documents and excerpts from publications issued by the following government agencies: Centers for Disease Control and Prevention (CDC); Child Welfare Information Gateway; Children's Bureau; Drug Enforcement Administration (DEA); National Institutes of Health (NIH); National Institute on Alcohol Abuse and Alcoholism (NIAAA); National Institute on Drug Abuse (NIDA); Substance Abuse and Mental Health Services Administration (SAMHSA); U.S. Department of Veterans Affairs (VA); and WhiteHouse.gov.

The photograph on the front cover is © Inspirestock International/123RF.com

About The *Teen Health Series*

At the request of librarians serving today's young adults, the *Teen Health Series* was developed as a specially focused set of volumes within Omnigraphics' *Health Reference Series*. Each volume deals comprehensively with a topic selected according to the needs and interests of people in middle school and high school.

Teens seeking preventive guidance, information about disease warning signs, medical statistics, and risk factors for health problems will find answers to their questions in the *Teen Health Series*. The *Series*, however, is not intended to serve as a tool for diagnosing illness, in prescribing treatments, or as a substitute for the physician/patient relationship. All people concerned about medical symptoms or the possibility of disease are encouraged to seek professional care from an appropriate health care provider.

If there is a topic you would like to see addressed in a future volume of the *Teen Health Series*, please write to:

Managing Editor
Teen Health Series
Omnigraphics, Inc.
155 W. Congress, Suite 200
Detroit, MI 48226

A Note About Spelling And Style

Teen Health Series editors use Stedman's Medical Dictionary as an authority for questions related to the spelling of medical terms and the Chicago Manual of Style for questions related to grammatical structures, punctuation, and other editorial concerns. Consistent adherence is not always possible, however, because the individual volumes within the *Series* include many documents from a wide variety of different producers, and the editor's primary goal is to present material from each source as accurately as is possible. This sometimes means that information in different chapters may follow other guidelines and alternate spelling authorities.

Our Advisory Board

We would like to thank the following advisory board members for providing guidance to the development of this Series:

Dr. Lynda Baker, Associate Professor of Library and Information Science, Wayne State University, Detroit, MI

Nancy Bulgarelli, William Beaumont Hospital Library, Royal Oak, MI

Karen Imarisio, Bloomfield Township Public Library, Bloomfield Township, MI

Karen Morgan, Mardigian Library, University of Michigan-Dearborn, Dearborn, MI

Rosemary Orlando, St. Clair Shores Public Library, St. Clair Shores, MI

Part One
General Information About Addiction And Substance Abuse

Chapter 1
The Science Of Addiction

How Science Has Revolutionized The Understanding Of Drug Addiction

For much of the past century, scientists studying drug abuse labored in the shadows of powerful myths and misconceptions about the nature of addiction. When scientists began to study addictive behavior in the 1930s, people addicted to drugs were thought to be morally flawed and lacking in willpower. Those views shaped society's responses to drug abuse, treating it as a moral failing rather than a health problem, which led to an emphasis on punishment rather than prevention and treatment. Today, thanks to science, our views and our responses to addiction and other substance use disorders have changed dramatically. Groundbreaking discoveries about the brain have revolutionized our understanding of compulsive drug use, enabling us to respond effectively to the problem.

As a result of scientific research, we know that addiction is a disease that affects both the brain and behavior. We have identified many of the biological and environmental factors and are beginning to search for the genetic variations that contribute to the development and progression of the disease. Scientists use this knowledge to develop effective prevention and treatment approaches that reduce the toll drug abuse takes on individuals, families, and communities.

What Is Drug Addiction?

Addiction is defined as a chronic, relapsing brain disease that is characterized by compulsive drug seeking and use, despite harmful consequences. It is considered a brain disease because

About This Chapter: Information in this chapter is excerpted from "Drugs, Brains, and Behavior: The Science of Addiction," NIDA for Teens, National Institute on Drug Abuse (NIDA), July 2014.

drugs change the brain—they change its structure and how it works. These brain changes can be long-lasting, and can lead to the harmful behaviors seen in people who abuse drugs.

Addiction is a lot like other diseases, such as heart disease. Both disrupt the normal, healthy functioning of the underlying organ, have serious harmful consequences, and are preventable and treatable, but if left untreated, can last a lifetime.

Why Do People Take Drugs?

In general, people begin taking drugs for a variety of reasons:

- **To feel good.** Most abused drugs produce intense feelings of pleasure. This initial sensation of euphoria is followed by other effects, which differ with the type of drug used. For example, with stimulants such as cocaine, the "high" is followed by feelings of power, self-confidence, and increased energy. In contrast, the euphoria caused by opiates such as heroin is followed by feelings of relaxation and satisfaction.

- **To feel better.** Some people who suffer from social anxiety, stress-related disorders, and depression begin abusing drugs in an attempt to lessen feelings of distress. Stress can play a major role in beginning drug use, continuing drug abuse, or relapse in patients recovering from addiction.

- **To do better.** Some people feel pressure to chemically enhance or improve their cognitive or athletic performance, which can play a role in initial experimentation and continued abuse of drugs such as prescription stimulants or anabolic/androgenic steroids.

- **"Curiosity and "because others are doing it."** In this respect adolescents are particularly vulnerable because of the strong influence of peer pressure. Teens are more likely than adults to engage in risky or daring behaviors to impress their friends and express their independence from parental and social rules.

If Taking Drugs Makes People Feel Good Or Better, What's The Problem?

When they first use a drug, people may perceive what seem to be positive effects; they also may believe that they can control their use. However, drugs can quickly take over a person's life. Over time, if drug use continues, other pleasurable activities become less pleasurable, and taking the drug becomes necessary for the user just to feel "normal." They may then compulsively seek and take drugs even though it causes tremendous problems for themselves and their loved ones. Some people may start to feel the need to take higher or more frequent doses, even in the early stages of their drug use. These are the telltale signs of an addiction.

Even relatively moderate drug use poses dangers. Consider how a social drinker can become intoxicated, get behind the wheel of a car, and quickly turn a pleasurable activity into a tragedy that affects many lives.

Is Continued Drug Abuse A Voluntary Behavior?

The initial decision to take drugs is typically voluntary. However, with continued use, a person's ability to exert self-control can become seriously impaired; this impairment in self-control is the hallmark of addiction. Brain imaging studies of people with addiction show physical changes in areas of the brain that are critical to judgment, decision making, learning and memory, and behavior control. Scientists believe that these changes alter the way the brain works and may help explain the compulsive and destructive behaviors of addiction.

Why Study Drug Abuse And Addiction?

Abuse of and addiction to alcohol, nicotine, and illicit and prescription drugs cost Americans more than $700 billion a year in increased health care costs, crime, and lost productivity. Every year, illicit and prescription drugs and alcohol contribute to the death of more than 90,000 Americans, while tobacco is linked to an estimated 480,000 deaths per year.

People of all ages suffer the harmful consequences of drug abuse and addiction.

- **Babies** exposed to drugs in the womb may be born premature and underweight. This exposure can slow the child's intellectual development and affect behavior later in life.

- **Adolescents** who abuse drugs often act out, do poorly academically, and drop out of school. They are at risk for unplanned pregnancies, violence, and infectious diseases.

- **Adults** who abuse drugs often have problems thinking clearly, remembering, and paying attention. They often develop poor social behaviors as a result of their drug abuse, and their work performance and personal relationships suffer.

- **Parents'** drug abuse often means chaotic, stress-filled homes, as well as child abuse and neglect. Such conditions harm the well-being and development of children in the home and may set the stage for drug abuse in the next generation.

How Does Science Provide Solutions For Drug Abuse And Addiction?

Scientists study the effects that drugs have on the brain and on people's behavior. They use this information to develop programs for preventing drug abuse and for helping people recover from addiction. Further research helps transfer these ideas into practice in our communities.

Chapter 2
Risk Factors For Addiction

Why Do Some People Become Addicted To Drugs, While Others Do Not?

As with any other disease, vulnerability to addiction differs from person to person, and no single factor determines whether a person will become addicted to drugs. In general, the more risk factors a person has, the greater the chance that taking drugs will lead to abuse and addiction. Protective factors, on the other hand, reduce a person's risk of developing addiction. Risk and protective factors may be either environmental (such as conditions at home, at school, and in the neighborhood) or biological (for instance, a person's genes, their stage of development, and even their gender or ethnicity).

Table 2.1. Risk And Protective Factors For Drug Abuse And Addiction

Risk Factors	Protective Factors
Aggressive behavior in childhood	Good self-control
Lack of parental supervision	Parental monitoring and support
Poor social skills	Positive relationships
Drug experimentation	Academic Competence
Availability of drugs at school	School anti-drug policies
Community poverty	Neighborhood pride

About This Chapter: Information in this chapter is excerpted from "Drugs, Brains, and Behavior: The Science of Addiction," National Institute on Drug Abuse (NIDA), July 2014.

What Environmental Factors Increase The Risk Of Addiction?

- **Home And Family.** The influence of the home environment, especially during childhood, is a very important factor. Parents or older family members who abuse alcohol or drugs, or who engage in criminal behavior, can increase children's risks of developing their own drug problems.

- **Peer And School.** Friends and acquaintances can have an increasingly strong influence during adolescence. Drug-using peers can sway even those without risk factors to try drugs for the first time. Academic failure or poor social skills can put a child at further risk for using or becoming addicted to drugs.

What Biological Factors Increase Risk Of Addiction?

Scientists estimate that genetic factors account for between 40 and 60 percent of a person's vulnerability to addiction; this includes the effects of environmental factors on the function and expression of a person's genes. A person's stage of development and other medical conditions they may have are also factors. Adolescents and people with mental disorders are at greater risk of drug abuse and addiction than the general population.

What Other Factors Increase The Risk Of Addiction?

- **Early Use.** Although taking drugs at any age can lead to addiction, research shows that the earlier a person begins to use drugs, the more likely he or she is to develop serious problems. This may reflect the harmful effect that drugs can have on the developing brain; it also may result from a mix of early social and biological vulnerability factors, including unstable family relationships, exposure to physical or sexual abuse, genetic susceptibility, or mental illness. Still, the fact remains that early use is a strong indicator of problems ahead, including addiction.

- **Method Of Administration.** Smoking a drug or injecting it into a vein increases its addictive potential. Both smoked and injected drugs enter the brain within seconds, producing a powerful rush of pleasure. However, this intense "high" can fade within a few minutes, taking the abuser down to lower, more normal levels. Scientists believe this starkly felt contrast drives some people to repeated drug taking in an attempt to recapture the fleeting pleasurable state.

The brain continues to develop into adulthood and undergoes dramatic changes during adolescence.

One of the brain areas still maturing during adolescence is the prefrontal cortex—the part of the brain that enables us to assess situations, make sound decisions, and keep our emotions and desires under control. The fact that this critical part of an adolescent's brain is still a work in progress puts them at increased risk for making poor decisions (such as trying drugs or continuing to take them). Also, introducing drugs during this period of development may cause brain changes that have profound and long-lasting consequences.

Chapter 3
How Drugs Affect The Brain

Your Brain

Your brain is who you are. It's what allows you to think, breathe, move, speak, and feel. It's just 3 pounds of gray-and-white matter that rests in your skull, and it is your own personal "mission control." Information from your environment—both outside (like what your eyes see and skin feels) and inside (like your heart rate and body temperature)—makes its way to the brain, which receives, processes, and integrates it so that you can survive and function under all sorts of changing circumstances and learn from experience. The brain is always working, even when you are sleeping.

The brain is made up of many parts that all work together as a team. Each of these different parts has a specific and important job to do.

When drugs enter the brain, they interfere with its normal processing and can eventually lead to changes in how well it works. Over time, drug use can lead to addiction, a devastating brain disease in which people can't stop using drugs even when they really want to and even after it causes terrible consequences to their health and other parts of their lives.

Drugs affect three primary areas of the brain:

- **The brain stem** is in charge of all the functions our body needs to stay alive—breathing, moving blood, and digesting food. It also links the brain with the spinal cord, which runs down the back and moves muscles and limbs as well as lets the brain know what's happening to the body.

About This Chapter: Information in this chapter is excerpted from "Brain and Addiction," NIDA for Teens, National Institute on Drug Abuse (NIDA), October 23, 2015; and information from "Effects of Drugs of Abuse on the Brain," NIDA for Teens, National Institute on Drug Abuse (NIDA), October 23, 2015.

- **The limbic system** links together a bunch of brain structures that control our emotional responses, such as feeling pleasure when we eat chocolate. The good feelings motivate us to repeat the behavior, which is good because eating is critical to our lives.

- **The cerebral cortex** is the mushroom-shaped outer part of the brain (the gray matter). In humans, it is so big that it makes up about three-fourths of the entire brain. It's divided into four areas, called lobes, which control specific functions. Some areas process information from our senses, allowing us to see, feel, hear, and taste. The front part of the cortex, known as the frontal cortex or forebrain, is the thinking center. It powers our ability to think, plan, solve problems, and make decisions.

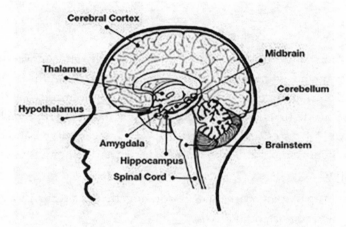

Figure 3.1. Primary Areas Of The Brain

How Does Your Brain Communicate?

The brain is a complex communications network of billions of neurons, or nerve cells. Networks of neurons pass messages back and forth thousands of times a minute within the brain, spinal column, and nerves. These nerve networks control everything we feel, think, and do. Understanding these networks helps in understanding how drugs affect the brain. The networks are made up of:

- **Neurons**

  Your brain contains about 100 billion neurons—nerve cells that work nonstop to send and receive messages. Within a neuron, messages travel from the cell body down the axon to the axon terminal in the form of electrical impulses. From there, the message is sent to other neurons with the help of neurotransmitters.

- **Neurotransmitters—The Brain's Chemical Messengers**

  To make messages jump from one neuron to another, the neuron creates chemical messengers, called neurotransmitters. The axon terminal releases neurotransmitters that travel across the space (called the synapse) to nearby neurons. Then the transmitter attaches to receptors on the nearby neuron.

- **Receptors—The Brain's Chemical Receivers**

  As the neurotransmitter approaches the nearby neuron, it attaches to a special site on that neuron called a receptor. A neurotransmitter and its receptor operate like a key and lock, in that a very specific mechanism makes sure that each receptor will forward the right message only after interacting with the right kind of neurotransmitter.

- **Transporters—The Brain's Chemical Recyclers**

  Once neurotransmitters do their job, they are pulled back into their original neuron by transporters. This recycling process shuts off the signal between the neurons.

How Do Drugs Affect Your Brain?

Drugs are chemicals. When someone puts these chemicals into their body, either by smoking, injecting, inhaling, or eating them, they tap into the brain's communication system and tamper with the way nerve cells normally send, receive, and process information. Different drugs—because of their chemical structures—work differently. We know there are at least two ways drugs work in the brain:

- Imitating the brain's natural chemical messengers
- Overstimulating the "reward circuit" of the brain

Some drugs, like marijuana and heroin, have chemical structures that mimic that of a neurotransmitter that naturally occurs in our bodies. In fact, these drugs can "fool" our receptors, lock onto them, and activate the nerve cells. However, they don't work the same way as a natural neurotransmitter, and the neurons wind up sending abnormal messages through the brain, which can cause problems both for our brains as well as our bodies.

Other drugs, such as cocaine and methamphetamine, cause nerve cells to release too much dopamine, which is a natural neurotransmitter, or prevent the normal recycling of dopamine. This leads to exaggerated messages in the brain, causing problems with communication channels. It's like the difference between someone whispering in your ear versus someone shouting in a microphone.

13

The "High" From Drugs/Pleasure Effect

Most drugs of abuse—nicotine, cocaine, marijuana, and others—affect the brain's "reward" circuit, which is part of the limbic system. Normally, the reward circuit responds to feelings of pleasure by releasing the neurotransmitter dopamine. Dopamine creates feelings of pleasure. Drugs take control of this system, causing large amounts of dopamine to flood the system. This flood of dopamine is what causes the "high" or intense excitement and happiness (sometimes called euphoria) linked with drug use.

The Repeat Effect

Our brains are wired to make sure we will repeat healthy activities, like eating, by connecting those activities with feeling good. Whenever this reward circuit is kick-started, the brain notes that something important is happening that needs to be remembered, and teaches us to do it again and again, without thinking about it. Because drugs of abuse come in and "hijack" the same circuit, people learn to use drugs in the same way.

After repeated drug use, the brain starts to adjust to the surges of dopamine. Neurons may begin to reduce the number of dopamine receptors or simply make less dopamine. The result is less dopamine signaling in the brain—like turning down the volume on the dopamine signal. Because some drugs are toxic, some neurons also may die.

As a result, the ability to feel any pleasure is reduced. The person feels flat, lifeless, and depressed, and is unable to enjoy things that once brought pleasure. Now the person needs drugs just to bring dopamine levels up to normal, and more of the drug is needed to create a dopamine flood, or "high"—an effect known as "tolerance."

Long-Term Effects

Drug use can eventually lead to dramatic changes in neurons and brain circuits. These changes can still be present even after the person has stopped taking drugs. This is more likely to happen when a drug is taken over and over.

The Pleasure Center

Pleasure, which scientists call reward, is a very powerful biological force for our survival. If you do something pleasurable, the brain is wired in such a way that you tend to do it again. Life sustaining activities, such as eating, activate a circuit of specialized nerve cells devoted to producing and regulating pleasure. One important set of these nerve cells, which uses a chemical neurotransmitter called dopamine, sits at the very top of the brainstem in the ventral

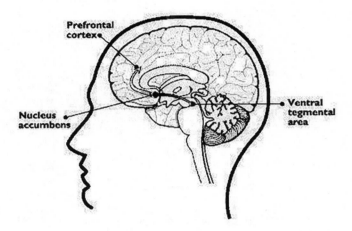

Figure 3.2. Involved In The Pleasure Circuit

tegmental area (VTA) (Figure 3.2). These dopamine-containing neurons relay messages about pleasure through their nerve fibers to nerve cells in a limbic system structure called the nucleus accumbens. Still other fibers reach to a related part of the frontal region of the cerebral cortex. So, the pleasure circuit, which is known as the mesolimbic dopamine system, spans the survival- oriented brainstem, the emotional limbic system, and the frontal cerebral cortex.

All drugs that are addicting can activate the brain's pleasure circuit. Drug addiction is a biological, pathological process that alters the way in which the pleasure center, as well as other parts of the brain, functions. To understand this process, it is necessary to examine the effects of drugs on neurotransmission. Almost all drugs that change the way the brain works do so by affecting chemical neurotransmission. Some drugs, like heroin and LSD, mimic the effects of a natural neurotransmitter. Others, like PCP, block receptors and thereby prevent neuronal messages from getting through. Still others, like cocaine, interfere with the molecules that are responsible for transporting neurotransmitters back into the neurons that released them (Figure 3.3). Finally, some drugs such as Methamphetamine, act by causing neurotransmitters to be released in greater amounts than normal.

Prolonged drug use changes the brain in fundamental and long-lasting ways. These long-lasting changes are a major component of the addiction itself. It is as though there is a figurative "switch" in the brain that "flips" at some point during an individual's drug use. The point at which this "flip" occurs varies from individual to individual, but the effect of this change is the transformation of a drug abuser to a drug addict.

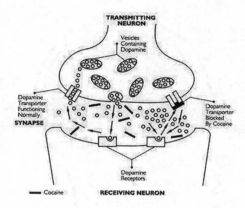

Figure 3.3. When cocaine enters the brain, it blocks the dopamine transporter from pumping dopamine back into the transmitting neuron, flooding the synapse with dopamine. This intensifies and prolongs the stimulation of receiving neurons in the brain's pleasure circuits, causing a cocaine "high."

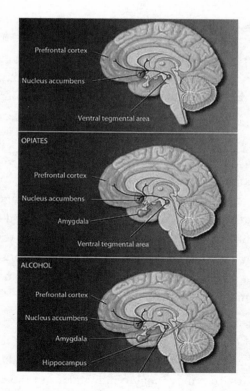

Figure 3.4. Drugs Change Critical Parts

Chapter 4
Preventing Drug Abuse

Preventing Drug Abuse: The Best Strategy

Why is adolescence a critical time for preventing drug addiction?

As noted previously, early use of drugs increases a person's chances of developing addiction. Remember, drugs change brains—and this can lead to addiction and other serious problems. So, preventing early use of drugs or alcohol may go a long way in reducing these risks. If we can prevent young people from experimenting with drugs, we can prevent drug addiction.

Risk of drug abuse increases greatly during times of transition. For an adult, a divorce or loss of a job may lead to drug abuse; for a teenager, risky times include moving or changing schools. In early adolescence, when children advance from elementary through middle school, they face new and challenging social and academic situations. Often during this period, children are exposed to abusable substances such as cigarettes and alcohol for the first time. When they enter high school, teens may encounter greater availability of drugs, drug use by older teens, and social activities where drugs are used.

At the same time, many behaviors that are a normal aspect of their development, such as the desire to try new things or take greater risks, may increase teen tendencies to experiment with drugs. Some teens may give in to the urging of drug-using friends to share the experience with them. Others may think that taking drugs (such as steroids) will improve their appearance or their athletic performance or that abusing substances such as alcohol or MDMA (ecstasy or "Molly") will ease their anxiety in social situations. A growing number of teens are abusing prescription ADHD stimulants such as Adderall® to help them study or lose weight.

About This Chapter: Information in this chapter is excerpted from "Drugs, Brains, and Behavior: The Science of Addiction," NIDA for Teens, National Institute on Drug Abuse (NIDA), July 2014.

Teens' still-developing judgment and decision-making skills may limit their ability to accurately assess the risks of all of these forms of drug use.

Using abusable substances at this age can disrupt brain function in areas critical to motivation, memory, learning, judgment, and behavior control. So, it is not surprising that teens who use alcohol and other drugs often have family and social problems, poor academic performance, health-related problems (including mental health), and involvement with the juvenile justice system.

Can research-based programs prevent drug addiction in youth?

Yes. The term "research-based" means that these programs have been rationally designed based on current scientific evidence, rigorously tested, and shown to produce positive results. Scientists have developed a broad range of programs that positively alter the balance between risk and protective factors for drug abuse in families, schools, and communities. Studies have shown that research-based programs, such as those described in NIDA's *Preventing Drug Use among Children and Adolescents: A Research-Based Guide for Parents, Educators, and Community Leaders,* can significantly reduce early use of tobacco, alcohol, and illicit drugs.

How do research-based prevention programs work?

These prevention programs work to boost protective factors and eliminate or reduce risk factors for drug use. The programs are designed for various ages and can be designed for individual or group settings, such as the school and home. There are three types of programs:

1. **Universal programs** address risk and protective factors common to all children in a given setting, such as a school or community.

2. **Selective programs** target groups of children and teens who have factors that put them at increased risk of drug use.

3. **Indicated programs** are designed for youth who have already begun using drugs.

Are all prevention programs effective in reducing drug abuse?

When research-based substance use prevention programs are properly implemented by schools and communities, use of alcohol, tobacco, and illegal drugs is reduced. Such programs help teachers, parents, and health care professionals shape youths' perceptions about the risks of substance use. While many social and cultural factors affect drug use trends, when young people perceive drug use as harmful, they reduce their level of use.

Chapter 5

Peer Pressure: Its Influence On Teens And Decision Making

Risk Versus Reward

New research shows that, when making a decision, teens think about both the risks and rewards of their actions and behaviors—but, unlike adults, teens are more likely to ignore the risk in favor of the reward.

In a NIDA-funded study, teens driving with their friends in the car were more likely to take risks—like speeding through yellow lights—if they knew that two or more of their friends were watching. Teens were also significantly more likely to act this way than adults in the same experiment.

Researchers monitored the brain activity of all the teen drivers in the study. Results showed that just knowing friends were watching activated brain regions linked with reward, especially when the teen drivers made risky decisions.

So, be aware: The desire to impress your friends may override your fear of taking risks. This could also apply to deciding whether to try drugs or alcohol—your decision might be influenced by who is around and if you think they'd be impressed.

Tell us: When you already know the risks, yet you want to impress your friends, do you run the light or slow down and stop? Do you accept a drink or turn it down? Do you go with

About This Chapter: Information in this chapter is excerpted from "Why Does Peer Pressure Influence Teens To Try Drugs?" NIDA for Teens, National Institute on Drug Abuse (NIDA), May 8, 2012; information from "6 Tactful Tips for Resisting Peer Pressure To Use Drugs and Alcohol," NIDA for Teens, National Institute on Drug Abuse (NIDA), March 9, 2015; and information from "Alcohol: The Friend Factor," NIDA for Teens, National Institute on Drug Abuse (NIDA), June 18, 2014.

the crowd or be your own person and impress others with your individuality? What are some ways you could put the brakes on long enough to think twice before making a decision to do something you know is risky?

Tactful Tips for Resisting Peer Pressure To Use Drugs and Alcohol

Even when you are confident in your decision not to use drugs or alcohol, it can be hard when it's your friend who is offering.

A lot of times, a simple "no thanks" may be enough. But sometimes it's not. It can get intense, especially if the people who want you to join in on a bad idea feel judged. If you're all being "stupid" together, then they feel less self-conscious and don't need to take all the responsibility.

But knowing they are just trying to save face doesn't end the pressure, so here are a few tips that may come in handy.

- Offer to be the designated driver. Get your friends home safely, and everyone will be glad you didn't drink or take drugs.If you're on a sports team, you can say you are staying healthy to maximize your athletic performance—besides, no one would argue that a hangover would help you play your best.
- "I have to [study for a big test / go to a concert / visit my grandmother / babysit / march in a parade, etc.]. I can't do that after a night of drinking/drugs."
- Keep a bottled drink like a soda or iced tea with you to drink at parties. People will be less likely to pressure you to drink alcohol if you're already drinking something. If they still offer you something, just say "I'm covered."
- Find something to do so that you look busy. Get up and dance. Offer to DJ.
- When all else fails…blame your parents. They won't mind! Explain that your parents are really strict, or that they will check up on you when you get home.
- If your friends aren't having it—then it's a good time to find the door. Nobody wants to leave the party or their friends, but if your friends won't let you party without drugs, then it's not going to be fun for you.

Sometimes these situations totally surprise us. But sometimes we know that the party we are going to has alcohol or that people plan to do drugs at a concert. These are the times when asking yourself what you could do differently is key to not having to go through this weekend after weekend.

Alcohol: The Friend Factor

Friends can influence your opinion about music, fashion—and alcohol.

Have you ever said "It's not me, it's my friends?" Turns out, this reasoning may not fly since what your friends do can have a big impact on you. Research studies show that teens whose best friends drink alcohol are twice as likely to try alcohol themselves. And, if teens get alcohol from friends, they're more likely to start drinking at a younger age.

It's a big deal. We know that a person who drinks alcohol early is more likely to abuse alcohol when he or she gets older.

So, if your friends drink and you don't want to, what are you supposed to do? Get a whole new set of friends? It depends. You may find that some people believe drinking alcohol is the only way to have fun. But lots of people find other ways to enjoy themselves. If you're not ready to give up on your friends just yet, take some time to learn a few key strategies for dealing with peer pressure.

- **It's brave to stand up for yourself.** Be that guy or girl who doesn't drink. It might be hard at first, but eventually people will respect you for sticking to your beliefs. You might even start to influence some of your friends to stay away from alcohol too.

- **Not everyone is doing it.** In fact, according to NIDA's *2013 Monitoring the Future* survey, nearly 75% of 10th graders reported NOT using alcohol in the past month.

- **It's okay to make up an excuse.** If someone is really hounding you, dodge the issue—you could say that you took medicine that will make you sick if you drink.

If you've said no and your friends still don't respect your choices, you have to ask yourself—are they really that good a friend?

Chapter 6
Drug Use Among U.S. Teens

The following are facts and statistics on substance use in the United States in 2013, the most recent year for National Survey on Drug Use and Health (NSDUH) survey results.

Illicit Drug Use

Illicit drug use in the United States has been increasing. In 2013, an estimated 24.6 million Americans aged 12 or older—9.4 percent of the population—had used an illicit drug in the past month. This number is up from 8.3 percent in 2002. The increase mostly reflects a recent rise in use of marijuana, the most commonly used illicit drug.

Marijuana use has increased since 2007. In 2013, there were 19.8 million current users—about 7.5 percent of people aged 12 or older—up from 14.5 million (5.8 percent) in 2007.

Use of most drugs other than marijuana has stabilized over the past decade or has declined. In 2013, 6.5 million Americans aged 12 or older (or 2.5 percent) had used prescription drugs nonmedically in the past month. Prescription drugs include pain relievers, tranquilizers, stimulants, and sedatives. And 1.3 million Americans (0.5 percent) had used hallucinogens (a category that includes ecstasy and LSD) in the past month.

Cocaine use has gone down in the last few years. In 2013, the number of current users aged 12 or older was 1.5 million. This number is lower than in 2002 to 2007 (ranging from 2.0 million to 2.4 million).

Methamphetamine use was higher in 2013, with 595,000 current users, compared with 353,000 users in 2010.

About This Chapter: Information in this chapter is excerpted from "DrugFacts: Nationwide Trends," NIDA for Teens, National Institute on Drug Abuse (NIDA), June 2015.

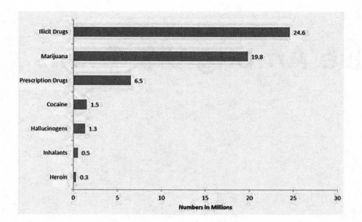

Figure 6.1. Illicit Drug Use (2013)

Most people use drugs for the first time when they are teenagers. There were just over 2.8 million new users of illicit drugs in 2013, or about 7,800 new users per day. Over half (54.1 percent) were under 18 years of age.

More than half of new illicit drug users begin with marijuana. Next most common are prescription pain relievers, followed by inhalants (which is most common among younger teens).

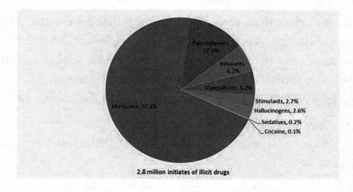

Figure 6.2. Intiation of Illicit Drug Use (2013)

Drug use is highest among people in their late teens and twenties. In 2013, 22.6 percent of 18- to 20-year-olds reported using an illicit drug in the past month.

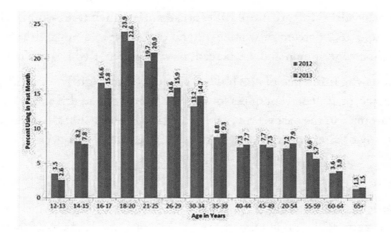

Figure 6.3. Illicit Drug Use By Age (2012 And 2013)

Drug use is increasing among people in their fifties and early sixties. This increase is, in part, due to the aging of the baby boomers, whose rates of illicit drug use have historically been higher than those of previous generations.

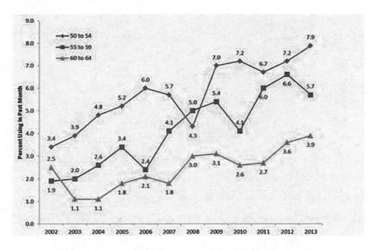

Figure 6.4. Illicit Drug Use Among Adults Aged 50 To 64

Alcohol

Drinking by underage persons (ages 12 to 20) has declined. Current alcohol use by this age group declined from 28.8 to 22.7 percent between 2002 and 2013, while binge drinking declined from 19.3 to 14.2 percent and the rate of heavy drinking went from 6.2 to 3.7 percent.

Binge and heavy drinking are more widespread among men than women. In 2013, 30.2 percent of men and 16.0 percent of women 12 and older reported binge drinking in the past month. And 9.5 percent of men and 3.3 percent of women reported heavy alcohol use.

Driving under the influence of alcohol has also declined slightly. In 2013, an estimated 28.7 million people, or 10.9 percent of persons aged 12 or older, had driven under the influence of alcohol at least once in the past year, down from 14.2 percent in 2002. Although this decline is encouraging, any driving under the influence remains a cause for concern.

Tobacco

Fewer Americans are smoking. In 2013, an estimated 55.8 million Americans aged 12 or older, or 21.3 percent of the population, were current cigarette smokers. This reflects a continual but slow downward trend from 2002, when the rate was 26 percent.

Teen smoking is declining more rapidly. The rate of past-month cigarette use among 12- to 17-year-olds went from 13 percent in 2002 to 5.6 percent in 2013.

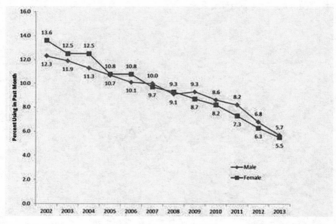

Figure 6.5. Cigarette Use Among Youths Aged 12 To 17 By Gender

Substance Dependence/Abuse And Treatment

Rates of alcohol dependence/abuse declined from 2002 to 2013. In 2013, 17.3 million Americans (6.6 percent of the population) were dependent on alcohol or had problems related to their alcohol use (abuse). This is a decline from 18.1 million (or 7.7 percent) in 2002.

After alcohol, marijuana has the highest rate of dependence or abuse among all drugs. In 2013, 4.2 million Americans met clinical criteria for dependence or abuse of marijuana in the past year—more than twice the number for dependence/abuse of prescription pain relievers (1.9 million) and nearly five times the number for dependence/abuse of cocaine (855,000).

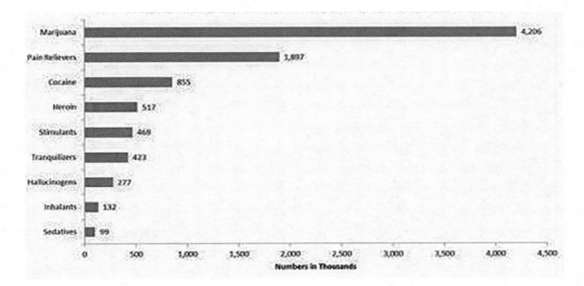

Figure 6.6. Specific Illicit Drug Dependence Or Abuse (2013)

There continues to be a large "treatment gap" in this country. In 2013, an estimated 22.7 million Americans (8.6 percent) needed treatment for a problem related to drugs or alcohol, but only about 2.5 million people (0.9 percent) received treatment at a specialty facility.

Chapter 7

The Controlled Substances Act

Controlling Drugs Or Other Substances Through Formal Scheduling

The Controlled Substances Act (CSA) places all substances which were in some manner regulated under existing federal law into one of five schedules. This placement is based upon the substance's medical use, potential for abuse, and safety or dependence liability. The Act also provides a mechanism for substances to be controlled (added to or transferred between schedules) or decontrolled (removed from control). The procedure for these actions is found in Section 201 of the Act.

Proceedings to add, delete, or change the schedule of a drug or other substance may be initiated by the Drug Enforcement Administration (DEA), the Department of Health and Human Services (HHS), or by petition from any interested party, including:

- The manufacturer of a drug

- A medical society or association

- A pharmacy association

- A public interest group concerned with drug abuse

- A state or local government agency

- An individual citizen

About This Chapter: Information in this chapter is excerpted from "Drugs of Abuse," Drug Enforcement Administration (DEA), 2015.

When a petition is received by the DEA, the agency begins its own investigation of the drug. The DEA also may begin an investigation of a drug at any time based upon information received from law enforcement laboratories, state and local law enforcement and regulatory agencies, or other sources of information.

Once the DEA has collected the necessary data, the DEA Administrator, by authority of the Attorney General, requests from HHS a scientific and medical evaluation and recommendation as to whether the drug or other substance should be controlled or removed from control. This request is sent to the Assistant Secretary for Health of HHS.

The Assistant Secretary, by authority of the Secretary, compiles the information and transmits back to the DEA: a medical and scientific evaluation regarding the drug or other substance, a recommendation as to whether the drug should be controlled, and in what schedule it should be placed.

The medical and scientific evaluations are binding on the DEA with respect to scientific and medical matters and form a part of the scheduling decision.

Once the DEA has received the scientific and medical evaluation from HHS, the Administrator will evaluate all available data and make a final decision whether to propose that a drug. or other substance should be removed or controlled and into which schedule it should be placed.

If a drug does not have a potential for abuse, it cannot be controlled. Although the term "potential for abuse" is not defined in the CSA, there is much discussion of the term in the legislative history of the Act. The following items are indicators that a drug or other substance has a potential for abuse:

1. There is evidence that individuals are taking the drug or other substance in amounts sufficient to create a hazard to their health or to the safety of other individuals or to the community.

2. There is significant diversion of the drug or other substance from legitimate drug channels.

3. Individuals are taking the drug or other substance on their own initiative rather than on the basis of medical advice from a practitioner.

4. The drug is a new drug so related in its action to a drug or other substance already listed as having a potential for abuse to make it likely that the drug will have the same potential for abuse as such drugs, thus making it reasonable to assume that there may be significant diversions from legitimate channels, significant use contrary to or without

medical advice, or that it has a substantial capability of creating hazards to the health of the user or to the safety of the community. Of course, evidence of actual abuse of a substance is indicative that a drug has a potential for abuse.

In determining into which schedule a drug or other substance should be placed, or whether a substance should be decontrolled or rescheduled, certain factors are required to be considered.

These factors are listed in Section 201 (c), of the CSA as follows:

1. **The drug's actual or relative potential for abuse.**

2. **Scientific evidence of the drug's pharmacological effect, if known.**

   The state of knowledge with respect to the effects of a specific drug is, of course, a major consideration. For example, it is vital to know whether or not a drug has a hallucinogenic effect if it is to be controlled due to that effect. The best available knowledge of the pharmacological properties of a drug should be considered.

3. **The state of current scientific knowledge regarding the substance.**

   Criteria (2) and (3) are closely related. However, (2) is primarily concerned with pharmacological effects and (3) deals with all scientific knowledge with respect to the substance.

4. **Its history and current pattern of abuse.** To determine whether or not a drug should be controlled, it is important to know the pattern of abuse of that substance.

5. **The scope, duration, and significance of abuse.** In evaluating existing abuse, the DEA Administrator must know not only the pattern of abuse, but whether the abuse is widespread.

6. **What, if any, risk there is to the public health.** If a drug creates dangers to the public health, in addition to or because of its abuse potential, then these dangers must also be considered by the Administrator.

7. **The drug's psychic or physiological dependence liability.** There must be an assessment of the extent to which a drug is physically addictive or psychologically habit forming.

8. **Whether the substance is an immediate precursor of a substance already controlled.**

   The CSA allows inclusion of immediate precursors on this basis alone into the appropriate schedule and thus safeguards against possibilities of clandestine manufacture. After considering the above listed factors, the Administrator must make specific findings concerning the drug or other substance. This will determine into which schedule the drug or other substance will be placed. These schedules are established by the CSA. They are as follows:

Schedule I

- The drug or other substance has a high potential for abuse.

- The drug or other substance has no currently accepted medical use in treatment in the United States.

- There is a lack of accepted safety for use of the drug or other substance under medical supervision.

- Examples of Schedule I substances include heroin, gamma hydroxybutyric acid (GHB), lysergic acid diethylamide (LSD), marijuana, and methaqualone.

Schedule II

- The drug or other substance has a high potential for abuse.

- The drug or other substance has a currently accepted medical use in treatment in the United States or a currently accepted medical use with severe restrictions.

- Abuse of the drug or other substance may lead to severe psychological or physical dependence.

- Examples of Schedule II substances include morphine, phencyclidine (PCP), cocaine, methadone, hydrocodone, fentanyl, and methamphetamine.

Schedule III

- The drug or other substance has less potential for abuse than the drugs or other substances in Schedules I and II.

- The drug or other substance has a currently accepted medical use in treatment in the United States.

- Abuse of the drug or other substance may lead to moderate or low physical dependence or high psychological dependence.

- Anabolic steroids, codeine and hydrocodone products with aspirin or Tylenol®, and some barbiturates are examples of Schedule III substances.

Schedule IV

- The drug or other substance has a low potential for abuse relative to the drugs or other substances in Schedule III.

- The drug or other substance has a currently accepted medical use in treatment in the United States.

- Abuse of the drug or other substance may lead to limited physical dependence or psychological dependence relative to the drugs or other substances in Schedule III.

- Examples of drugs included in Schedule IV are alprazolam, clonazepam, and diazepam.

Schedule V

- The drug or other substance has a low potential for abuse relative to the drugs or other substances in Schedule IV.

- The drug or other substance has a currently accepted medical use in treatment in the United States.

- Abuse of the drug or other substances may lead to limited physical dependence or psychological dependence relative to the drugs or other substances in Schedule IV.

- Cough medicines with codeine are examples of Schedule V drugs.

When the DEA Administrator has determined that a drug or other substance should be controlled, decontrolled, or rescheduled, a proposal to take action is published in the Federal Register. The proposal invites all interested persons to file comments with the DEA and may also request a hearing with the DEA. If no hearing is requested, the DEA will evaluate all comments received and publish a final order in the Federal Register, controlling the drug as proposed or with modifications based upon the written comments filed. This order will set the effective dates for imposing the various requirements of the CSA.

If a hearing is requested, the DEA will enter into discussions with the party or parties requesting a hearing in an attempt to narrow the issue for litigation. If necessary, a hearing will then be held before an Administrative Law Judge. The judge will take evidence on factual issues and hear arguments on legal questions regarding the control of the drug. Depending on the scope and complexity of the issues, the hearing may be brief or quite extensive. The Administrative Law Judge, at the close of the hearing, prepares findings of fact and conclusions of law and a recommended decision that is submitted to the DEA Administrator. The DEA Administrator will review these documents, as well as the underlying material, and prepare his/her own findings of fact and conclusions of law (which may or may not be the same as those drafted by the Administrative Law Judge). The DEA Administrator then publishes a final order in the Federal Register either scheduling the drug or other substance or declining to do so.

Once the final order is published in the Federal Register, interested parties have 30 days to appeal to a U.S. Court of Appeals to challenge the order. Findings of fact by the Administrator are deemed conclusive if supported by "substantial evidence." The order imposing controls is not stayed during the appeal, however, unless so ordered by the Court

Emergency Or Temporary Scheduling

The CSA was amended by the Comprehensive Crime Control Act of 1984. This Act included a provision which allows the DEA Administrator to place a substance, on a temporary basis, into Schedule I, when necessary, to avoid an imminent hazard to the public safety.

This emergency scheduling authority permits the scheduling of a substance which is not currently controlled, is being abused, and is a risk to the public health while the formal rule-making procedures described in the CSA are being conducted. This emergency scheduling applies only to substances with no accepted medical use.

A temporary scheduling order may be issued for one year with a possible extension of up to six months if formal scheduling procedures have been initiated. The notice of intent and order are published in the Federal Register, as are the proposals and orders for formal scheduling.

Controlled Substance Analogues

A new class of substances was created by the Anti-Drug Abuse Act of 1986. Controlled substance analogues are substances that are not controlled substances, but may be found in illicit trafficking. They are structurally or pharmacologically similar to Schedule I or II controlled substances and have no legitimate medical use. A substance that meets the definition of a controlled substance analogue and is intended for human consumption is treated under the CSA as if it were a controlled substance in Schedule I.

International Treaty Obligations

U.S. treaty obligations may require that a drug or other substance be controlled under the CSA, or rescheduled if existing controls are less stringent than those required by a treaty. The procedures for these scheduling actions are found in Section 201.

The United States is a party to the Single Convention on Narcotic Drugs of 1961, which was designed to establish effective control over international and domestic traffic in narcotics, coca leaf, cocaine, and cannabis. A second treaty, the Convention on Psychotropic Substances of 1971, which entered into force in 1976 and was ratified by Congress in 1980, is designed to establish comparable control over stimulants, depressants, and hallucinogens.

Part Two
Alcohol

Chapter 8
Alcoholism And Alcohol Abuse

What Is Alcohol?

Ethyl alcohol, or ethanol, is an intoxicating ingredient found in beer, wine, and liquor. Alcohol is produced by the fermentation of yeast, sugars, and starches.

Why Do Some People React Differently To Alcohol Than Others?

Individual reactions to alcohol vary, and are influenced by many factors; such as:

- Age
- Gender
- Race or ethnicity
- Physical condition (weight, fitness level, etc.)
- Amount of food consumed before drinking
- How quickly the alcohol was consumed
- Use of drugs or prescription medicines
- Family history of alcohol problems

What Does It Mean To Be Above The Legal Limit For Drinking?

The legal limit for drinking is the alcohol level above which an individual is subject to legal penalties (e.g., arrest or loss of a driver's license).

About This Chapter: Information in this chapter is excerpted from "Frequently Asked Questions," Centers for Disease Control and Prevention (CDC), November 7, 2014; and information from "Facts About Alcohol," Substance Abuse and Mental Health Services Administration (SAMHSA), November 19, 2014.

- Legal limits are measured using either a blood alcohol test or a breathalyzer.

- Legal limits are typically defined by state law, and may vary based on individual characteristics, such as age and occupation.

All states in the United States have adopted 0.08% (80 mg/dL) as the legal limit for operating a motor vehicle for drivers aged 21 years or older. However, drivers younger than 21 are not allowed to operate a motor vehicle with any level of alcohol in their system.

> Legal limits do not define a level below which it is safe to operate a vehicle or engage in some other activity. Impairment due to alcohol use begins to occur at levels well below the legal limit.

How Do I Know If It's Okay To Drink?

The current *Dietary Guidelines for Americans* recommend that if you choose to drink alcoholic beverages, do not exceed 1 drink per day for women or 2 drinks per day for men. According to the guidelines, people who **should not** drink alcoholic beverages at all include the following:

- Children and adolescents.

- Individuals of any age who cannot limit their drinking to low level.

- Women who may become pregnant or who are pregnant.

- Individuals who plan to drive, operate machinery, or take part in other activities that require attention, skill, or coordination.

- Individuals taking prescription or over-the-counter medications that can interact with alcohol.

- Individuals with certain medical conditions.

- Persons recovering from alcoholism.

According to the Dietary Guidelines for Americans, it is not recommended that anyone begin drinking or drink more frequently on the basis of potential health benefits because moderate alcohol intake also is associated with increased risk of breast cancer, violence, drowning, and injuries from falls and motor vehicle crashes.

What Is The Difference Between Alcoholism And Alcohol Abuse?

Alcohol abuse is a pattern of drinking that results in harm to one's health, interpersonal relationships, or ability to work.

Manifestations of alcohol abuse include the following:

- Failure to fulfill major responsibilities at work, school or home.

- Drinking in dangerous situations, such as drinking while driving or operating machinery.

- Legal problems related to alcohol, such as being arrested for drinking while driving or for physically hurting someone while drunk.

- Continued drinking despite ongoing relationship problems that are caused or worsened by drinking.

- Long-term alcohol abuse can turn into alcohol dependence.

Dependency on alcohol, also known as alcohol addiction and alcoholism, is a chronic disease. The signs and symptoms of alcohol dependence include—

- A strong craving for alcohol.

- Continued use despite repeated physical, psychological or interpersonal problems.

- The inability to limit drinking.

What Does It Mean To Get Drunk?

"Getting drunk" or intoxicated is the result of consuming excessive amounts of alcohol. Binge drinking typically results in acute intoxication.

Alcohol intoxication can be harmful for a variety of reasons, including—

- Impaired brain function resulting in poor judgment, reduced reaction time, loss of balance and motor skills, or slurred speech.

- Dilation of blood vessels causing a feeling of warmth but resulting in rapid loss of body heat.

- Increased risk of certain cancers, stroke, and liver diseases (e.g., cirrhosis), particularly when excessive amounts of alcohol are consumed over extended periods of time.

- Damage to a developing fetus if consumed by pregnant women.

- Increased risk of motor-vehicle traffic crashes, violence, and other injuries.

Coma and death can occur if alcohol is consumed rapidly and in large amounts.

How Do I Know If I Have A Drinking Problem?

Drinking is a problem if it causes trouble in your relationships, in school, in social activities, or in how you think and feel. If you are concerned that either you or someone in your family might have a drinking problem, consult your personal health care provider.

I'm Young. Is Drinking Bad For My Health?

Yes. Studies have shown that alcohol use by youth and young adults increases the risk of both fatal and nonfatal injuries. Research has also shown that youth who use alcohol before age 15 are five times more likely to become alcohol dependent than adults who begin drinking at age 21. Other consequences of youth alcohol use include increased risky sexual behaviors, poor school performance, and increased risk of suicide and homicide.

Is It Okay To Drink When Pregnant?

No. There is no safe level of alcohol use during pregnancy. Women who are pregnant or plan on becoming pregnant should refrain from drinking alcohol. Several conditions, including Fetal Alcohol Spectrum Disorders have been linked to alcohol use during pregnancy. Women of child bearing age should also avoid Binge drinking to reduce the risk of unintended pregnancy and potential exposure of a developing fetus to alcohol.

What Is Underage Drinking?

Underage drinking occurs when anyone under age 21 drinks alcohol in any amount or form.

Underage drinking is not smart because:

• It's dangerous; and

• It's against the law, except in special cases, such as when it is part of a religious ceremony.

In 1984, the federal government enacted the National Minimum Drinking Age Act, which calls for reduced federal transportation funds—the money that states use to build and repair their highways—to those states that did not raise the minimum legal drinking age to 21. At present, drinking by anyone under age 21 is against the law in every state, the District of Columbia, and Guam (a U.S. territory).

Why Is Underage Drinking Dangerous?

Underage drinking is a major cause of death from injuries among young people. Each year, approximately 4,700 people under age 21 die as a result of underage drinking. Causes include alcohol poisoning; suicide; homicide; traffic crashes; and injuries from burns, falls, and other harms.

It can harm the growing brain. Today we know that the brain continues to develop from birth through the adolescent years and into the mid-twenties.

It can affect the body in many ways. The effects of alcohol range from hangovers to death from alcohol poisoning.

It can lead to other problems. Young people who use alcohol also are more likely to smoke and use other drugs. Those who begin drinking before age 15 also are far more likely to develop alcohol problems as adults.

It affects how well a young person judges risk and makes sound decisions. For example, after drinking, a teen may see nothing wrong with driving a car or riding with a driver who has been drinking. But, before drinking, the teen might realize the riskiness involved.

It plays a role in risky sexual activity. People do things when they are under the influence of alcohol—even a small amount—that they would not do when they are sober, including having sex even when they didn't want to and had not planned to do so. This behavior can increase the chance of teen pregnancy and sexually transmitted diseases, including HIV/AIDS.

How Many Tweens and Teens Are Drinking?

The vast majority of tweens and teens do not use alcohol. In 2012, only 2.2 percent of 12- or 13-year-olds, 11.1 percent of 14- or 15-year-olds, 24.8 percent of 16- or 17-year-olds, and 45.8 percent of 18- to 20-year-olds reported any use of alcohol during the past month.

Don't be taken in by myths, rumors, and the opinions of others about how many youth drink. Get the facts from sources you can trust.

What Is Binge Drinking?

Binge alcohol use is defined as drinking five or more drinks on the same occasion on at least 1 day in the past 30 days. Heavy drinking is defined as binge drinking on at least 5 days in the past month.

As more youth recognize the risks of binge drinking, fewer are doing so. For example, about 41 percent of 12th-grade students engaged in binge drinking in 1983. In 2011, this percentage had dropped to 22 percent—or almost cut in half.

What Is A Drink?

A drink can come in many forms. It can be a shot of hard liquor or a mixed drink containing vodka, rum, tequila, gin, scotch, or some other liquor. It can also be wine, a wine cooler, beer, or malt liquor.

A standard drink is any drink that contains about 14 grams of pure alcohol (about 0.6 fluid ounces or 1.2 tablespoons). This is the amount of alcohol usually found in:

- One 12-ounce beer;

- One 4- to 5-ounce glass of wine; and

- One 1.5-ounce shot of 80-proof liquor.

Below are U.S. standard drink equivalents. These are approximate, since different brands and types of beverages vary in their actual alcohol content.

Figure 8.1. A Drink Defined

Are Beer And Wine Safer Than Liquor?

No. Alcohol is alcohol. It can cause you problems no matter how you consume it. One 12-ounce bottle of beer or a 5-ounce glass of wine (about a half cup) has as much alcohol as a 1.5-ounce shot of liquor.

How Can I Say No?

Resisting peer pressure to drink isn't always easy. But you have the right to say no, the right not to give a reason why, and the right to just walk away from a situation.

Chapter 9
Recent Trends in Underage Drinking

Underage Drinking

Alcohol use by persons under age 21 years is a major public health problem. Alcohol is the most commonly used and abused drug among youth in the United States, more than tobacco and illicit drugs, and is responsible for more than 4,300 annual deaths among underage youth. Although drinking by persons under the age of 21 is illegal, people aged 12 to 20 years drink 11% of all alcohol consumed in the United States. More than 90% of this alcohol is consumed in the form of binge drinks. On average, underage drinkers consume more drinks per drinking occasion than adult drinkers. There were approximately 189,000 emergency rooms visits by persons under age 21 for injuries and other conditions linked to alcohol.

Drinking Levels Among Youth

The *2013 Youth Risk Behavior Survey* found that among high school students, during the past 30 days:

- 35% drank some amount of alcohol.

- 21% binge drank.

- 10% drove after drinking alcohol.

- 22% rode with a driver who had been drinking alcohol.

About This Chapter: Information in this chapter is excerpted from "Fact Sheets – Underage Drinking," Centers for Disease Control and Prevention (CDC), October 31, 2014; information from "Trends In Underage Drinking In The United States, 1991–2013," National Institute on Alcohol Abuse and Alcoholism (NIAAA), a component of the National Institutes of Health (NIH), March 2015; information from "Trends in the Prevalence of Alcohol Use National YRBS: 1991–2013," Centers for Disease Control and Prevention (CDC), June 13, 2014; and information from "Underage Drinking," National Institute on Alcohol Abuse and Alcoholism (NIAAA), a component of the National Institutes of Health (NIH), September 2015.

Other national surveys:

- In 2012, the National Survey on Drug Use and Health reported that 24% of youth aged 12 to 20 years drink alcohol and 15% reported binge drinking.

- In 2013, the *Monitoring the Future* survey reported that 28% of 8th graders and 68% of 12th graders had tried alcohol, and 10% of 8th graders and 39% of 12th graders drank during the past month.

Underage Drinking Statistics

Many, many young people drink alcohol

- By age 15, about 35 percent of teens have had at least 1 drink.

- By age 18, about 65 percent of teens have had at least 1 drink.

- In 2013, 8.7 million young people ages 12–20 reported that they drank alcohol beyond "just a few sips" in the past month.

Youth ages 12 to 20 often binge drink

People ages 12 through 20 drink 11 percent of all alcohol consumed in the United States. Although youth drink less often than adults do, when they do drink, they drink more. That is because young people consume more than 90 percent of their alcohol by binge drinking. Binge drinking is consuming many drinks on an occasion. Drinking alcohol and binge drinking become more prevalent as young people get older.

- 5.4 million young people had 5 or more drinks on the same occasion, within a few hours, at least once in the past month.

- 1.4 million young people had 5 or more drinks on the same occasion on 5 or more days over the past month.

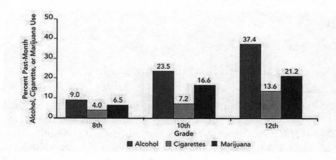

Figure 9.1. More Adolescents Use Alcohol Than Cigarettes Or Marijuana

Recent Trends In Teen Drinking

This surveillance report, prepared by the Alcohol Epidemiologic Data System (AEDS), National Institute on Alcohol Abuse and Alcoholism (NIAAA), presents data on underage drinking among youth ages 12–20 for 1991–2013. This is the sixth of a series of reports to be published every two years on underage drinking and related attitudes and risk behaviors. Data for this series are compiled from three separate nationally representative surveys: the National Survey on Drug Use and Health (NSDUH), the Monitoring the Future (MTF) survey, and the Youth Risk Behavior Survey (YRBS).

The following are highlights of trends from 1991 through 2013.

Prevalence Of Use

- Although there are marked differences in absolute values of estimates, the trends across all three survey data sources show an overall decline in the prevalence of alcohol consumption in the past 30 days between 1991 and 2013. In 2013, 22.8 percent of youth ages 12–20 reported consuming alcohol in the past 30 days (NSDUH).

- Overall, the rate of decline in the past-30 day alcohol consumption is greater in males than in females in the last few years, resulting in converging trends. However, gender differences have been smaller at the younger ages than ages 18–20 (NSDUH).

- Throughout this period, rates of underage drinking remained highest among non-Hispanic whites, followed by Hispanics and non-Hispanic blacks. Rates were also higher among youth ages 12–20 not enrolled in school as compared with those enrolled in school (NSDUH), although rates among full-time college students ages 18–20 remained higher than among their same-age peers not enrolled or enrolled part-time.

Drinking Patterns

- The median age of initiation of drinking alcohol has increased from 13.65 years in 1991–1993 to 14.47 years in 2011–2013 (NSDUH). In addition, there has been a gradual decline in the proportion of youth reporting initiating drinking at age 12 years or younger (NSDUH, YRBS).

- Over the course of the study period, males have generally maintained higher average frequency, quantity, and volume of consumption in the past 30 days than females. In 2011–2013, youth drinkers ages 12–20 reported drinking on an average of 5.09 days in the past 30 days. They consumed an average of 4.45 drinks on the days that they drank. Their average total volume of consumption was 28 drinks in the past 30 days (NSDUH).

- According to NSDUH, a household-based survey, overall rates of binge drinking have increased between 1993 and 2001, from 12.1 to 18.6 percent, but have trended down to 13.8 percent in 2013. Data from the secondary school-based surveys (MTF and YRBS), by contrast, show an overall decline in binge drinking rates; the recent downward trends appear to have started in 1999 (MTF) and possibly as early as 1997 (YRBS). Persistent gender gaps in binge drinking rates are observed over time.

Alcohol-Related Attitudes

- The percentages of youth who strongly disapprove others regularly consuming alcohol or binge drinking and who consider regular or binge drinking a great risk (MTF) show a declining trend during the 1990s, particularly in the early 1990s. The trend was reversed in the 2000s showing a gradual increase for ten years or so. However, the percentages started to show a sign of plateauing in the last few years.

Alcohol-Related Risk Behaviors

- Between 1991 and 2013, trends from the YRBS show an overall decline in the prevalence of secondary school youth driving while under the influence of alcohol, and similar downward trends are observed in the NSDUH data for the prevalence since 2003. Although the NSDUH data show an increase in the prevalence between 1995 and 2002, the difference is due to the large increase in rates among 18- to 20-year-olds—from 15.6 percent in 1995 to 22.2 percent in 2002, as the rates among younger youth remained relatively stable (NSDUH).

Trends In The Prevalence Of Alcohol Use National YRBS: 1991–2013

The national Youth Risk Behavior Survey (YRBS) monitors priority health risk behaviors that contribute to the leading causes of death, disability, and social problems among youth and adults in the United States. The national YRBS is conducted every two years during the spring semester and provides data representative of 9th through 12th grade students in public and private schools throughout the United States.

Table 9.1. Teen Drug Information

Percentages												Changes From 1991-2013[1]	Changes From 1991-2013[2]
1991	1993	1995	1997	1999	2001	2003	2005	2007	2009	2011	2013		
Ever had at least one drink of alcohol (on at least 1 day during their life)													
81.6	80.9	80.4	79.1	81	78.2	74.9	74.3	75	72.5	70.8	66.2	Decreased 1991—2013 No change 1991—1999 Decreased 1999—2013	Decreased
Drank alcohol before age 13 years (for the first time other than a few sips)													
32.7	32.9	32.4	31.1	32.2	29.1	27.8	25.6	23.8	21.1	20.5	18.6	Decreased 1991—2013 No change 1991—1999 Decreased 1999—2013	Decreased
Currently drank alcohol (at least one drink of alcohol on at least 1 day during the 30 days before the survey)													
50.8	48	51.6	50.8	50	47.1	44.9	43.3	44.7	41.8	38.7	34.9	Decreased 1991—2013 No change 1991—1999 Decreased 1999—2013	Decreased
Had five or more drinks of alcohol in a row (within a couple of hours on at least 1 day during the 30 days before the survey)													
31.3	30	32.6	33.4	31.5	29.9	28.3	25.5	26	24.2	21.9	20.8	Decreased 1991—2013 Increased 1991—1999 Decreased 1999—2013	No change

[1] Based on linear and quadratic trend analyses using logistic regression models controlling for sex, race/ethnicity, and grade, $p < 0.05$.

[2] Based on t-test analysis, $p < 0.05$.

Chapter 10

Underage Drinking: Reasons, Risks, And Prevention

Underage Drinking

Underage drinking is a serious public health problem in the United States. Alcohol is the most widely used substance of abuse among America's youth, and drinking by young people poses enormous health and safety risks.

The consequences of underage drinking can affect everyone— regardless of age or drinking status. We all feel the effects of the aggressive behavior, property damage, injuries, violence, and deaths that can result from underage drinking. This is not simply a problem for some families—it is a nationwide concern.

> **How Much Is A Drink?**
> A standard drink is roughly 14 grams of pure alcohol, which is found in:
> - 12 ounces of beer
> - 5 ounces of wine
> - 1.5 ounces of distilled spirits

Consequences Of Underage Drinking

Youth who drink alcohol are more likely to experience:

- School problems, such as higher absence and poor or failing grades.

About This Chapter: Information in this chapter is excerpted from "Underage Drinking," National Institute on Alcohol Abuse and Alcoholism (NIAAA), a component of the National Institutes of Health (NIH), September 2015.

- Social problems, such as fighting and lack of participation in youth activities.

- Legal problems, such as arrest for driving or physically hurting someone while drunk.

- Physical problems, such as hangovers or illnesses.

- Unwanted, unplanned, and unprotected sexual activity.

- Disruption of normal growth and sexual development.

- Physical and sexual assault.

- Higher risk for suicide and homicide.

- Alcohol-related car crashes and other unintentional injuries, such as burns, falls, and drowning.

- Memory problems.

- Abuse of other drugs.

- Changes in brain development that may have life-long effects.

- Death from alcohol poisoning.

In general, the risk of youth experiencing these problems is greater for those who binge drink than for those who do not binge drink.

Youth who start drinking before age 15 years are five times more likely to develop alcohol dependence or abuse later in life than those who begin drinking at or after age 21 years.

Underage Drinking Is Dangerous

Underage drinking poses a range of risks and negative consequences. It is dangerous because it:

Causes many deaths

Based on data from 2006–2010, the Centers for Disease Control and Prevention (CDC) estimates that, on average, alcohol is a factor in the deaths of 4,358 young people under age 21 each year.5 This includes:

- 1,580 deaths from motor vehicle crashes

- 1,269 from homicides

- 245 from alcohol poisoning, falls, burns, and drowning

- 492 from suicides

Causes many injuries

Drinking alcohol can cause kids to have accidents and get hurt. In 2010 alone, about 189,000 people under age 21 visited an emergency room for alcohol-related injuries.

Impairs judgment

Drinking can lead to poor decisions about engaging in risky behavior, including drinking and driving, sexual activity (such as unprotected sex), and aggressive or violent behavior.

Increases the risk of physical and sexual assault

Underage youth who drink are more likely to carry out or be the victim of a physical or sexual assault after drinking than others their age who do not drink.

Can lead to other problems

Drinking may cause youth to have trouble in school or with the law. Drinking alcohol also is associated with the use of other drugs.

Increases the risk of alcohol problems later in life

Research shows that people who start drinking before the age of 15 are 4 times more likely to meet the criteria for alcohol dependence at some point in their lives.

Interferes with brain development

Research shows that young people's brains keep developing well into their 20s. Alcohol can alter this development, potentially affecting both brain structure and function. This may cause cognitive or learning problems and/or make the brain more prone to alcohol dependence. This is especially a risk when people start drinking young and drink heavily.

Why Do So Many Young People Drink?

As children mature, it is natural for them to assert their independence, seek new challenges, and try taking risks. Underage drinking is a risk that attracts many developing adolescents and teens. Many want to try alcohol, but often do not fully recognize its effects on their health and behavior. Other reasons young people drink alcohol include:

- Peer pressure
- Increased independence, or desire for it
- Stress

In addition, many youth have easy access to alcohol. A 2013 study showed that 93.7 percent of adolescents ages 12–14 who drank alcohol got it for free the last time they drank. In many cases, adolescents have access to alcohol through family members, or find it at home.

What is "binge drinking?"

For adults, binge drinking means drinking so much within about 2 hours that blood alcohol concentration (BAC) levels reach 0.08g/dL, the legal limit of intoxication. For women, this typically takes about 4 drinks, and for men, about 5. But, according to recent research estimates, it takes fewer drinks for children to reach these BAC levels.

For boys:

- Ages 9–13: About 3 drinks
- Ages 14–15: About 4 drinks
- Ages 16–17: About 5 drinks

For girls:

- Ages 9–17: About 3 drinks

Preventing Underage Drinking

Preventing underage drinking is a complex challenge. Any successful approach must consider many factors, including:

- Genetics
- Personality
- Rate of maturation and development
- Level of risk
- Social factors
- Environmental factors

Several key approaches have been found to be successful. They are:

Environmental interventions

This approach makes alcohol harder to get—for example, by raising the price of alcohol and keeping the minimum drinking age at 21. Enacting zero-tolerance laws that outlaw driving after any amount of drinking for people under 21 also can help prevent problems.

Individual-level interventions

This approach seeks to change the way young people think about alcohol, so they are better able to resist pressures to drink.

School-based interventions

These are programs that provide students with the knowledge, skills, motivation, and opportunities they need to remain alcohol free.

Family-based interventions

These are efforts to empower parents to set and enforce clear rules against drinking, as well as improve communication between children and parents about alcohol.

The Role Parents Play

Parents and teachers can play a big role in shaping young people's attitudes toward drinking. Parents in particular can have either a positive or negative influence.

- Parents can help their children avoid alcohol problems by:

- Talking about the dangers of drinking

- Drinking responsibly, if they choose to drink

- Serving as positive role models in general

- Not making alcohol available

- Getting to know their children's friends

- Having regular conversations about life in general

- Connecting with other parents about sending clear messages about the importance of not drinking alcohol

- Supervising all parties to make sure there is no alcohol

- Encouraging kids to participate in healthy and fun activities that do not involve alcohol

Research shows that children whose parents are actively involved in their lives are less likely to drink alcohol.

On the other hand, research shows that a child with a parent who binge drinks is much more likely to binge drink than a child whose parents do not binge drink.

Warning Signs of Underage Drinking

Adolescence is a time of change and growth, including behavior changes. These changes usually are a normal part of growing up but sometimes can point to an alcohol problem.

Parents and teachers should pay close attention to the following warning signs that may indicate underage drinking:

- Changes in mood, including anger and irritability
- Academic and/or behavioral problems in school
- Rebelliousness
- Changing groups of friends
- Low energy level
- Less interest in activities and/or care in appearance
- Finding alcohol among a young person's things
- Smelling alcohol on a young person's breath
- Problems concentrating and/or remembering
- Slurred speech
- Coordination problems

Treating Underage Drinking Problems

Some young people can experience serious problems as a result of drinking, including alcohol use disorder. These problems require intervention by trained professionals. Professional treatment options include:

- Seeing a counselor, psychologist, psychiatrist, or other trained professional
- Participating in outpatient or inpatient treatment at a substance abuse treatment facility or other

Chapter 11
Drinking Too Much Can Kill You

Drinking To Excess
Recognize And Treat Alcohol Problems

Some people enjoy an occasional glass of wine with dinner. Others might grab a beer while watching a football game. Most people drink alcohol moderately, within their limits. Others overdo it occasionally. But some people find they can't control their drinking. How do you know when drinking is becoming a problem? And what can you do if it is?

About 18 million Americans have an alcohol use disorder. Drinking too much alcohol raises your risk of injury and accidents, disease, and other health problems. Heavy drinking is one of the leading causes of preventable deaths in this country, contributing to nearly 88,000 deaths each year.

How much is too much? Men shouldn't have more than 14 drinks per week and 4 drinks on any single day. Women shouldn't have more than 7 drinks per week and no more than 3 drinks on any day. But you might be surprised at what counts as a drink. A 5-ounce glass of table wine, a 12-ounce glass of regular beer, and 1½ ounces of hard liquor each contain the same amount of alcohol, and each counts as 1 drink. You may need to adjust the amount you drink depending on how alcohol affects you. Some people—such as pregnant women or people taking certain medications—shouldn't drink alcohol at all.

Alcohol problems come from drinking too much, too fast, or too often. People with alcohol dependence are addicted to alcohol, and they can't control their drinking. When alcohol-

About This Chapter: Information in this chapter is excerpted from "Drinking to Excess," National Institutes of Health (NIH), September 2014.

dependent people try to stop drinking, they may feel anxious and irritable—so they may drink some more, and it becomes a vicious cycle.

Rethink That Drink

Drinking too much alcohol? Here are some tips to help cut back:

- **Pace yourself.** Sip slowly. Drink a glass of water after each alcoholic drink.
- **Include food.** Don't drink on an empty stomach.
- **Avoid triggers.** If certain people, places, or activities tempt you to drink, try to avoid them.
- **Seek healthy alternatives.** Look for new hobbies, interests or friendships to help fill your time and manage your stress.
- **Track and control how much you drink.** If offered a drink you don't want, have a polite, convincing "no thanks" reply ready.
- **Get help.** To find an alcoholism treatment specialist in your area, visit this NIH's Support and Treatment webpage.

"Addiction has 3 major problems: You lose your ability to feel good, you get more stressed, and you have a hard time making proper decisions," says Dr. George Koob, director of NIH's National Institute on Alcohol Abuse and Alcoholism. "That's a recipe for disaster."

Signs of an alcohol problem include drinking more, or more often, than you intended, or making unsuccessful attempts to cut back or quit. People with alcohol problems often have trouble functioning at work, home, or school.

"A good indicator is that something is out of whack. Is your personal life deteriorating because of your drinking? Are people starting to shun you? If you're feeling generally miserable, that's a warning sign," Koob says. "You don't have to hit bottom. You'll save yourself a lot of damage socially, professionally, and probably in your own body if you attend to an alcohol problem a lot earlier."

"People shouldn't wait for a physical problem like liver disease," says Dr. Lorenzo Leggio, an NIH researcher studying new alcoholism treatments. "People develop an alcohol disorder before liver problems get bad. The goal is to identify an alcohol disorder sooner. The sooner you act can help prevent medical consequences."

Studies show that most people with an alcohol use disorder can benefit from some form of treatment. If you or someone you care about may have an alcohol problem, help is available. The first step is to talk to a primary care doctor. In some cases, a brief intervention, or an honest conversation about drinking habits and risks, is all the person needs. If the problem is more serious, the doctor can help create a treatment plan, prescribe medications, or refer the person to a specialist. In more severe cases, the doctor might recommend a treatment clinic or in-patient addiction center.

"Alcohol dependence is a complex, diverse disorder. There's not one treatment that works for everybody," says Dr. Raye Litten, an alcohol treatment and recovery expert at NIH. "If one treatment doesn't work, you can try another one. Sometimes a combination of these will work."

Medications can help people stop or reduce their drinking. Three medications are approved by the U.S. Food and Drug Administration for treating alcohol use disorders. One of these, disulfiram, causes unpleasant side effects such as nausea, vomiting, and a racing heart rate if you consume any alcohol while taking the drug. Understandably, some people don't want to take this medication for that reason. The two other drugs, naltrexone and acamprosate, also have been shown effective at reducing alcohol craving in many heavy drinkers.

Additional medications are under study as possible treatments for alcohol use disorders. These include a handful of medicines already approved to treat other medical conditions. For example, the drug gabapentin is now used to treat pain and other conditions, but it also has shown promise for reducing heavy drinking in clinical research trials. Gabapentin may reduce alcohol cravings as well as anxiety, trouble sleeping, and other symptoms associated with alcohol use disorders.

NIH researchers are working to develop other approaches as well. Some are exploring a possible connection between appetite and alcohol craving. Leggio is studying a hormone in the stomach called ghrelin. His research suggests that when ghrelin is elevated, people feel hungry and also crave more alcohol. His lab is testing an experimental drug designed to block this hormone to help reduce alcohol craving. The drug is now being assessed in early trials at the NIH Clinical Center in Maryland.

"There's not going to be a drug that cures you of alcoholism," Koob says. "I think that drugs can help you along the way, so that some of the chemical changes in the brain can return to normal. Strengthen that with behavioral therapy to make recovery as permanent as you can."

Behavioral therapy, such as counseling or support groups, can help people develop skills to avoid or overcome stress and other triggers that could lead to drinking. The approach can help people set realistic goals, identify the feelings and situations that might lead to heavy drinking, and offer tips to manage stress. It also helps to build a strong social support network.

If the treatment plan created by your health care team is working, it's important to stick to that plan. Many people repeatedly try to cut back or quit drinking, have a setback, then try to quit again. Think of an alcohol relapse as a temporary setback and keep persisting toward full recovery.

"You always have to be aware there's a possibility of relapse and temptation," says Koob. "Any recovering alcoholic will tell you it's a daily fight for a long time."

Chapter 12
Binge Drinking

Binge drinking is the most common pattern of excessive alcohol use in the United States. The National Institute on Alcohol Abuse and Alcoholism defines binge drinking as a pattern of drinking that brings a person's blood alcohol concentration (BAC) to 0.08 grams percent or above. This typically happens when men consume 5 or more drinks, and when women consume 4 or more drinks, in about 2 hours.

Most people who binge drink are not alcohol dependent.

According to national surveys:

- One in six U.S. adults binge drinks about four times a month, consuming about eight drinks per binge.

- While binge drinking is more common among young adults aged 18–34 years, binge drinkers aged 65 years and older report binge drinking more often—an average of five to six times a month.

- Binge drinking is more common among those with household incomes of $75,000 or more than among those with lower incomes.

- Approximately 92% of U.S. adults who drink excessively report binge drinking in the past 30 days.

- Although college students commonly binge drink, 70% of binge drinking episodes involve adults age 26 years and older.

About This Chapter: Information in this chapter is excerpted from "Fact Sheets - Binge Drinking," Centers for Disease Control and Prevention (CDC), January 16, 2014.

- The prevalence of binge drinking among men is twice the prevalence among women.

- Binge drinkers are 14 times more likely to report alcohol-impaired driving than non-binge drinkers.

- About 90% of the alcohol consumed by youth under the age of 21 in the United States is in the form of binge drinks.

- More than half of the alcohol consumed by adults in the United States is in the form of binge drinks.

Binge drinking is associated with many health problems, including—

- Unintentional injuries (e.g., car crashes, falls, burns, drowning)

- Intentional injuries (e.g., firearm injuries, sexual assault, domestic violence)

- Alcohol poisoning

- Sexually transmitted diseases

- Unintended pregnancy

- Children born with Fetal Alcohol Spectrum Disorders

- High blood pressure, stroke, and other cardiovascular diseases

- Liver disease

- Neurological damage

- Sexual dysfunction

- Poor control of diabetes

Binge drinking costs everyone.

- Drinking too much, including binge drinking, cost the United States $249 billion in 2010, or $2.05 a drink, from losses in productivity, health care, crime, and other expenses. Binge drinking was responsible for 77% of these costs, or $191 billion.

Evidence-based interventions to prevent binge drinking and related harms include:

- Increasing alcoholic beverage costs and excise taxes.

- Limiting the number of retail alcohol outlets that sell alcoholic beverages in a given area.

- Holding alcohol retailers responsible for the harms caused by their underage or intoxicated patrons (dram shop liability).

- Restricting access to alcohol by maintaining limits on the days and hours of alcohol retail sales.

- Consistent enforcement of laws against underage drinking and alcohol-impaired driving.

- Maintaining government controls on alcohol sales (avoiding privatization).

- Screening and counseling for alcohol misuse.

Chapter 13
Questions And Answers About Alcoholism

Is Drinking No Big Deal?

My friends say that drinking alcohol is no big deal. Everybody is doing it, and I should, too. What should I do?

First, the **great majority** (75.7 percent) of 12- to 20-year-olds **do not** drink, and the percentage who do has been steadily decreasing for more than a decade.

Second, underage drinking affects every organ in your body, including your developing brain. Alcohol use also is linked to several risky behaviors; various types of injuries; and deaths from homicide, suicide, and impaired driving.

Remember, too, that underage drinking is illegal. If you are caught drinking, you could delay your chance of getting a driver's license or lose the one you already have. You could also be barred from playing on an athletic team.

What's Right?

People try to get me to drink at parties. I don't want to break the law or violate my parents' trust, but I don't want to look lame and like I don't fit in. How can I do the right thing?

Make sure you know what the consequences will be if parents, police, and other adults find out that you have been drinking.

About This Chapter: Information in this chapter is excerpted from "Need Advice?" Substance Abuse and Mental Health Services Administration (SAMHSA), November 19, 2014.

Why Should I Wait Until I Am of Legal Age To Drink?

I feel that I am mature for my age. I have great grades and a part-time job. A drink here and there shouldn't hurt, right? I can drink responsibly.

No matter how mature you feel, your body and brain are still developing. In fact, research shows that brain development continues well into a person's twenties. Alcohol can affect this development and contribute to a range of problems.

Will Alcohol Make Me Less Shy?

I'm shy and have a hard time making friends. The idea of going out on a date makes me nervous. Someone told me that a drink or two would give me more confidence and help me relax around others. Is this true?

Some drinkers feel less shy and ill at ease with others temporarily. However, alcohol impairs judgment so that drinkers often do things they wouldn't consider doing if sober. Their behavior can lead to embarrassment, regret, serious trouble, and even tragedy.

"Just about everybody feels shy sometimes," says Dr. Colleen Sherman in an article on shyness. If you're looking for more information on shyness, healthfinder.gov is a good place to go when you want reliable information on any health topic. Just type "shy" or "shyness" into the Search box.

Talk with a parent or another adult you trust about your feelings. School counselors and nurses know where you can find help. So do ministers, priests, rabbis, and other faith leaders.

I Did Something Stupid. What Now?

I did something stupid when I was drinking with my friends recently. Now some of them treat me differently and aren't as friendly as they used to be. What should I do?

Perhaps you said or did something that was embarrassing or unkind or annoying. Friends will probably accept your apology and your sincere promise not to do anything like this again.

Maybe you broke something. You need to repair the damage, pay for someone else to fix it, or replace the item. And you should offer a sincere apology.

Doing "something stupid" under the influence of alcohol can also mean something much more serious, such as driving under the influence or having risky sex. Talk with your parent or another adult you trust and ask for help.

Or call this 24-hour toll-free helpline: 1–800–662–HELP (1–800–662–4357).

How Can I Help My Friends?

Some friends of mine do things I know they don't mean to do whenever they drink. I don't want to get them in trouble or be a snitch. What can I do to help them?

It isn't snitching to get help for someone who may be in trouble because of drinking. About 4,700 underage drinkers die every year. A lot of them die in highway crashes. But many others die from alcohol poisoning or from trying to do something dangerous while they are impaired.

If you have a friend with a drinking problem, he or she is in trouble already and needs help before the problem worsens or leads to tragedy.

How Do I Handle Adults Who Drink Too Much?

Some adults in my family drink too much and act badly. They don't think their drinking is a problem, but I do. Their drinking bothers me a lot. What can I do?

Get the facts about alcoholism so you will understand that you are not the reason it's going on and that you are not responsible for your family's problems.

Alcoholism tends to run in families. If you are a member of a family with a history of alcohol problems, you need to avoid underage drinking. Children of alcoholics are two to four times more likely to become alcoholics themselves than children from families with no alcoholic adults. You need to be familiar with your family history and aware of your risks.

Chapter 14
Alcohol Use And Health Risks

Negative Consequences Of Underage Drinking

Adolescence can be a wonderful time filled with physical and emotional growth. For some youth, however, adolescence takes a dark turn, especially when underage alcohol use is involved.

Underage alcohol use increases the risk of academic failure, illicit drug use, and tobacco use. It can cause a range of physical consequences, from hangovers to death from alcohol poisoning, suicide, homicide, and traffic crashes. Annually, about 4,700 people under age 21 die from injuries involving underage drinking.

Underage alcohol use also can alter the structure and function of the developing brain, which continues to mature into the mid- to late-twenties, and may have consequences reaching far beyond adolescence. For example, those who start using alcohol while young are at greater risk of developing alcohol problems as adults. In 2012, adults who had first used alcohol before age 15 were more than seven times as likely to experience alcohol dependence or abuse as those who waited until age 21 for their first drink (15.2 vs. 2.1 percent).

Alcohol's Effects On The Body

Drinking too much—on a single occasion or over time—can take a serious toll on your health.

Here's how alcohol can affect your body:

About This Chapter: Information in this chapter is excerpted from "Negative Consequences Of Underage Drinking," Substance Abuse and Mental Health Services Administration (SAMHSA), May 21, 2014; information from "Alcohol's Effects on the Body," National Institute on Alcohol Abuse and Alcoholism (NIAAA), May 17, 2012; information from "Alcohol And The Developing Brain," Substance Abuse and Mental Health Services Administration (SAMHSA), May 21, 2014; and information from "Fact Sheets – Alcohol Use and Your Health," Centers for Disease Control and Prevention (CDC), November 7, 2014.

Brain:

Alcohol interferes with the brain's communication pathways, and can affect the way the brain looks and works. These disruptions can change mood and behavior, and make it harder to think clearly and move with coordination.

Heart:

Drinking a lot over a long time or too much on a single occasion can damage the heart, causing problems including:

- Cardiomyopathy – Stretching and drooping of heart muscle
- Arrhythmias – Irregular heart beat
- Stroke
- High blood pressure

Research also shows that drinking moderate amounts of alcohol may protect healthy adults from developing coronary heart disease.

Liver:

Heavy drinking takes a toll on the liver, and can lead to a variety of problems and liver inflammations including:

- Steatosis, or fatty liver
- Alcoholic hepatitis
- Fibrosis
- Cirrhosis

Pancreas:

Alcohol causes the pancreas to produce toxic substances that can eventually lead to pancreatitis, a dangerous inflammation and swelling of the blood vessels in the pancreas that prevents proper digestion.

Cancer:

Drinking too much alcohol can increase your risk of developing certain cancers, including cancers of the:

- Mouth
- Esophagus

- Throat
- Liver
- Breast

Immune System:

Drinking too much can weaken your immune system, making your body a much easier target for diseases. Chronic drinkers are more liable to contract diseases like pneumonia and tuberculosis than people who do not drink too much. Drinking a lot on a single occasion slows your body's ability to ward off infections—even up to 24 hours after getting drunk.

Alcohol And The Developing Brain

Alcohol can cause alterations in the structure and function of the developing brain, which continues to mature into a person's mid-20s, and it may have consequences reaching far beyond adolescence.

In adolescence, brain development is characterized by dramatic changes to the brain's structure, neuron connectivity (i.e., "wiring"), and physiology. These changes in the brain affect everything from emerging sexuality to emotionality and judgment.

Not all parts of the adolescent brain mature at the same time, which may put an adolescent at a disadvantage in certain situations. For example, the limbic areas of the brain mature earlier than the frontal lobes. The limbic areas regulate emotions and are associated with an adolescent's lowered sensitivity to risk. The frontal lobes are responsible for self-regulation, judgment, reasoning, problem-solving, and impulse control. Differences in maturation among parts of the brain can result in impulsive decisions or actions and a disregard for consequences.

How Alcohol Affects The Brain

Alcohol affects an adolescent's brain development in many ways. The effects of underage drinking on specific brain activities are explained below:

Alcohol is a central nervous system depressant. Alcohol can appear to be a stimulant because, initially, it depresses the part of the brain that controls inhibitions.

CEREBRAL CORTEX—Alcohol slows down the cerebral cortex as it works with information from a person's senses.

CENTRAL NERVOUS SYSTEM—When a person thinks of something he wants his body to do, the central nervous system—the brain and the spinal cord—sends a signal to that part of the body. Alcohol slows down the central nervous system, making the person think, speak, and move slower.

FRONTAL LOBES—The brain's frontal lobes are important for planning, forming ideas, making decisions, and using self-control.

When alcohol affects the frontal lobes of the brain, a person may find it hard to control his or her emotions and urges. The person may act without thinking or may even become violent.

Drinking alcohol over a long period of time can damage the frontal lobes forever.

HIPPOCAMPUS—The hippocampus is the part of the brain where memories are made.

- When alcohol reaches the hippocampus, a person may have trouble remembering something he or she just learned, such as a name or a phone number. This can happen after just one or two drinks.

- Drinking a lot of alcohol quickly can cause a blackout—not being able to remember entire events, such as what he or she did last night.

- If alcohol damages the hippocampus, a person may find it hard to learn and to hold on to knowledge.

CEREBELLUM—The cerebellum is important for coordination, thoughts, and awareness. A person may have trouble with these skills when alcohol enters the cerebellum. After drinking alcohol, a person's hands may be so shaky that they can't touch or grab things normally, and they may lose their balance and fall.

HYPOTHALAMUS—The hypothalamus is a small part of the brain that does an amazing number of the body's housekeeping chores. Alcohol upsets the work of the hypothalamus. After a person drinks alcohol, blood pressure, hunger, thirst, and the urge to urinate increase while body temperature and heart rate decrease.

MEDULLA—The medulla controls the body's automatic actions, such as a person's heartbeat. It also keeps the body at the right temperature. Alcohol actually chills the body. Drinking a lot of alcohol outdoors in cold weather can cause a person's body temperature to fall below normal. This dangerous condition is called *hypothermia*.

Alcohol Use and Health Risks

Short-Term Health Risks

Excessive alcohol use has immediate effects that increase the risk of many harmful health conditions. These are most often the result of binge drinking and include the following:

- Injuries, such as motor vehicle crashes, falls, drownings, and burns.

- Violence, including homicide, suicide, sexual assault, and intimate partner violence.

- Alcohol poisoning, a medical emergency that results from high blood alcohol levels.

- Risky sexual behaviors, including unprotected sex or sex with multiple partners. These behaviors can result in unintended pregnancy or sexually transmitted diseases, including HIV.

- Miscarriage and stillbirth or fetal alcohol spectrum disorders (FASDs) among pregnant women.

Long-Term Health Risks

Over time, excessive alcohol use can lead to the development of chronic diseases and other serious problems including:

- High blood pressure, heart disease, stroke, liver disease, and digestive problems.

- Cancer of the breast, mouth, throat, esophagus, liver, and colon.

- Learning and memory problems, including dementia and poor school performance.

- Mental health problems, including depression and anxiety.

- Social problems, including lost productivity, family problems, and unemployment.

- Alcohol dependence, or alcoholism.

By not drinking too much, you can reduce the risk of these short- and long-term health risks.

Chapter 15
A Family History Of Alcoholism

If you are among the millions of people in this country who have a parent, grandparent, or other close relative with alcoholism, you may have wondered what your family's history of alcoholism means for you. Are problems with alcohol a part of your future? Is your risk for becoming an alcoholic greater than for people who do not have a family history of alcoholism? If so, what can you do to lower your risk?

What Is Alcoholism?

Alcoholism, or alcohol dependence, is a disease that includes four symptoms:

1. Craving—A strong need, or urge, to drink.
2. Loss Of Control—Not being able to stop drinking once drinking has begun.
3. Physical Dependence—Withdrawal symptoms, such as upset stomach, sweating, shakiness, and anxiety after stopping drinking.
4. Tolerance—The need to drink greater amounts of alcohol to get "high."

Many scientific studies, including research conducted among twins and children of alcoholics, have shown that genetic factors influence alcoholism. These findings show that children of alcoholics are about four times more likely than the general population to develop alcohol problems. Children of alcoholics also have a higher risk for many other behavioral and emo-

About This Chapter: Information in this chapter is excerpted from "A Family History of Alcoholism," Centers for Disease Control and Prevention (CDC), NIH Publication No. 03–5340, June 2012.

tional problems. But alcoholism is not determined only by the genes you inherit from your parents. In fact, more than one–half of all children of alcoholics do not become alcoholic. Research shows that many factors influence your risk of developing alcoholism. Some factors raise the risk while others lower it.

Genes are not the only things children inherit from their parents. How parents act and how they treat each other and their children has an influence on children growing up in the family. These aspects of family life also affect the risk for alcoholism. Researchers believe a person's risk increases if he or she is in a family with the following difficulties:

- an alcoholic parent is depressed or has other psychological problems;

- both parents abuse alcohol and other drugs;

- the parents' alcohol abuse is severe; and

- conflicts lead to aggression and violence in the family.

The good news is that many children of alcoholics from even the most troubled families do not develop drinking problems. Just as a family history of alcoholism does not guarantee that you will become an alcoholic, neither does growing up in a very troubled household with alcoholic parents. Just because alcoholism tends to run in families does not mean that a child of an alcoholic parent will automatically become an alcoholic too. The risk is higher but it does not have to happen.

If you are worried that your family's history of alcohol problems or your troubled family life puts you at risk for becoming alcoholic, here is some common–sense advice to help you:

Avoid underage drinking—First, underage drinking is illegal. Second, research shows that the risk for alcoholism is higher among people who begin to drink at an early age, perhaps as a result of both environmental and genetic factors.

Drink moderately as an adult—Even if they do not have a family history of alcoholism, adults who choose to drink alcohol should do so in moderation—no more than one drink a day for most women, and no more than two drinks a day for most men, according to guidelines from the U.S. Department of Agriculture and the U.S. Department of Health and Human Services. Some people should not drink at all, including women who are pregnant or who are trying to become pregnant, recovering alcoholics, people who plan to drive or engage in other activities that require attention or skill, people taking certain medications, and people with certain medical conditions.

People with a family history of alcoholism, who have a higher risk for becoming dependent on alcohol, should approach moderate drinking carefully. Maintaining moderate drinking habits may be harder for them than for people without a family history of drinking problems. Once a person moves from moderate to heavier drinking, the risks of social problems (for example, drinking and driving, violence, and trauma) and medical problems (for example, liver disease, brain damage, and cancer) increase greatly.

Talk to a health care professional—Discuss your concerns with a doctor, nurse, nurse practitioner, or other health care provider. They can recommend groups or organizations that could help you avoid alcohol problems. If you are an adult who already has begun to drink, a health care professional can assess your drinking habits to see if you need to cut back on your drinking and advise you about how to do that.

Chapter 16
Coping With An Alcoholic Parent

Impact Of Parental Substance Use On Children

The way parents with substance use disorders behave and interact with their children can have a multifaceted impact on the children. The effects can be both indirect (e.g., through a chaotic living environment) and direct (e.g., physical or sexual abuse). Parental substance use can affect parenting, prenatal development, and early childhood and adolescent development. It is important to recognize, however, that not all children of parents with substance use issues will suffer abuse, neglect, or other negative outcomes.

Parenting

A parent's substance use disorder may affect his or her ability to function effectively in a parental role. Ineffective or inconsistent parenting can be due to the following:

- Physical or mental impairments caused by alcohol or other drugs
- Reduced capacity to respond to a child's cues and needs
- Difficulties regulating emotions and controlling anger and impulsivity
- Disruptions in healthy parent-child attachment
- Spending limited funds on alcohol and drugs rather than food or other household needs
- Spending time seeking out, manufacturing, or using alcohol or other drugs
- Incarceration, which can result in inadequate or inappropriate supervision for children
- Estrangement from family and other social supports

About This Chapter: Information in this chapter is excerpted from "Parental Substance Use and the Child Welfare System," Child Welfare Information Gateway, a component of the Children's Bureau, October 2014.

Family life for children with one or both parents that abuse drugs or alcohol often can be chaotic and unpredictable. Children's basic needs—including nutrition, supervision, and nurturing—may go unmet, which can result in neglect. These families often experience a number of other problems such as mental illness, domestic violence, unemployment, and housing instability—that also affect parenting and contribute to high levels of stress. A parent with a substance abuse disorder may be unable to regulate stress and other emotions, which can lead to impulsive and reactive behavior that may escalate to physical abuse.

Different substances may have different effects on parenting and safety. For example, the threats to a child of a parent who becomes sedated and inattentive after drinking excessively differ from the threats posed by a parent who exhibits aggressive side effects from methamphetamine use. Dangers may be posed not only from use of illegal drugs, but also, and increasingly, from abuse of prescription drugs (pain relievers, anti-anxiety medicines, and sleeping pills). Polysubstance use (multiple drugs) may make it difficult to determine the specific and compounded effects on any individual. Further, risks for the child's safety may differ depending upon the level and severity of parental substance use and associated adverse effects.

Prenatal And Infant Development

The effects of parental substance use disorders on a child can begin before the child is born. Maternal drug and alcohol use during pregnancy have been associated with premature birth, low birth weight, slowed growth, and a variety of physical, emotional, behavioral, and cognitive problems. Research suggests powerful effects of legal drugs, such as tobacco, as well as illegal drugs on prenatal and early childhood development.

Fetal alcohol spectrum disorders (FASDs) are a set of conditions that affect an estimated 40,000 infants born each year to mothers who drank alcohol during pregnancy. Children with FASD may experience mild to severe physical, mental, behavioral, and/or learning disabilities, some of which may have lifelong implications (e.g., brain damage, physical defects, attention deficits). In addition, increasing numbers of newborns— approximately 3 per 1,000 hospital births each year—are affected by neonatal abstinence syndrome (NAS), a group of problems that occur in a newborn who was exposed prenatally to addictive illegal or prescription drugs.

The full impact of prenatal substance exposure depends on a number of factors. These include the frequency, timing, and type of substances used by pregnant women; co-occurring environmental deficiencies; and the extent of prenatal care. Research suggests that some of the negative outcomes of prenatal exposure can be improved by supportive home environments and positive parenting practices.

Child And Adolescent Development

Children and youth of parents who use or abuse substances and have parenting difficulties have an increased chance of experiencing a variety of negative outcomes:

- Poor cognitive, social, and emotional development

- Depression, anxiety, and other trauma and mental health symptoms

- Physical and health issues

- Substance use problems

Parental substance use can affect the well-being of children and youth in complex ways. For example, an infant who receives inconsistent care and nurturing from a parent engaged in addiction- elated behaviors may suffer from attachment difficulties that can then interfere with the growing child's emotional development. Adolescent children of parents with substance use disorders, particularly those who have experienced child maltreatment and foster care, may turn to substances themselves as a coping mechanism. In addition, children of parents with substance use issues are more likely to experience trauma and its effects, which include difficulties with concentration and learning, controlling physical and emotional responses to stress, and forming trusting relationships.

Innovative Prevention And Treatment Approaches

While parental substance abuse continues to be a major challenge in child welfare, the past two decades have witnessed some new and more effective approaches and innovative programs to address child protection for families where substance abuse is an issue. Some examples of promising and innovative prevention and treatment approaches include the following:

Promotion of protective factors, such as social connections, concrete supports, and parenting knowledge, to support families and buffer risks.

Early identification of at-risk families in substance abuse treatment programs and through expanded prenatal screening initiatives so that prevention services can be provided to promote child safety and well-being in the home.

Priority and timely access to substance abuse treatment slots for mothers involved in the child welfare system.

Gender-sensitive treatment and support services that respond to the specific needs, characteristics, and co-occurring issues of women who have substance use disorders.

Family-centered treatment services, including inpatient treatment for mothers in facilities where they can have their children with them and programs that provide services to each family member **Recovery coaches or mentoring** of parents to support treatment, recovery, and parenting.

Shared family care in which a family experiencing parental substance use and child maltreatment is placed with a host family for support and mentoring. Find more information on specific programs and service models:

- National Center on Substance Abuse and Child Welfare (NCSACW), Regional Partnership Grant (RPG) Program: Overview of Grantees' Services and Interventions
- NRC for In-Home Services, In-Home Programs for Drug Affected Families
- SAMHSA's National Registry of Evidence-Based Programs and Practices

Part Three
Tobacco, Nicotine, And
E-Cigarettes

Chapter 17
Tobacco And Nicotine Addiction

What Are Tobacco, Nicotine, And E-Cigarette Products?

Cigarettes: Also known as: "smokes," "cigs," or "butts"

Smokeless tobacco: Also known as: "chew," "dip," "spit tobacco," "snus," or "snuff"

Hookah: Also known as: "narghile," "argileh," "shisha," "hubble-bubble," or "goza"

Tobacco is a leafy plant grown around the world, including in parts of the United States. There are many chemicals found in tobacco or created by burning it (as in cigarettes), but nicotine is the ingredient that can lead to addiction. Other chemicals produced by smoking, such as tar, carbon monoxide, acetaldehyde, and nitrosamines, also can cause harm to the body. For example, tar causes lung cancer and other serious diseases that affect breathing. Carbon monoxide causes heart problems, which is one reason why people who smoke are at high risk for heart disease.

Tobacco use is the leading preventable cause of disease, disability, and death in the United States. According to the Centers for Disease Control and Prevention (CDC), cigarettes cause more than 480,000 premature deaths in the United States each year—from smoking or exposure to secondhand smoke—about 1 in every 5 U.S. deaths, or 1,300 deaths every day. An additional 16 million people suffer with a serious illness caused by smoking. Thus, for every 1 person who dies from smoking, 33 more suffer from at least 1 serious tobacco-related illness.

How Are Tobacco And Nicotine Products Used?

Tobacco and nicotine products come in many forms. People either smoke, chew, or sniff them, or inhale their vapors.

About This Chapter: Information in this chapter is excerpted from "Tobacco, Nicotine, & E-Cigarettes," NIDA for Teens, National Institute on Drug Abuse (NIDA), October 23, 2015.

- **Smoked tobacco products.**

  - Cigarettes (regular, light, and menthol). No evidence exists that "lite" or menthol cigarettes are safer than regular cigarettes.

  - Cigars and pipes.

  - Bidis and kreteks (clove cigarettes). Bidis are small, thin, hand-rolled cigarettes primarily imported to the United States from India and other Southeast Asian countries. Kreteks—sometimes referred to as clove cigarettes—contain about 60–80% tobacco and 20–40% ground cloves. Flavored bidis and kreteks are banned in the United States because of the ban on flavored cigarettes.

  - Hookahs or water pipes. Practiced for centuries in other countries, smoking hookahs has become popular among teens in the United States. Hookah tobacco comes in many flavors, and the pipe is typically passed around in groups. As with smoking cigarettes, water pipe smoking still delivers the addictive drug nicotine and is at least as toxic as cigarette smoking.

- **Smokeless tobacco products.** The tobacco is not burned with these products:

  - Chewing tobacco, which is placed between the cheek and gums.

  - Snuff, ground tobacco that can be sniffed if dried or placed between the cheek and gum.

  - Dip, moist snuff that is used like chewing tobacco.

  - Snus, a small pouch of moist snuff.

  - Dissolvable products, including lozenges, orbs, sticks, and strips.

- **Electronic cigarettes.** Also called e-cigarettes, electronic nicotine delivery systems, or e-cigs, electronic cigarettes are smokeless, battery-operated devices that deliver flavored nicotine to the lungs without burning tobacco (the usual source of nicotine). In most e-cigarettes, puffing activates the battery-powered heating device, which vaporizes the liquid in the cartridge. The resulting vapor is then inhaled (called "vaping").

How Do Tobacco And Nicotine Affect The Brain?

Like cocaine, heroin, and marijuana, nicotine increases levels of a neurotransmitter called dopamine. Dopamine is released normally when you experience something pleasurable like good food, your favorite activity, or spending time with people you care about. When a person uses tobacco products, the release of dopamine causes similar effects. This effect wears off quickly, causing people who smoke to get the urge to light up again for more of that good feeling, which can lead to addiction.

Studies suggest that other chemicals in tobacco smoke, such as acetaldehyde, may enhance the effects of nicotine on the brain.

When smokeless tobacco is used, nicotine is absorbed through the mouth tissues directly into the blood, where it goes to the brain. Even after the tobacco is removed from the mouth, nicotine continues to be absorbed into the bloodstream. Also, the nicotine stays in the blood longer for users of smokeless tobacco than for smokers.

Can You Get Addicted To Tobacco Or Nicotine Products?

Yes. It is the nicotine in tobacco that is addictive. Each cigarette contains about 10 milligrams of nicotine. A person inhales only some of the smoke from a cigarette, and not all of each puff is absorbed in the lungs. Therefore, a person gets about 1 to 2 milligrams of the drug from each cigarette.

Studies of widely used brands of smokeless tobacco showed that the amount of nicotine per gram of tobacco ranged from 4.4 milligrams to 25.0 milligrams. Holding an average-size dip in your mouth for 30 minutes gives you as much nicotine as smoking 3 cigarettes.

A 2-can-a-week snuff dipper gets as much nicotine as a person who smokes 1½ packs a day.

Whether a person smokes tobacco products or uses smokeless tobacco, the amount of nicotine absorbed in the body is enough to make someone addicted. When this happens, the person compulsively seeks out the tobacco even though he or she understands the harm it causes. Nicotine addiction can cause:

- **Tolerance.** Over the course of a day, someone who uses tobacco products develops tolerance—more nicotine is required to produce the same initial effects. Some of this tolerance is lost overnight. In fact, people who smoke often report that the first cigarette of the day is the strongest or the "best."

- **Withdrawal.** When people quit using tobacco products, they usually experience withdrawal symptoms, which often drive them back to tobacco use. Nicotine withdrawal symptoms include:

  - Irritability

  - Problems with thinking and paying attention

  - Sleep problems

- Increased appetite

- Craving, which may last 6 months or longer, and can be a major stumbling block to quitting

Treatments can help people who use tobacco products manage these symptoms and improve the likelihood of successfully quitting. For now, smokers who want to quit have other good options with proven effectiveness.

Most people (nearly 70%) who smoke want to quit. Most who try to quit on their own relapse—often within a week. However, most former smokers have had several failed quit attempts before they succeed.

Can You Die If You Use Tobacco And Nicotine?

Yes. Tobacco use (both smoked and smokeless tobacco use) is the leading preventable cause of death in the United States. It is a known cause of human cancer. Smoking tobacco also can lead to early death from heart disease, health problems in children, and accidental fires caused by dropped cigarettes. In addition, the nicotine in smokeless tobacco may increase the risk for sudden death from a condition where the heart does not beat properly (ventricular arrhythmias); as a result, the heart pumps little or no blood to the body's organs.

According to the Centers for Disease Control and Prevention (CDC), cigarette smoking results in more than 480,000 premature deaths in the United States each year—about 1 in every 5 U.S. deaths, or 1,300 deaths every day. People who smoke are at increased risk of death from cancer, particularly lung cancer, heart disease, lung diseases, and accidental injury from fires started by dropped cigarettes.

Chapter 18
Child And Teen Tobacco Use

Background

Preventing tobacco use among youth is critical to ending the tobacco epidemic in the United States.

- Tobacco use is started and established primarily during adolescence.

- Nearly 9 out of 10 cigarette smokers first tried smoking by age 18, and 99% first tried smoking by age 26.

- Each day in the United States, more than 3,800 youth aged 18 years or younger smoke their first cigarette, and an additional 2,100 youth and young adults become daily cigarette smokers.

- Flavorings in tobacco products can make them more appealing to youth.

- In 2014, 73% of high school students and 56% of middle school students who used tobacco products in the past 30 days reported using a flavored tobacco product during that time.

Youth use of tobacco in any form is unsafe.

If smoking continues at the current rate among youth in this country, 5.6 million of today's Americans younger than 18 will die early from a smoking-related illness. That's about 1 of every 13 Americans aged 17 years or younger alive today.

About This Chapter: Information in this chapter is excerpted from "Youth and Tobacco Use," Centers for Disease Control and Prevention (CDC), October 14, 2015.

Estimates Of Current Tobacco Use Among Youth

Cigarette smoking has declined among U.S. youth in recent years, but the use of some other tobacco products has increased.

Cigarettes

- From 2011 to 2014, current cigarette smoking declined among middle and high school students.

- Nearly 3 of every 100 middle school students (2.5%) reported in 2014 that they smoked cigarettes in the past 30 days—a decrease from 4.3% in 2011.

- About 9 of every 100 high school students (9.2%) reported in 2014 that they smoked cigarettes in the past 30 days—a decrease from 15.8% in 2011.

E-cigarettes

- Current use of e-cigarettes increased among middle and high school students from 2011 to 2014.

- Nearly 4 of every 100 middle school students (3.9%) reported in 2014 that they used e-cigarettes in the past 30 days—an increase from 0.6% in 2011.

- More than 13 of every 100 high school students (13.4%) reported in 2014 that they used e-cigarettes in the past 30 days—an increase from 1.5% in 2011.

Hookahs

- From 2011 to 2014, current use of hookahs increased among middle and high school students.

- Nearly 3 of every 100 middle school students (2.5%) reported in 2014 that they had used hookah in the past 30 days—an increase from 1.0% in 2011.

- More than 9 of every 100 high school students (9.4%) reported in 2014 that they had used hookah in the past 30 days—an increase from 4.1% in 2011.

Smokeless Tobacco

In 2014:

- More than 5 of every 100 high school students (5.5%) reported current use of smokeless tobacco.

- Nearly 2 of every 100 middle school students (1.6%) reported current use of smokeless tobacco.

All Tobacco Product Use

- In 2014, nearly 25 of every 100 high school students (24.6%) and nearly 8 of every 100 middle school students (7.7%) used some type of tobacco product.

- In 2013, nearly half (46.0%) of high school students and nearly 18 of every 100 middle school students (17.7%) said they had ever tried a tobacco product.

Use of multiple tobacco products is prevalent among youth.

- In 2013, more than 31 of every 100 high school students (31.4%) said they had ever tried two or more tobacco products.

- In 2014, more than 12 of every 100 high school students (12.7%) and approximately 3 of every 100 middle school students (3.1%) reported use of two or more tobacco products in the past 30 days.

Youth who use multiple tobacco products are at higher risk for developing nicotine dependence and might be more likely to continue using tobacco into adulthood.

Table 18.1. Tobacco Use* Among High School Students In 2014

Tobacco Product	Overall	Females	Males
Any tobacco product†	24.60%	20.90%	28.30%
Electronic cigarettes	13.40%	11.90%	15.00%
Hookahs	9.40%	9.80%	8.90%
Cigarettes	9.20%	7.90%	10.60%
Cigars	8.20%	5.50%	10.80%
Smokeless tobacco	5.50%	1.20%	9.90%
Snus	1.90%	0.80%	3.00%
Pipes	1.50%	0.90%	2.10%
Bidis	0.90%	0.60%	1.20%
Dissolvable tobacco	0.60%	0.40%	0.80%

Table 18.2. Tobacco Use* Among Middle School Students In 2014

Tobacco Product	Overall	Females	Males
Any tobacco product[†]	7.70%	6.60%	8.80%
Electronic cigarettes	3.90%	3.30%	4.50%
Hookahs	2.50%	2.60%	2.40%
Cigarettes	2.50%	2.00%	3.00%
Cigars	1.90%	1.40%	2.40%
Smokeless tobacco	1.60%	-§	2.10%
Snus	0.50%	–	0.70%
Pipes	0.60%	–	0.60%
Bidis	0.50%	0.30%	–
Dissolvable tobacco	0.30%	–	0.40%

* "Use" is determined by respondents indicating that they have used a tobacco product on at least 1 day during the past 30 days.

[†] "Any tobacco product" includes cigarettes, cigars, smokeless tobacco, tobacco pipes, bidis, hookah, snus, dissolvable tobacco, and/or electronic cigarettes.

§ Where percentages are missing, sample sizes were less than 50 and not considered reliable.

Factors Associated With Youth Tobacco Use

Factors associated with youth tobacco use include the following:

- Social and physical environments:

    - The way mass media show tobacco use as a normal activity can promote smoking among young people.

    - Youth are more likely to use tobacco if they see that tobacco use is acceptable or normal among their peers.

    - High school athletes are more likely to use smokeless tobacco than their peers who are non-athletes.

    - Parental smoking may promote smoking among young people.

- Biological and genetic factors:

    - There is evidence that youth may be sensitive to nicotine and that teens can feel dependent on nicotine sooner than adults.

- Genetic factors may make quitting smoking more difficult for young people.

- A mother's smoking during pregnancy may increase the likelihood that her offspring will become regular smokers.

- Mental health: There is a strong relationship between youth smoking and depression, anxiety, and stress.

- Personal perceptions: Expectations of positive outcomes from smoking, such as coping with stress and controlling weight, are related to youth tobacco use.

- Other influences that affect youth tobacco use include:

  - Lower socioeconomic status, including lower income or education

  - Lack of skills to resist influences to tobacco use

  - Lack of support or involvement from parents

  - Accessibility, availability, and price of tobacco products

  - Low levels of academic achievement

  - Low self-image or self-esteem

  - Exposure to tobacco advertising

Chapter 19
E-Cigarettes

What About E-Cigarettes?

E-cigarettes have emerged over the past decade and researchers are in the early stage of investigating what the health effects are for people who use these products or who are exposed to the aerosol (vapor) secondhand.

E-cigarettes are designed to deliver nicotine without the other chemicals produced by burning tobacco leaves. Puffing on the mouthpiece of the cartridge activates a battery-powered inhalation device (called a vaporizer). The vaporizer heats the liquid inside the cartridge which contains nicotine, flavors, and other chemicals. The heated liquid turns into an aerosol (vapor) that the user inhales—referred to as "vaping."

There are conflicting studies about whether or not e-cigarettes help smokers to quit. For tobacco cigarette smokers, e-cigarettes may be a safer alternative, if the goal is not to quit nicotine all together. However, health experts have raised many questions about the safety of these products, particularly for teens:

- Testing of some e-cigarette products found the aerosol (vapor) to contain known cancer-causing and toxic chemicals, and particles from the vaporizing mechanism that may be harmful. The health effects of repeated exposure to these chemicals are not yet clear.

- There is an animal research that shows that nicotine exposure may cause changes in the brain that make other drugs more rewarding. If this is true in humans, as some experts

About This Chapter: Information in this chapter is excerpted from "Tobacco, Nicotine, & E-Cigarettes," NIDA for Teens, National Institute on Drug Abuse (NIDA), October 23, 2015; and information from "Are E-Cigarettes Harmful?" NIDA for Teens, National Institute on Drug Abuse (NIDA), October 30, 2015.

believe, it would mean that using nicotine would increase the risk of other drug use and for addiction.

- There is an established link between e-cigarette use and tobacco cigarette use in teens. Researchers are investigating this relationship. The concern is that e-cigarette use may serve as a "gateway" or introductory product for youth to try other tobacco products, including regular cigarettes, which are known to cause disease and lead to early death.

- The liquid in e-cigarettes can cause nicotine poisoning if someone drinks, sniffs or touches it. Recently, there has been a surge of poisoning cases in children under age 5. There is also concern for users changing cartridges and for pets.

Are E-Cigarettes Regulated?

The U.S. government's Food and Drug Administration (FDA) may start to regulate how e-cigarettes are made and sold. Currently, they only regulate e-cigarettes that have a therapeutic benefit, but at this time no products qualify. If the FDA moves to regulate all e-cigarettes, this will likely result in there being rules on safety, advertising, and warning labels, similar to those that currently govern tobacco cigarettes and other tobacco products. For now, e-cigarettes are not guaranteed to be safe. Consumers should not assume that the health claims made in advertisements by manufactures are scientifically proven.

Are E-Cigarettes Harmful?

Have you been to a mall lately? Or maybe your local convenience store? You may have seen electronic cigarettes (known as e-cigarettes or e-cigs) on sale. There is definitely no shortage in supply: e-cigarettes have grown to be a billion-dollar industry with an estimated 460 brands.

And as it turns out, this supply has a sizeable demand—including more and more teens. The Centers for Disease Control and Prevention in May 2015 estimated that 2 million high school students and 450,000 middle school students have used an e-cigarette in the previous month. (That's triple the number of teens using them in 2014.)

Doesn't Vaping Beat Smoking?

The thinking goes, "If they're not as bad as cigarettes, then maybe they're OK." But your health isn't a "rock-paper-scissors" game. We still don't know if e-cigarettes can hurt your lungs. And we do know that they are made to deliver the same highly addictive nicotine as regular cigarettes. This means by using them you can get hooked on nicotine. And, by the way, it's a very hard drug to quit once you are addicted. Just ask the 90% of current smokers that started while they were teens.

But Don't People Use e-Cigarettes To Quit Smoking?

You may have heard that e-cigarettes are a great way to kick a smoking habit. But we just don't have enough research to know. And no e-cigarettes on the market are approved for this purpose.

Plus, some studies have found that as many as 75% of adults who use them still smoke regular cigarettes. And most teens who use e-cigarettes also smoke regular cigarettes too.

What's The Harm in Nicotine Addiction (If You Don't Smoke)?

Well, first (and yes, you've heard us say this before), the teen brain is still developing. This means that the teen brain is more vulnerable to addiction. Researchers worry that once you get hooked on nicotine through e-cigarettes you'll start using regular cigarettes. Plus, research suggests that once addicted to nicotine, it may be easier to get addicted to other drugs, such as cocaine.

Still, in the years to come, researchers will learn a lot more about e-cigarettes. But in the meantime, take a page out of the history books and remember that it wasn't so long ago that doctors didn't think cigarette smoking was dangerous.

Chapter 20

Smoking's Immediate Effects On The Body

Here And Now

Smoking may stain your teeth and turn your fingers yellow. It can also harm your skin by destroying its elastic fibers and weakening its ability to repair itself. This can lead to wrinkles and other signs of premature aging—we've all seen it before, but it can come on a lot faster when you smoke.

Smoking also causes inflammation and cell damage throughout the body, and can weaken your immune system, making it less efficient at fighting off disease. As a result, smokers have more lung infections than nonsmokers. They are also more likely to have a serious gum infection that can lead to tooth loss.

Oh, by the way, you don't have to be a long-time smoker to have an asthma attack that is triggered by tobacco smoke.

Under Attack

Every time you smoke, your body is under attack. Your lungs become inflamed and damaged. Your body recognizes this, and your immune system kicks into high gear to repair the damage. When you keep smoking, it's like spilling an irritant on your skin — if you did this many times a day, your skin would not have a chance to heal. It would stay red, irritated, and inflamed.

About This Chapter: Information in this chapter is excerpted from "Health Costs," U.S. Department of Health and Human Services (HHS), December 9, 2013.

The organs in your body also have a lining of cells similar to skin. Chemicals in cigarette smoke can inflame and damage these cells and when you keep smoking, the damage cannot heal. Making your immune system work overtime can leave you vulnerable to disease in almost every part of your body.

Catch Your Breath

So smoking is bad for your lungs, no surprise there. What might surprise you is how bad it is for lungs that are still developing. **If you're under 20, your lungs are still growing, and smoking can stunt that growth**. We're not talking about just being short of breath now—teens who smoke may end up as adults with lungs that never grow to their potential or perform at full capacity. Such damage is permanent and increases the risk of chronic bronchitis and emphysema.

Over Time

Even young adults under age 30 who started smoking in their teens and early twenties can develop smoking-related health problems, such as:

- Smaller lungs that don't function properly
- Wheezing that can lead to being diagnosed with asthma
- DNA damage that can cause cancer almost anywhere in the body
- Early cardiovascular disease (e.g., heart attacks and stroke)

Smoking longer means more damage. Scientists now know that your disease risk surges even higher after you have smoked for about 20 years. Because of nicotine addiction, smokers often have difficulty quitting and continue smoking for many years. Those who smoke die, on average, at least 10 years younger than nonsmokers. Did you know that smoking is the leading cause of preventable deaths in the United States? Every day, more than 1,300 people in this country die from smoking-related causes—and almost all of them started before age 18. This accounts for 1 out of 5 deaths.

Quitting isn't easy but it can be done and will benefit your health at any age. The sooner you quit, the sooner your body will begin to heal. In fact, research shows that if you quit when you are still young, your health could become almost as good as a nonsmoker's.

Chapter 21
Health Harms From Smoking And Other Tobacco Use

Why Smoking Tobacco Products Is So Deadly

The danger of smoking comes from inhaling chemical compounds, some in the tobacco and some that are created when tobacco is burned. The tobacco in cigarettes is a blend of dried tobacco leaf and tobacco sheet made from stems, ribs, and other tobacco leaf waste. The process used to make modern cigarettes includes the use of many chemicals. In all, scientists have identified more than 7,000 chemicals and chemical compounds in tobacco smoke. At least 70 of them are known specifically to cause cancer. All cigarettes are harmful, and any exposure to tobacco smoke can cause both immediate and long-term damage to the body. There is no safe level of exposure to tobacco smoke, and there is no safe cigarette. To reduce cancer risk, quitting smoking entirely is an important strategy that has been proven to work.

Smoking—The Cancer Trigger

Cancer is a serious disease that happens when cells grow uncontrollably in the body. These cells grow into tumors that damage organs and can spread to other parts of the body. Smoking can cause cancer almost anywhere in the body. Nearly all lung cancer—the number-one cancer killer of both men and women—is caused by smoking. **If no one in the United States smoked, we could prevent one out of three cancer deaths**.

About This Chapter: Information in this chapter is excerpted from "Let's Make The Next Generation Tobacco-Free," Centers for Disease Control and Prevention (CDC), July 2015.

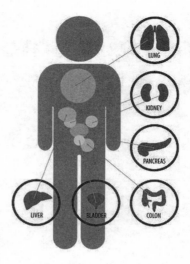

Figure 21.1. Diseases And Health Problems Linked To Smoking

DNA Damage

Deoxyribonucleic acid (DNA) is the "blueprint" for every cell in the human body—the cell's "instruction manual." DNA controls a cell's growth and the work each cell does. When tobacco smoke damages DNA, cells can begin growing abnormally. Typically, the body releases special cells to attack and kill cells that are growing out of control. However, toxic chemicals in cigarette smoke weaken this process and make it easier for the abnormal cells to keep growing and dividing.

Lung Cancer

At present, lung cancer is the number-one cause of cancer death for both men and women. Nearly 9 out of 10 lung cancers are caused by smoking. In fact, smokers today are much more likely to develop lung cancer than smokers were in 1964, when the first Surgeon General's *Report on Smoking and Health* linked smoking to lung cancer.

Smoking Linked To Two Additional Cancers

Evidence now proves that smoking causes liver cancer, and colorectal cancer, which is the second deadliest cancer among those that affect both men and women. Studies suggest a link between smoking and breast cancer, but the evidence is not as firm. Studies also suggest that men with prostate cancer who smoke may be more likely to die from the disease than nonsmokers.

Cancer Treatment

People who continue to smoke after being diagnosed with cancer raise their risk for future cancers and death. They're more likely to die from their original cancer, secondary cancers, and all other causes than are former smokers and people who have never smoked.

Smoking—The Breath Blocker

Respiratory Diseases

The chemicals in cigarette smoke cause immediate damage to cells and tissue in the human body, including those on the path from the mouth to the lung's air sacs—the final target of the smoke. Delicate lung tissue damaged by chemicals in cigarette smoke doesn't have a chance to heal if it is exposed to these chemicals in large amounts day after day. The result is a wide range of deadly lung conditions.

Smoking—The Heart Stopper

More than 16 million Americans have heart disease, almost 8 million already have had a heart attack and 7 million have had a stroke. Cardiovascular disease (CVD) is the single largest cause of all deaths in the United States, killing more than 800,000 people a year.

CVD includes narrow or blocked arteries in and around the heart (coronary heart disease), high blood pressure (hypertension), heart attack (acute myocardial infarction), stroke and heart-related chest pain (angina pectoris). Smoking is a major cause of CVD.

Even people who smoke fewer than five cigarettes a day show signs of early stages of CVD. The risk of CVD increases when more cigarettes a day are smoked, and when smoking continues for many years.

Exposure to secondhand smoke can increase the risk for a heart attack or stroke. More than 33,000 nonsmokers die every year in the United States from coronary heart disease caused by exposure to secondhand smoke.

Smoking And Reproduction

For many reasons, men and women who want to have children should not smoke. Studies suggest that smoking affects hormone production. This could make it more difficult for women smokers to become pregnant. Pregnant women who smoke or who are exposed to secondhand smoke endanger their unborn babies, as well as their own health. Babies whose mothers smoked during pregnancy or who are exposed to secondhand smoke after birth are more likely to die of sudden infant death syndrome (SIDS) than are babies who are not exposed. More than 100,000 of the smoking-caused deaths over the last 50 years were of babies who died from SIDS or other health conditions. Deadly chemicals in cigarette smoke reached these infants before they were born, or when they were exposed to cigarette smoke during infancy.

Smoking And Diabetes

Diabetes—a disease that causes blood sugar levels in the body to be too high—is a growing health crisis around the world. In the United States, more than 25 million adults suffer from diabetes. We now know that smoking causes type 2 diabetes, also known as adult-onset diabetes. Smokers are 30% to 40% more likely to develop type 2 diabetes than nonsmokers. The more cigarettes an individual smokes, the higher the risk for diabetes.

Diabetes can cause serious health problems, including heart disease, blindness, kidney failure, and nerve and blood vessel damage of the feet and legs, which can lead to amputation. A person with diabetes who smokes is more likely to have trouble regulating insulin and controlling the disease than nonsmokers with diabetes. Both smoking and diabetes cause problems with blood flow, which raises the risk of blindness and amputations. Smokers with diabetes are also more likely to have kidney failure than nonsmokers with diabetes. Diabetes is the seventh leading cause of death in the United States.

Smoking And The Immune System

The immune system is the body's way of protecting itself from infection and disease. The immune system fights everything from cold and flu viruses to serious conditions such as cancer. Smoking compromises the immune system and can make the body less successful at fighting disease. Smokers have more respiratory infections than nonsmokers, in part because the chemicals in cigarettes make it harder for their immune systems to successfully attack the viruses and bacteria that can cause respiratory infections. In fact, smokers generally are much less healthy than nonsmokers. Their overall health is worse, they need to go to the doctor more often, and they are admitted to the hospital more often.

Smoking also causes autoimmune disorders. Autoimmune disorders occur when the immune system attacks the body's healthy cells. For example, in rheumatoid arthritis, or RA, the immune system attacks the joints and tissue around the joints, causing swelling and pain. As a result, people with RA have a harder time getting around and doing normal daily activities. We now know RA can be caused by smoking, and smoking makes some RA treatments less effective.

Smoking And Death

Cigarette smoking is the leading preventable cause of death in the United States.

- Cigarette smoking causes more than 480,000 deaths each year in the United States. This is nearly one in five deaths.
- Smoking causes more deaths each year than the following causes combined:
  - Human immunodeficiency virus (HIV)
  - Illegal drug use
  - Alcohol use
  - Motor vehicle injuries
  - Firearm-related incidents
- More than 10 times as many U.S. citizens have died prematurely from cigarette smoking than have died in all the wars fought by the United States during its history.
- Smoking causes about 90% (or 9 out of 10) of all lung cancer deaths in men and women. More women die from lung cancer each year than from breast cancer.
- About 80% (or 8 out of 10) of all deaths from chronic obstructive pulmonary disease (COPD) are caused by smoking.
- Cigarette smoking increases risk for death from all causes in men and women.
- The risk of dying from cigarette smoking has increased over the last 50 years in men and women in the United States.

Chapter 22

Facts About Smoking Cessation

What You Need to Know About Quitting Smoking

- Tobacco use can lead to tobacco/nicotine dependence and serious health problems. **Quitting smoking greatly reduces the risk of developing smoking-related diseases.**

- Tobacco/nicotine dependence is a condition that often requires repeated treatments, but **there are helpful treatments and resources for quitting.**

- Smokers can and do quit smoking. In fact, **today there are more former smokers than current smokers.**

Nicotine Dependence

- Most smokers become addicted to nicotine, a drug that is found naturally in tobacco.

- More people in the United States are addicted to nicotine than to any other drug. Research suggests that nicotine may be as addictive as heroin, cocaine, or alcohol.

- Quitting smoking is hard and may require several attempts. People who stop smoking often start again because of withdrawal symptoms, stress, and weight gain.

- Nicotine withdrawal symptoms may include:

  - Feeling irritable, angry, or anxious

  - Having trouble thinking

About This Chapter: Information in this chapter is excerpted from "Quitting Smoking," Centers for Disease Control and Prevention (CDC), May 21, 2015; information from "Benefits of Quitting," Centers for Disease Control and Prevention (CDC), July 20, 2015; and information from "Quit Smoking," U.S. Department of Health and Human Services (HHS), July 29, 2015.

- Craving tobacco products

- Feeling hungrier than usual

Health Benefits Of Quitting

Tobacco smoke contains a deadly mix of more than 7,000 chemicals; hundreds are harmful, and about 70 can cause cancer. Smoking increases the risk for serious health problems, many diseases, and death.

People who stop smoking greatly reduce their risk for disease and early death. Although the health benefits are greater for people who stop at earlier ages, there are benefits at any age. **You are never too old to quit.**

Stopping smoking is associated with the following health benefits:

- Lowered risk for lung cancer and many other types of cancer.

- Reduced risk for heart disease, stroke, and peripheral vascular disease (narrowing of the blood vessels outside your heart).

- Reduced heart disease risk within 1 to 2 years of quitting.

- Reduced respiratory symptoms, such as coughing, wheezing, and shortness of breath. While these symptoms may not disappear, they do not continue to progress at the same rate among people who quit compared with those who continue to smoke.

- Reduced risk of developing some lung diseases (such as chronic obstructive pulmonary disease, also known as COPD, one of the leading causes of death in the United States).

- Reduced risk for infertility in women of childbearing age. Women who stop smoking during pregnancy also reduce their risk of having a low birth weight baby.

Smokers' Attempts To Quit

Among all current U.S. adult cigarette smokers, nearly 7 out of every 10 (68.8%) reported in 2010 that they wanted to quit completely.

- Since 2002, the number of former smokers has been greater than the number of current smokers.

Percentage of adult daily cigarette smokers who stopped smoking for more than 1 day in 2012 because they were trying to quit:

- More than 4 out of 10 (**42.7%**) of all **adult** smokers

- Nearly 5 out of 10 (**48.5%**) smokers aged **18–24** years

- More than 4 out of 10 (**46.8%**) smokers aged **25–44** years

- Nearly 4 out of 10 (**38.8%**) smokers aged **45–64** years

- More than 3 out of 10 (**34.6%**) smokers aged **65 years or older**

Percentage of high school cigarette smokers who tried to stop smoking in the past 12 months:

- Nearly 5 out of 10 (**48%**) of all high school students who smoke

Will Quitting Make Me Gain Weight?

Some people worry about gaining weight when they quit smoking. The average weight gain after quitting smoking is small—about 6 to 10 pounds.

To help control your weight as you quit smoking:

- Get active. Aim for 2 hours and 30 minutes a week of moderate aerobic activity, like walking fast or dancing.
- Eat healthy snacks, like vegetables or fruit.
- Talk with your doctor about ways to control your weight.

Other Benefits Of Quitting

- Health benefits for people with diabetes who quit smoking begin immediately and include having better control over blood sugar levels.

- If you quit smoking, you will breathe better and it will be easier to be active.

- By not smoking, you help protect family, friends, and coworkers from health risks associated with breathing secondhand smoke. These include an increased risk for heart disease and lung cancer among adults. For babies and children, risks include respiratory infections, ear infections, and sudden infant death syndrome (SIDS).

Chapter 23

How Can I Quit Smoking?

Prepare To Quit

We get it, quitting is hard. But it is easier if you prepare ahead of time. When you feel like you are ready to quit, **START** by following these five steps:

1. Set a Quit Date

Pick a date within the next two weeks to quit smoking. This will give you enough time to prepare. Really think about your quit date. Avoid choosing a day where you know you will be busy, stressed, or tempted to smoke (for example, a night out with friends, days where you may smoke at work).

2. Tell Family and Friends You Plan to Quit

Quitting smoking is easier when the people in your life support you. Let them know you are planning to quit. Explain how they can help you quit. We all need different things, so be sure you let friends and family know exactly how they can help. Not sure what you need? Here are a few ways to start the conversation:

- Tell family and friends your reasons for quitting.

- Ask your friends and family to check in with you to see how things are going.

- Identify your smoking triggers, and ask your friends and family to help you deal with them.

About This Chapter: Information in this chapter is excerpted from "Steps to Prepare," Centers for Disease Control and Prevention (CDC), March 15, 2015; information from "Making a Quit Plan," Centers for Disease Control and Prevention (CDC), March 15, 2015; information from "Getting Support as You Quit," Centers for Disease Control and Prevention (CDC), March 15, 2015; and information from "Quit Tips," Centers for Disease Control and Prevention (CDC), July 20, 2015.

- Ask your friends and family to help you think of smokefree activities you can do together (like going to the movies or a nice restaurant).

- Know a friend or family member who smokes? Ask them to quit with you, or at least not smoke around you.

- You are going to be tempted to smoke. Ask your friends and family not to let you have a cigarette—no matter what.

- Let your friends and family know that you may be in a bad mood while quitting; ask them to be patient and help you through it.

- Do you take any medicines? Tell your doctor or pharmacist you are quitting. You may need to change your prescriptions after you quit.

3. Anticipate and Plan for Challenges While Quitting

Quitting smoking is hardest during the first few weeks. You will deal with uncomfortable feelings, temptations to smoke, withdrawal symptoms, and cigarette cravings. An important part of preparing to quit is anticipating these challenges. To get a head start, be aware of the following:

Uncomfortable Feelings

The first few weeks after quitting, a lot of people may feel uncomfortable and will crave a cigarette. This is because of withdrawal. Withdrawal is when your body gets used to not having nicotine from cigarettes. Nicotine is the chemical found in cigarettes that makes you want to keep smoking. Some of the more common feelings that come with withdrawal are:

- Feeling a little depressed
- Not being able to sleep
- Getting cranky, frustrated, or mad
- Feeling anxious, nervous, or restless
- Having trouble thinking clearly

You may be tempted to smoke to relieve these feelings. Just remember that they are temporary, no matter how powerful they feel at the time.

Smoking Triggers

Triggers are specific persons, places, or activities that make you feel like smoking. It is important to know your smoking triggers so you can learn to deal with them.

Cravings

Cravings are short but intense urges to smoke. They usually only last a few minutes. Plan ahead and come up with a list of short activities you can do when you get a craving.

4. Remove Cigarettes and Other Tobacco From Your Home' Car' and Work

You will be tempted to smoke during your quit. Stay strong; you can do it! Removing things that remind you of smoking will get you ready to quit. Try these tips:

- Throw away all your cigarettes and matches. Give or throw away your lighters and ash-trays. Remember the ashtray and lighter in your car!
- Don't save one pack of cigarettes "just in case." Keeping one pack just makes it easier to start smoking again.
- Remove the smell of cigarettes from your life. Make things clean and fresh at work' in your car' and at home. Clean your drapes and clothes. Shampoo your car. You will be less tempted to light up if you don't smell smoke.
- Have your dentist clean your teeth to get rid of smoking stains. Your teeth will look amazing. When you quit smoking, they will always look that way.

Don't Use Other Products with Tobacco

Thinking about using other tobacco products instead of cigarettes? Think again. All tobacco products contain harmful chemicals and poisons. Despite their name, light or low-tar cigarettes are just as bad as regular cigarettes. Smokeless tobacco' pipes' cigars' cigarillos' hookahs (waterpipes)' bidi cigarettes' clove cigarettes' and herbal cigarettes also hurt your health.

No matter how they are presented in advertisements' all tobacco products are dangerous.

5. Talk to Your Doctor or Pharmacist About Quit Options

It is difficult to quit smoking on your own, but quitting "cold turkey" is not your only choice. Talk to your doctor or pharmacist about other support options. Most doctors and pharmacists can answer your questions, give advice, and tell you where to get quit smoking help.

Quit smoking medications are also an effective quit option. Many quit smoking medicines, especially Nicotine Replacement Therapy (NRT), are available without a prescription. This includes the nicotine patch, nicotine gum, or nicotine lozenge. Read the instructions before using any medications. If you have questions about a medication, ask your pharmacist. If you are pregnant or planning to become pregnant, consult your doctor before using any type of medication. If you plan on using quit smoking medications, remember to have them available on your quit day.

If you need help right away, you can talk to a quit smoking counselor by phone or online.

Have You Built A Quit Plan?

One of the keys to a successful quit is preparation. A great way to prepare to quit smoking is to create a quit plan. Quit plans:

- Combine quit smoking strategies to keep you focused, confident, and motivated to quit

- Help you identify challenges you will face as you quit and ways to overcome them

- Can improve your chances of quitting smoking for good

The following steps will help you to create your own customized quit plan. As you move through the steps, keep a record of your plan and have it readily available during your quit.

Pick A Quit Date

When it comes to choosing a quit date, sooner is better than later. Many smokers choose a date within two weeks to quit smoking. This will give you enough time to prepare. Really think about your quit date. Avoid choosing a day where you know you will be busy, stressed, or tempted to smoke (e.g., a night out with friends or days where you may smoke at work).

Next Step: Circle your quit day on your calendar. Write it out somewhere where you will see it every day. This will remind you of your decision to become smokefree and give you time to prepare to quit.

Let Loved Ones Know You Are Quitting

Quitting smoking is easier with support from important people in your life. Let them know ahead of your quit date that you are planning to quit. Explain how they can help you quit. We all need different things, so be sure you let friends and family know exactly how they can help.

Next Step: Support is one of the keys to successfully quitting. However, it can be hard to ask for help, even from the people closest to you. Review tips on getting support to make sure you get the help you need.

Remove Reminders Of Smoking

Getting rid of smoking reminders can keep you on track during your quit. Smoking reminders can include your cigarettes, matches, ashtrays, and lighters. It may also help to make things clean and fresh at work' in your car' and at home. Even the smell of cigarettes can cause a cigarette craving.

Next Step: Throw away all your cigarettes and matches. Give or throw away your lighters and ashtrays. Don't save one pack of cigarettes "just in case."

Identify Your Reasons To Quit Smoking

Everyone has their own reasons for quitting smoking. Maybe they want to be healthier, save some money, or keep their family safe. As you prepare to quit, think about your own reasons for quitting. Remind yourself of them every day. They can inspire you to stop smoking for good.

Next Step: Make a list of all the reasons you want to quit smoking. Keep it in a place where you can see it every day. Any time you feel the urge to smoke, review your list. It will keep you motivated to stay smokefree.

Identify Your Smoking Triggers

When you smoke, it becomes tied to many parts of your life. Certain activities, feelings, and people are linked to your smoking. When you come across these things, they may "trigger" or turn on your urge to smoke. Try to anticipate these smoking triggers and develop ways to deal with them.

Next Step: Make a list of everything that makes you feel like smoking. Now, write down one way you can deal with or avoid each item on your list. Keep this list nearby during your quit.

Develop Coping Strategies

Nicotine is the chemical in cigarettes that makes you addicted to smoking. When you stop smoking, your body has to adjust to no longer having nicotine in its system. This is called withdrawal. Withdrawal can be unpleasant, but you can get through it. Developing strategies to cope with withdrawal ahead of your quit can help ensure you stay smokefree for good!

Next Steps: Medications and behavior changes can help you manage the symptoms of withdrawal. Many quit smoking medications are available over the counter. Make sure you have them on hand prior to your quit. While medications will help, they can't do all the work for you. Develop other quit smoking strategies to use with medications. Remember that withdrawal symptoms' including cravings' will fade with every day that you stay smokefree.

Have Places You Can Turn To For Immediate Help

Quitting smoking is hardest during the first few weeks. You will deal with uncomfortable feelings, temptations to smoke, withdrawal symptoms, and cigarette cravings. Whether it is a quitline, support group, or good friend, make sure you have quit smoking support options available at all times.

Next Steps: Plan on using multiple quit smoking support options. Keep them handy in case you need them during your quit. Here a few options you may want to consider:

- SmokefreeTXT: A mobile text messaging service designed for adults and young adults across the United States who are trying to quit smoking.

- Quitlines: If you want to talk to a quit smoking counselor right away, call 1–800–QUIT–NOW (1–800–784–8669).

- Quit Smoking Apps: Mobile phone applications can help you prepare to quit, provide support, and track your progress.

- Support Groups: Visit your county or state government's website to see if they offer quit smoking programs in your area.

- Friends and Family: Getting support from the important people in your life can make a big difference during your quit.

- Medications: If you are using a quit smoking medication, such as the patch, gum, or lozenges, make sure you have them on hand.

Set Up Rewards For Quit Milestones

Quitting smoking happens one minute, one hour, one day at a time. Reward yourself throughout your quit. Celebrate individual milestones, including being 24 hours smokefree, one week smokefree, and one month smokefree. Quitting smoking is hard, be proud of your accomplishments.

Next Steps: You should be proud every time you hit a quit smoking milestone. Treat yourself with a nice dinner, day at the movies, or any other smokefree activity. Plan out your milestones ahead of time and set up a smokefree reward for each one.

Tips To Get Support As You Quit

Getting support from the important people in your life can make a big difference as your quit. In fact, two out of five former smokers felt that support from others mattered a lot in their success. Remember that you are not in this alone. Your friends and family are there for you, in both good times and bad.

Are you one of the more than 70% of smokers who want to quit? Then try following this advice.

1. Don't smoke any cigarettes. Each cigarette you smoke damages your lungs, your blood vessels, and cells throughout your body. Even occasional smoking is harmful.

2. Write down why you want to quit. Do you want to—
   - Be around for your loved ones?
   - Have better health?
   - Set a good example for your children?
   - Protect your family from breathing other people's smoke?

   Really wanting to quit smoking is very important to how much success you will have in quitting.

3. Know that it will take commitment and effort to quit smoking. Nearly all smokers have some feelings of nicotine withdrawal when they try to quit. Nicotine is addictive. Knowing this will help you deal with withdrawal symptoms that can occur, such as bad moods and really wanting to smoke.

   There are many ways smokers quit, including using nicotine replacement products (gum and patches) or FDA-approved, non-nicotine cessation medications. Some people do not experience any withdrawal symptoms. For most people, symptoms only last a few days to a couple of weeks. Take quitting one day at a time, even one minute at a time—whatever you need to succeed.

4. Get help if you want it. Smokers can receive free resources and assistance to help them quit by calling the 1-800-QUIT-NOW quitline (1-800-784-8669) or by visiting CDC's *Tips From Former Smokers*. Your health care providers are also a good source for help and support.

   Concerned about weight gain? It's a common concern, but not everyone gains weight when they stop smoking. Learn ways to help you control your weight as you quit smoking.

5. Remember this good news! More than half of all adult smokers have quit, and you can, too. Millions of people have learned to face life without a cigarette. Quitting smoking is the single most important step you can take to protect your health and the health of your family.

Follow These Tips To Get The Support You Need:

- **Surround Yourself With People You Trust**

  Think of the people you trust the most—people you can talk to about anything and who have been there for you when you needed them. They could be friends, significant others, parents, co-workers, or other family members. Whoever they are, spend more time with them.

Tip: Bring friends along for your daily activities. Grab lunch with a friend, get a group together to go shopping, or meet up at a sporting event.

- **Focus On People Who Can Help**

  If a friendship doesn't feel right anymore, it might be time to let it go. Don't be afraid to try a little distance with people who aren't giving you the support you need. Letting go can be hard, but it is sometimes for the best.

  Tip: Focus your energy on spending time with people who make you feel good about yourself and want you to succeed.

- **Invest In Your Relationships**

  Make a point to invest time and effort in important relationships. People are more willing to provide support when they know you are there for them. You will also feel more comfortable calling on them for support if the relationship is strong.

  Tip: Go to that movie your friend really wants to see, even if it's not your top choice. Or go out of your way to call a friend just to chat and see how things are going.

- **Ask For Help**

  You might like to solve problems on your own, but the truth is we all need a little help from time to time. Go ahead and ask the people you trust. It doesn't mean you're weak. Your true friends will be there, ready and willing to help.

  Tip: Not sure how to ask? Send a text or email to get the conversation started (e.g., I want to quit smoking. Can you help me?). Know an ex-smoker? Ask them why and how they quit.

- **Be Specific About Your Wants**

  Your friends and family won't always be able to predict what you need during your quit. Be specific about what support you want (and don't want). Try to be nice about it. They are just trying to do what is best for you.

  Tip: Feeling stressed after a long day at work and craving a cigarette? Tell a friend and ask them to help plan a smokefree night out to distract you.

- **Say Thank You**

  Don't let acts of kindness go unnoticed. Tell your friends you appreciate them, whether you speak it, text it, or show it with your actions. Saying thanks doesn't take a lot of time, so do it in the moment before you forget.

Tip: Have a friend who gave up their last piece of gum to help you beat a cigarette craving? Buy some gum and give it to them with a note that says, "Thanks for helping me stay quit!"

- **Avoid Stressful Situations**

  Steer clear of the things that add unneeded stress to your day and look for more positive things to do.

  Tip: Identify what stresses you out and come up with ways to deal with that stress. Stress can make you feel like you want to smoke. Ask friends and family to be aware of your stressors. They can help make your life easier during your quit.

- **Grow Your Social Circle**

  Give your social circle a boost by connecting with other people who share your interests. Start by thinking about the things you like to do. Then look for ways to get more involved in them. Get talking with the people around you, and chances are, you'll find you have stuff in common.

  Tip: Strike up a conversation with someone new at work, join an intramural sport league, or volunteer. You never know who you will meet!

- **Be Approachable**

  How you present yourself to others is a big part of branching out and strengthening friendships. Make yourself approachable by making eye contact when talking with others. Smile. Sit and stand straight. Give compliments. People will be drawn to your confidence and positive attitude.

  Tip: Say hi and smile to co-workers as you pass them at work, compliment a family member on how great their shirt looks, or tell your friend you like their new haircut.

- **Be Hands-On**

  Don't wait around for others to come to you. Create opportunities to spend time with friends by suggesting things to do. Join in conversations and give your opinion.

  Tip: Reach out to the people you care about. Have lunch with a co-worker or friend. Invite friends over to your place for a game night.

- **Listen**

  Listening is a great way to strengthen and build friendships. Get people to open up by asking questions that can't be answered in just one word, like yes or no. Let them talk. Resist the urge to interrupt with your own comments and stories.

Tip: Are your friend's eyes glazing over when you talk? Take a breath and give them a chance to say something. Ask what they think of a new song you heard or if they have any plans for the weekend.

- **Support Others**

Support is a two-way street. If you want others to be there for you, you have to be there for them, too. Check in with your friends and help them out when you can. Sometimes small favors mean the most.

Tip: Do something small to brighten someone's day. Make a friend smile by emailing or texting them a joke, get someone a small treat for their birthday, or call a family member to see how they are doing.

Part Four
Marijuana

Chapter 24
What Is Marijuana?

Marijuana

Also known as: "weed," "pot," "bud," "grass," "herb," "Mary Jane," "MJ," "reefer," "skunk," "boom," "gangster," "kif," "chronic," and "ganja."

Marijuana is a mixture of the dried and shredded leaves, stems, seeds, and flowers of *Cannabis sativa*—the hemp plant. The mixture can be green, brown, or gray. Stronger forms of the drug include sinsemilla (sin-seh-me-yah), hashish ("hash" for short), and hash oil.

Of the approximately 400 chemicals in marijuana, delta-9-tetrahydrocannabinol, known as THC, is responsible for many of the drug's psychotropic (mind-altering) effects. It's this chemical that changes how the brain works, distorting how the mind perceives the world.

Smoked Marijuana Is Not Medicine

In 1970, Congress enacted laws against marijuana based in part on its conclusion that marijuana has no scientifically proven medical value. Likewise, the U.S. Food and Drug Administration (FDA), which is responsible for approving drugs as safe and effective medicine, has thus far declined to approve smoked marijuana for any condition or disease. Indeed, the FDA has noted that "there is currently sound evidence that smoked marijuana is harmful," and "that no sound scientific studies support medical use of marijuana for treatment in the United States, and no animal or human data support the safety or efficacy of marijuana for general medical use."

The United States Supreme Court has also declined to carve out an exception for marijuana under a theory of medical viability. In 2001, for example, the Supreme Court decided

About This Chapter: Information in this chapter is excerpted from "Marijuana," National Institute on Drug Abuse (NIDA), October 23, 2015.

that a 'medical necessity' defense against prosecution was unavailable to defendants because Congress had purposely placed marijuana into Schedule I, which enumerates those controlled substances without any medical benefits.

Legal Issues

It is illegal to buy, sell, or carry marijuana under federal law. The federal government considers marijuana a Schedule I substance—having no medicinal uses and high risk for abuse. However, across the United States, marijuana state laws for adult use are changing. As of 2014, 23 states and the District of Columbia have passed laws allowing the use of marijuana as a treatment for certain medical conditions.

In addition, four states and the District of Columbia have legalized marijuana for adult recreational use. Because of concerns over the possible harm to the developing teen brain and the risk of driving under the influence, marijuana use by people under age 21 is prohibited in all states.

Strength And Potency

The amount of THC in marijuana has increased over the past few decades—from an average of about 4 percent for marijuana and 7.5 percent for sinsemilla in the early 1990s to almost 10 percent for marijuana and 16 percent for sinsemilla in 2013. Scientists don't yet know what this increase in potency means for a person's health. It could be that users take in higher amounts of THC, or they may adjust how they consume marijuana (like smoke or eat less) to compensate for the greater potency.

Hash Oil

The honey-like resin from the marijuana plant has 3 to 5 times more THC than the plant itself. Smoking it (also called "dabbing") can potentially lead to dangerous levels of intoxication requiring emergency treatment. People have been burned in fires and explosions caused by attempts to extract hash oil using butane (lighter fluid).

How Is Marijuana Used?

Marijuana is commonly smoked using pipes, water pipes called "bongs," or hand-rolled cigarettes called "joints" or "nails." It is sometimes also combined with tobacco in partially hollowed-out cigars, known as "blunts." Recently vaporizers, that use heat without burning to produce a vapor, have increased in popularity. Marijuana can also be brewed as tea or mixed with food, sometimes called edibles.

In addition, concentrated resins containing high doses of marijuana's active ingredients, including honey-like "hash oil," waxy "budder," and hard amber-like "shatter," are increasingly popular among both recreational and medical users.

Does Marijuana Make You More Creative? What Does Science Say?

Many studies over the years have found that marijuana indeed makes users perceive themselves as having more creative thoughts and ideas—which would help explain why so many artists and musicians tout its benefits. But perception isn't always the same as reality—and we know that marijuana alters perceptions. In fact, the research on cannabis and creativity suggests that even if users feel more creative, it's actually an illusion. People may even be less creative after using it.

For example, a new study of almost 60 cannabis users in The Netherlands looked at the effects of the drug on a measure of creativity called divergent thinking—which means the ability to brainstorm, think flexibly, and come up with original solutions to problems. After inhaling a high or low dose of vaporized cannabis or a vapor with the same odor and taste but no THC (the chemical that causes the high), the participants took a test that asked them to come up with as many creative uses for two common items (like a pen or a shoe) as they could.

The results surprised even the researchers: Low doses of cannabis did not have any effect on the participants' ability to think creatively, compared to not taking cannabis. And high doses actually lowered their creativity—by a lot.

It seems that feeling creative and being creative really aren't the same thing.

Yet it is also true that your expectations about a drug do matter. Different studies have shown that people who are unknowingly given a placebo instead of a drug (or alcohol) will act or perform in ways that correspond to how they expect the drug to affect them.

Marijuana on Your Mind

One study, for example, found that regular marijuana users who ate biscuits containing marijuana were less creative than a control group who didn't eat any biscuits, and that both of those groups were less creative than a group who ate biscuits they thought contained marijuana but were actually a placebo.

It goes to show that your mind, including your beliefs about drugs, have a lot more power than you think. You don't have to take the drug to get the effect you expect—in fact it works best if you don't!

Can You Get Addicted To Marijuana?

Yes, marijuana is addictive. A user may feel the urge to smoke marijuana again and again to re-create the "high." Repeated use could lead to addiction—which means the person has trouble controlling their drug use and often cannot stop even though they want to.

It is estimated that about 1 in 6 people who start using as a teen, and 25% to 50% percent of those who use it every day, become addicted to marijuana. What causes one person to become addicted to marijuana and another not to depends on many factors—including their family history (genetics), the age they start using, whether they also use other drugs, their family and friend relationships, and whether they take part in positive activities like school or sports (environment).

People who use marijuana may also feel withdrawal when they stop using the drug. Withdrawal symptoms may include:

- Irritability

- Sleeplessness

- Lack of appetite, which can lead to weight loss

- Anxiety

- Drug cravings

These effects can last for several days to a few weeks after drug use is stopped. Relapse (returning to the drug after you've quit) is common during this period because people also crave the drug to relieve these symptoms.

Marijuana Use Among Youth Is Rising As Perception Of Risk Decreases

- Historical drug trends from the national *Monitoring the Future* Survey show that when antidrug attitudes soften there is a corresponding increase in drug use in the coming years. An adolescent's perception of risks associated with substance use is an important determinant of whether he or she engages in substance abuse. Youths who perceive high risk of harm are less likely to use drugs than youths who perceive low risk of harm.

- The *2011 Monitoring the Future* Survey noted that daily or near daily marijuana use, defined as use on 20 or more occasions in the past 30 days rose significantly in the 8th, 10th, and 12th grades in 2010 and rose slightly higher again in 2011. This translates to one in every 15 high school seniors smoking pot on a daily or near daily basis, the highest rates that has been seen in 30 years—since 1981.

- One explanation for the resurgence is that perceived risk of harm from use of the marijuana, even on a daily basis, has fallen sharply for marijuana over the past five years, and it declined in all three grades in 2011. Teens' disapproval of marijuana use also has fallen over the past three or four years, suggesting a lowering of peer norms against use.

Chapter 25

Marijuana Abuse Among U.S. Teens

What Is The Scope Of Marijuana Use In The United States?

Marijuana is the most commonly used illicit drug (19.8 million past-month users) according to the 2013 National Survey on Drug Use and Health (NSDUH). That year, marijuana was used by 81.0 percent of current illicit drug users (defined as having used a drug at some time in the 30 days before the survey) and was the only drug used by 64.7 percent of them.

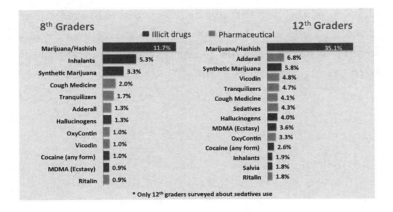

Figure 25.1. Top Drugs Among 8th And 12th Graders (2012)

About This Chapter: Information in this chapter is excerpted from "Marijuana," NIDA for Teens, National Institute on Drug Abuse (NIDA), September 2015.

Marijuana Use Adolescents And Young Adults

Marijuana use is widespread among adolescents and young adults. According to the *Monitoring the Future* survey—an annual survey of drug use and attitudes among the Nation's middle and high school students—most measures of marijuana use by 8th-, 10th-, and 12th-graders have held steady in the past few years following several years of increase in the previous decade.

Teens' perceptions of the risks of marijuana use have steadily declined over the past decade, possibly related to increasing public debate about legalizing or loosening restrictions on marijuana for medicinal and recreational use. In 2014, 11.7 percent of 8th-graders reported marijuana use in the past year and 6.5 percent were current users.

Among 10th-graders, 27.3 percent had used marijuana in the past year and 16.6 percent were current users. Rates of use among 12th-graders were higher still: 35.1 percent had used marijuana during the year prior to the survey and 21.2 percent were current users; 5.8 percent said they used marijuana daily or near-daily.

Medical emergencies possibly related to marijuana use have also increased. The Drug Abuse Warning Network (DAWN), a system for monitoring the health impact of drugs, estimated that in 2011, there were nearly 456,000 drug-related emergency department visits in the United States in which marijuana use was mentioned in the medical record (a 21 percent increase over 2009). About two-thirds of patients were male and 13 percent were between the ages of 12 and 17. It is unknown whether this increase is due to increased use, increased *potency* of marijuana (amount of THC it contains), or other factors. It should be noted, however, that mentions of marijuana in medical records do not necessarily indicate that these emergencies were directly related to marijuana intoxication.

Chapter 26
Health Effects Of Marijuana

How Does Marijuana Affect The Brain?

The main chemical in marijuana that affects the brain is delta-9-tetrahydrocannabinol (THC). When marijuana is smoked, THC quickly passes from the lungs into the bloodstream, which carries it to organs throughout the body, including the brain. As it enters the brain, THC attaches to cells, or neurons, with specific kinds of receptors called cannabinoid receptors. Normally, these receptors are activated by chemicals that occur naturally in the body. They are part of a communication network in the brain called the endocannabinoid system. This system is important in normal brain development and function.

Most of the cannabinoid receptors are found in parts of the brain that influence pleasure, memory, thinking, concentration, sensory and time perception, and coordinated movement. Marijuana triggers an increase in the activity of the endocannabinoid system, which causes the release of dopamine in the brain's reward centers, creating the pleasurable feelings or "high." Other effects include changes in perceptions and mood, lack of coordination, difficulty with thinking and problem solving, and disrupted learning and memory.

- **Learning and memory.** The hippocampus plays a critical role in certain types of learning. Disrupting its normal functioning can lead to problems studying, learning new things, and recalling recent events. A recent study followed people from age 13 to 38 and found that those who used marijuana a lot in their teens had up to an 8 point drop in IQ, even if they quit in adulthood.

About This Chapter: Information in this chapter is excerpted from "Marijuana," NIDA for Teens, National Institute on Drug Abuse (NIDA), October 23, 2015; and information from "Marijuana Use & Educational Outcomes," National Institute on Drug Abuse (NIDA), November 2014.

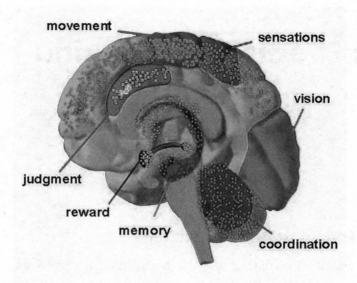

Figure 26.1. Marijuana's Effect on Brain. Certain parts of the brain have a lot of cannabinoid receptors. These areas are the hippocampus, the cerebellum, the basal ganglia, and the cerebral cortex. The functions that these brain areas control are the ones most affected by marijuana.

- **Coordination.** THC affects the cerebellum, the area of our brain that controls balance and coordination, and the basal ganglia, another part of the brain that helps control movement. These effects can influence performance in such activities as sports, driving, and video games.

- **Judgment.** Since THC affects areas of the frontal cortex involved in decision making, using it can cause you to do things you might not do when you are not under the influence of drugs—such as engaging in risky sexual behavior, which can lead to sexually transmitted diseases (STDs) like HIV, the virus that causes AIDS—or getting in a car with someone who's been drinking or is high on marijuana.

When marijuana is smoked, its effects begin almost immediately and can last from 1 to 3 hours. Decision making, concentration, and memory can suffer for days after use, especially in regular users.

If marijuana is consumed in foods or beverages, the effects of THC appear later—usually in 30 minutes to 1 hour—but can last over 4 hours.

Long-term, regular use of marijuana—starting in the teen years—may impair brain development and lower IQ, meaning the brain may not reach its full potential.

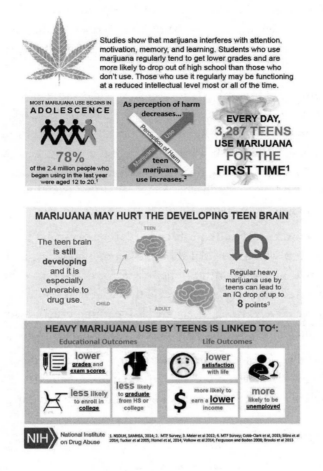

Figure 26.2. Marijuana Use And Educational Outcomes

What Are The Other Effects Of Marijuana?

The changes that take place in the brain when a person uses marijuana can cause serious health problems and affect a person's daily life.

Effects On Health

Within a few minutes after inhaling marijuana smoke, a person's heart rate speeds up, the bronchial passages (the pipes that let air in and out of your lungs) relax and become enlarged, and blood vessels in the eyes expand, making the eyes look red. While these and other effects seem harmless, they can take a toll on the body.

- **Increased heart rate.** When someone uses marijuana, heart rate—normally 70 to 80 beats per minute—may increase by 20 to 50 beats per minute or, in some cases, even double. This effect can be greater if other drugs are taken with marijuana. The increased heart rate forces the heart to work extra hard to keep up.

- **Respiratory (lung and breathing) problems.** Smoke from marijuana irritates the lungs, causing breathing and lung problems among regular users similar to those experienced by people who smoke tobacco—like a daily cough and a greater risk for lung infections such as pneumonia. While research has not found a strong association between marijuana and lung cancer, many people who smoke marijuana also smoke cigarettes, which do cause cancer. And, some studies have suggested that smoking marijuana could make it harder to quit cigarette smoking.

- **Increased risk for mental health problems.** Marijuana use has been linked with depression and anxiety, as well as suicidal thoughts among adolescents. In addition, research has suggested that in people with a genetic risk for developing schizophrenia, smoking marijuana during adolescence may increase the risk for developing psychosis and developing it at an earlier age. Researchers are still learning exactly what the relationship is between these mental health problems and marijuana use.

- **Increased risk of problems for an unborn baby.** Pregnant women who use marijuana may risk changing the developing brain of the unborn baby. These changes could contribute to problems with attention, memory, and problem solving.

Effects On School And Social Life

The effects of marijuana on the brain and body can have a serious impact on a person's life.

- **Reduced school performance.** Students who smoke marijuana tend to get lower grades and are more likely to drop out of high school than their peers who do not use. The effects of marijuana on attention, memory, and learning can last for days or weeks. These effects have a negative impact on learning and motivation. In fact, people who use marijuana regularly for a long time are less satisfied with their lives and have more problems with friends and family compared to people who do not use marijuana.

- **Impaired driving.** It is unsafe to drive while under the influence of marijuana. Marijuana affects a number of skills required for safe driving—alertness, concentration, coordination, and reaction time—so it's not safe to drive high or to ride with someone who's been smoking. Marijuana makes it hard to judge distances and react to signals and sounds on the road. Marijuana is the most common illegal drug involved in auto fatalities. High school seniors who smoke marijuana are 2 times more likely to receive a traffic ticket and 65% more likely to get into an accident than those who don't smoke. In 2011, among 12th graders, 12.5% reported that within the past 2 weeks they had driven after using marijuana. And combining marijuana with drinking even a small amount of alcohol greatly increases driving danger, more than either drug alone.

- **Potential gateway to other drugs.** Most young people who use marijuana do not go on to use other drugs. However, those who use marijuana, alcohol, or tobacco during their teen years are more likely to use other illegal drugs. It isn't clear why some people do go on to try other drugs, but researchers have a few theories. The human brain continues to develop into the early 20s. Exposure to addictive substances, including marijuana, may cause changes to the developing brain that make other drugs more appealing. Animal research supports this possibility—for example, early exposure to marijuana makes opioid drugs (like Vicodin or heroin) more pleasurable. In addition, someone who uses marijuana is more likely to be in contact with people who use and sell other drugs, increasing the risk for being encouraged or tempted to try them. Finally, people at high risk for using drugs may use marijuana first because it is easy to get (like cigarettes and alcohol).

Secondhand Marijuana Smoke

In concerts, at house parties, even in the hallway of apartment buildings, you may have come into contact and been exposed to secondhand marijuana smoke.

In situations like these, people often worry how breathing someone else's marijuana smoke affects them. A couple of common questions and the answers may help you see through the fog of this smoky situation.

Can you get high from inhaling secondhand marijuana smoke?

Probably not.

You may have heard the phrase "contact high," about someone breathing secondhand marijuana smoke and feeling a buzz. There have been studies that show in extreme conditions, with lots of smoke blown directly into your face, you can feel the high and it can even show up in a urine test. But this is not a normal circumstance.

Studies show that very little THC is exhaled back into the air when a smoker exhales. So little, in fact, that if you sat in a room while people exhaled the smoke of four marijuana cigarettes (sometimes called joints) in one hour, you wouldn't get high. You would have to be trapped in a room breathing the smoke of 16 burning joints before it you started to show signs of being high.

What are the health effects of inhaling secondhand marijuana smoke?

Researchers are still working to figure this out. We still don't know how a person is affected if they live with a regular marijuana smoker. We also don't know how higher amounts of THC in today's marijuana cigarettes affects secondhand smoke.

A recent study on rats suggests that secondhand marijuana smoke can do as much damage to your heart and blood vessels as secondhand tobacco smoke. But that study has not yet been done on humans.

We also know marijuana smoke contains harmful and cancer-causing chemicals, the same way tobacco smoke does. But we still don't know how it affects a person's health in the long run. Lots more research still needs to be done.

Can You Die If You Use Marijuana?

It is very unlikely for a person to overdose and die from marijuana use. However, people can and do injure themselves and die because of marijuana's effects on judgment, perception, and coordination, for example, when driving under the influence of the drug. Also, people can experience extreme anxiety (panic attacks) or psychotic reactions (where they lose touch with reality and may become paranoid).

Chapter 27

Marijuana Abuse And Mental Illness

Is There A Link Between Marijuana Use And Mental Illness?

Several studies have linked marijuana use to increased risk for mental illnesses, including psychosis (schizophrenia), depression, and anxiety, but whether and to what extent it actually causes these conditions is not always easy to determine. The amount of drug used, the age at first use, and genetic vulnerability have all been shown to influence this relationship.

Marijuana And Psychosis

You may know that smoking marijuana can pose risks for a person's physical health and brain development, especially for teens. But did you know that, for some people, it carries risks for their mental health, too?

We don't just mean short-term memory problems or poor judgment—those can happen for anybody who smokes marijuana. We're talking about serious mental illness.

Researchers have found that some marijuana users have an increased risk for psychosis, a serious mental disorder where people have false thoughts (delusions) or see or hear things that aren't there (hallucinations). But there is still a lot to learn about whether marijuana use may lead to this loss of touch with reality, or if having a mental illness makes people more likely to use marijuana. And as with other drugs, things like the age of users, how early they started

About This Chapter: Information in this chapter is excerpted from "Marijuana," National Institute on Drug Abuse (NIDA), September 2015; and information from "Marijuana & Psychosis," National Institute on Drug Abuse (NIDA), October 30, 2015.

smoking pot, the amount of the drug they used, and their genetics all could make a difference in whether or not long-term problems develop.

It's not your jeans that matter—it's your genes

Regular marijuana users with a specific version of a particular gene, AKT1, are at a greater risk of developing psychosis than those who smoke it less often or not at all. How much greater? For people who smoke marijuana daily, the risk is up to seven times greater.

The reason is that the AKT1 gene affects how much dopamine is released in your brain. Dopamine is one of our brain's "feel-good" chemicals; it affects important brain functions such as behavior, motivation, and reward. When your brain releases dopamine (for example, after a beautiful bike ride or when you eat a delicious piece of chocolate), the release "teaches" your brain to seek out the same experience (reward) again. Some researchers believe that changes in dopamine levels are linked to psychosis.

Another study found that adults who used marijuana when they were teenagers and who carried a specific form of another gene for the enzyme COMT (which also impacts dopamine signaling) were at a higher risk of becoming psychotic.

Are you at risk?

Right now, unless you've had your DNA tested for those specific genes, you don't know. Many health professionals believe that in the future most of us will know much more about our genetic makeup, but for now and for regular marijuana users, it's an unknown risk—and you won't know until you've developed an addiction.

Even if you don't have those specific genes, there's still a risk

A psychotic event can even happen to pot smokers without these specific genes that put them at risk for long-term serious mental illness. Although rare, marijuana-induced psychosis is becoming more common as people use higher potency forms, including edibles and oil extracts.

The bottom line? It's important to know *all* the risks that can come with using marijuana.

Chapter 28
Spice (Synthetic Marijuana)

"Spice" refers to a wide variety of herbal mixtures that produce experiences similar to marijuana (cannabis) and that are marketed as "safe," legal alternatives to that drug. Sold under many names, including K2, fake weed, Yucatan Fire, Skunk, Moon Rocks, and others—and labeled "not for human consumption"—these products contain dried, shredded plant material and chemical additives that are responsible for their psychoactive (mind-altering) effects.

For several years, Spice mixtures have been easy to purchase in head shops and gas stations and via the Internet. Because the chemicals used in Spice have a high potential for abuse and no medical benefit, the Drug Enforcement Administration (DEA) has designated the five active chemicals most frequently found in Spice as Schedule I controlled substances, making it illegal to sell, buy, or possess them. Manufacturers of Spice products attempt to evade these legal restrictions by substituting different chemicals in their mixtures, while the DEA continues to monitor the situation and evaluate the need for updating the list of banned cannabinoids.

Spice products are popular among young people; of the illicit drugs most used by high-school seniors, they are second only to marijuana. (They are more popular among boys than girls — in 2012, nearly twice as many male 12th graders reported past-year use of synthetic marijuana as females in the same age group.) Easy access and the misperception that Spice products are "natural" and therefore harmless have likely contributed to their popularity. Another selling point is that the chemicals used in Spice are not easily detected in standard drug tests.

About This Chapter: Information in this chapter is excerpted from "DrugFacts: K2/Spice (Synthetic Marijuana)," National Institute on Drug Abuse (NIDA), December 2012.

False Advertising

Labels on Spice products often claim that they contain "natural" psycho-active material taken from a variety of plants. Spice products do contain dried plant material, but chemical analyses show that their active ingredients are *synthetic* (or designer) cannabinoid compounds.

How Is Spice Abused?

Some Spice products are sold as "incense," but they more closely resemble potpourri. Like marijuana, Spice is abused mainly by smoking. Sometimes Spice is mixed with marijuana or is prepared as an herbal infusion for drinking.

How Does Spice Affect The Brain?

Spice users report experiences similar to those produced by marijuana—elevated mood, relaxation, and altered perception—and in some cases the effects are even stronger than those of marijuana. Some users report psychotic effects like extreme anxiety, paranoia, and hallucinations.

So far, there have been no scientific studies of Spice's effects on the human brain, but we do know that the cannabinoid compounds found in Spice products act on the same cell receptors as THC, the primary psychoactive component of marijuana. Some of the compounds found in Spice, however, bind more strongly to those receptors, which could lead to a much more powerful and unpredictable effect. Because the chemical composition of many products sold as Spice is unknown, it is likely that some varieties also contain substances that could cause dramatically different effects than the user might expect.

What Are The Other Health Effects Of Spice?

Spice abusers who have been taken to Poison Control Centers report symptoms that include rapid heart rate, vomiting, agitation, confusion, and hallucinations. Spice can also raise blood pressure and cause reduced blood supply to the heart (myocardial ischemia), and in a few cases it has been associated with heart attacks. Regular users may experience withdrawal and addiction symptoms.

We still do not know all the ways Spice may affect human health or how toxic it may be, but one public health concern is that there may be harmful heavy metal residues in Spice mixtures. Without further analyses, it is difficult to determine whether this concern is justified.

Chapter 29
Medical Marijuana And The Law

What Is Medical Marijuana?

The term *medical marijuana* refers to using the whole unprocessed marijuana plant or its basic extracts to treat a disease or symptom. The U.S. Food and Drug Administration (FDA) has not recognized or approved the marijuana plant as medicine.

However, scientific study of the chemicals in marijuana, called *cannabinoids*, has led to two FDA-approved medications that contain cannabinoid chemicals in pill form. Continued research may lead to more medications.

Because the marijuana plant contains chemicals that may help treat a range of illnesses or symptoms, many people argue that it should be legal for medical purposes. In fact, a growing number of states have legalized marijuana for medical use.

Why Is The Federal Government Opposed To Medical Marijuana?

It is the federal government's position that marijuana be subjected to the same rigorous clinical trials and scientific scrutiny that the U.S. Food and Drug Administration (FDA) applies to all other new medications, a comprehensive process designed to ensure the highest standards of safety and efficacy.

It is this rigorous FDA approval process, not popular vote, that should determine what is, and what is not medicine. The raw marijuana plant, which contains nearly 500 different chemical compounds, has not met the safety and efficacy standards of this process. Accord-

About This Chapter: Information in this chapter is excerpted from "DrugFacts: Is Marijuana Medicine?" National Institute on Drug Abuse (NIDA), July 2015; and information from "Answers to Frequently Asked Questions about Marijuana," WhiteHouse.gov, April 20, 2014; and information from "Marijuana Resource Center: State Laws Related to Marijuana," WhiteHouse.gov, April 30, 2015.

ing to the Institute of Medicine (IOM), smoking marijuana is an unsafe delivery system that produces harmful effects.

The FDA has, however, recognized and approved the medicinal use of isolated components of the marijuana plant and related synthetic compounds. Dronabinol is one such synthetically produced compound, used in the FDA-approved medicine Marinol, which is already legally available for prescription by physicians whose patients suffer from nausea and vomiting related to cancer chemotherapy and wasting (severe weight loss) associated with AIDS. Another FDA-approved medicine, Cesamet, contains the active ingredient Nabilone, which has a chemical structure similar to THC, the active ingredient of marijuana. And Sativex, an oromucosal spray approved in Canada, the UK, and other parts of Europe for the treatment of multiple sclerosis spasticity and cancer pain, is currently in late-stage clinical trials with the FDA. It combines THC and another active ingredient in marijuana, cannabidiol (CBD), and provides therapeutic benefits without the "high" from the drug.

State Laws Related To Marijuana

Since 1996, 23 states and Washington, DC have passed laws allowing smoked marijuana to be used for a variety of medical conditions. It is important to recognize that these state marijuana laws do not change the fact that using marijuana continues to be an offense under federal law. Nor do these state laws change the criteria or process for FDA approval of safe and effective medications.

These state laws vary greatly in their criteria and implementation, and many states are experiencing vigorous internal debates about the safety, efficacy, and legality of their marijuana laws. Many local governments are even creating zoning and enforcement ordinances that prevent marijuana dispensaries from operating in their communities. Regulation of marijuana for purported medical use may also exist at the county and city level, in addition to state laws.

Voters in Alaska, Colorado, Oregon, and Washington state also passed initiatives legalizing the sale and distribution of marijuana for adults 21 and older under state law. District of Columbia voters approved Initiative 71, which permits adults 21 years of age or older to grow and possess (but not sell) limited amounts of marijuana. There are critical differences in marijuana laws from one state, county, or city to another. For more information, refer to the the National Conference of State Legislatures (NCSL).

It is important to note that Congress has determined that marijuana is a dangerous drug and that the illegal distribution and sale of marijuana is a serious crime. The Department of Justice (DOJ) is committed to enforcing the Controlled Substances Act (CSA) consistent with these determinations. On August 29, 2013, DOJ issued guidance to federal prosecutors concerning marijuana enforcement under the CSA.

Does The Federal Government Block Medical Marijuana Research?

No. The federal government supports studies that meet accepted scientific standards and successfully compete for research funding based on peer review and potential public health significance. The federal government will continue to call for research that may result in the development of products to effectively treat debilitating diseases and chronic pain. Already, there are DEA-registered researchers eligible to study marijuana, and currently there are Phase III clinical trials underway examining the medical utility of a spray containing a mixture of two active ingredients in marijuana (i.e., Sativex). A number of government-funded research projects involving marijuana or its component compounds have been completed or are currently in progress. of abuse potential, physical/psychological effects, adverse effects, therapeutic potential, and detection. It is worth noting that a number of these studies include research with smoked marijuana on human subjects. The federal government is committed to the highest standards for basic science and clinical research on wide array of substances, including marijuana, that show promise.

Part Five
Abuse Of Legally Available Substances

Chapter 30

Facts About The Abuse Of Prescription And Over-The-Counter (OTC) Medications

What Is Prescription Drug Abuse?

Prescription drug abuse is when someone takes a medication that was prescribed for someone else or takes their own prescription in a way not intended by a doctor or for a different reason—like to get high.

It has become a big health issue because of the dangers, particularly the danger of abusing prescription pain medications. For teens, it is a growing problem:

- After marijuana and alcohol, prescription drugs are the most commonly abused substances by Americans age 14 and older.

- Teens abuse prescription drugs for a number of reasons, such as to get high, to stop pain, or because they think it will help them with school work.

- Most teens get prescription drugs they abuse from friends and relatives, sometimes without the person knowing.

- Boys and girls tend to abuse some types of prescription drugs for different reasons. For example, boys are more likely to abuse prescription stimulants to get high, while girls tend to abuse them to stay alert or to lose weight.

About This Chapter: Information in this chapter is excerpted from "Prescription Drugs," NIDA for Teens, National Institute on Drug Abuse (NIDA), October 23, 2015; information from "Types of Prescription Drugs," NIDA for Teens, National Institute on Drug Abuse (NIDA), October 23, 2015; and information from "Surprising Facts," NIDA for Teens, National Institute on Drug Abuse (NIDA), October 26, 2015.

When prescription drugs are taken as directed, they are usually safe. It requires a trained health care clinician, such as a doctor or nurse, to determine if the benefits of taking the medication outweigh any risks for side effects. But when abused and taken in different amounts or for different purposes than as prescribed, they affect the brain and body in ways very similar to illicit drugs.

When prescription drugs are abused, they can be addictive and put the person at risk for other harmful health effects, such as overdose (especially when taken along with other drugs or alcohol). And, abusing prescription drugs is illegal—and that includes sharing prescriptions with family members or friends.

Types Of Prescription Drugs

Prescription Drugs Are Also Known As:

Opioids: Hillbilly heroin, oxy, OC, oxycotton, percs, happy pills, vikes

Depressants: barbs, reds, red birds, phennies, tooies, yellows, yellow jackets; candy, downers, sleeping pills, tranks; A-minus, zombie pills

Stimulants: Skippy, the smart drug, Vitamin R, bennies, black beauties, roses, hearts, speed, uppers

Prescription Painkillers

Prescription painkillers are powerful drugs that reduce pain. These drugs attach to particular sites in the brain called opioid receptors, which carry messages about pain.

With proper use of prescription painkillers, the pain messages sent to the brain are changed and are no longer perceived as painful. Patients who are prescribed painkillers for a long period of time may develop a "physical dependence" on them. This is not the same as addiction. Physical dependence happens because the body adapts to having the drug around, and when its use is stopped abruptly, the person can experience symptoms of withdrawal. That is why these drugs are carefully monitored and should be taken or stopped only under a doctor's orders.

Prescription painkillers can be highly addictive when used improperly—without a doctor's prescription or in doses higher than prescribed. Addiction means that a person will strongly crave the drug and continue to use it despite severe consequences to their health and their life. Prescription painkillers also affect the brain areas controlling respiration, and when used improperly (or mixed with other drugs) can cause a severe decrease in breathing that can lead to death.

Prescription Drugs For Sleep Disorders

Prescription drugs for sleep disorders increase levels of a neurotransmitter named gamma-aminobutyric acid (GABA). GABA sends messages that slow down bodily functions and make a person feel drowsy.

Prescription drugs for sleep disorders may have side effects, including headache, muscle aches, daytime sleepiness, trouble concentrating, and dizziness. Prescription drugs for sleep disorders should never be mixed with any other drugs that cause drowsiness, such as over-the-counter cold medicine, alcohol, or painkillers. If combined, they can slow a person's heart rate and respiration, which can be fatal.

Prescription Anti-Anxiety Drugs

Doctors may prescribe drugs to help people with anxiety disorders. Some anti-anxiety drugs affect the neurotransmitter GABA.

After taking anti-anxiety drugs for a long time and suddenly stopping, a person may experience withdrawal symptoms such as anxiety, shakiness, headache, dizziness, and, in extreme cases, seizures. Abusing prescription anti-anxiety drugs can result in addiction or overdose.

Prescription Stimulants

Prescription stimulants cause neurons to release two neurotransmitters: dopamine and norepinephrine. Dopamine carries messages in the brain about feeling good. Norepinephrine is a chemical in the brain that helps people pay attention and focus.

Doctors often prescribe stimulants to help people with attention-deficit hyperactivity disorder (ADHD). Many scientists believe that in people with ADHD, the dopamine system works slightly differently than in people without the disorder. Prescription stimulants can bring brain dopamine function back to normal and help people with ADHD focus better and pay more attention.

Stimulants can be addictive and dangerous when abused. In fact, abusing stimulants can cause chest pain, stomach aches, and feelings of fear or anger. They can also cause seizures and irregular heartbeats that can cause death.

Surprising Facts
- Prescription painkillers can cause nausea and vomiting.
- Mixing anti-anxiety or sleep disorder drugs with other drugs, particularly alcohol, can slow breathing, slow heart rate, and possibly lead to death.
- Abusing stimulants while taking a cold medicine with decongestants can cause dangerous increases in blood pressure and irregular heart rhythms.

But Aren't Prescription Drugs Safe?

Prescription drugs are often strong medications, which is why they require a prescription in the first place. When they are abused, they can be just as dangerous as drugs that are made illegally. Even when they are not abused, every medication has some risk for harmful effects, sometimes serious ones. Doctors consider the potential benefits and risks to each patient before prescribing medications and take into account a lot of different factors, described below. People who abuse drugs might not understand how these factors interact and put them at risk.

- **Personal information.** Doctors take into account a person's weight, how long they've been prescribed the medication, and what other medications they are taking. Someone abusing prescription drugs may overload their system or put themselves at risk for dangerous drug interactions that can cause seizures, coma, or even death.

- **Form and dose.** Doctors know how long it takes for a pill or capsule to dissolve in the stomach, release drugs to the blood, and reach the brain. When abused, prescription drugs may be taken in larger amounts or in ways that change the way the drug works in the body and brain, putting the person at greater risk for an overdose. For example, when people who abuse OxyContin crush and inhale the pills, a dose that normally works over the course of 12 hours hits the central nervous system all at once. This effect increases the risk for addiction and overdose.

- **Side effects.** Prescription drugs are designed to treat a specific illness or condition, but they often affect the body in other ways, some of which can be dangerous. These are called side effects. For example, OxyContin stops pain, but it also causes constipation and sleepiness. Stimulants, such as Adderall, increase a person's ability to pay attention, but they also raise blood pressure and heart rate, making the heart work harder. These side effects can be worse when prescription drugs are not taken as prescribed or are abused in combination with other substances—including alcohol, other prescription drugs, and even over-the-counter drugs, such as cold medicines. For instance, some people mix alcohol and depressants, like Valium, both of which can slow breathing. This combination could stop breathing altogether.

How Are Prescription Drugs Abused?

People abuse prescription drugs by taking medication in a way that is not intended, such as:

- **Taking someone else's prescription medication.** Even when someone takes another person's medication for its intended purposes (such as to relieve pain, to stay awake, or to fall asleep) it is considered abuse.

- **Taking a prescription medication in a way other than prescribed.** Taking your own prescription in a way that it is not meant to be taken is also abuse. This includes taking more of the medication than prescribed or changing its form—for example, breaking or crushing a pill or capsule and then snorting the powder.

- **Taking a prescription medication to get high.** Some types of prescription drugs also can produce pleasurable effects or "highs." Taking the medication only for the purpose of getting high is considered prescription drug abuse.

How Does Prescription Drug Abuse Affect Your Brain?

In the brain, neurotransmitters such as dopamine send messages by attaching to receptors on nearby cells. The actions of these neurotransmitters and receptors cause the effects from prescription drugs. Each class of prescription drugs works a bit differently in the brain:

- Prescription opioid pain medications bind to molecules on cells known as opioid receptors—the same receptors that respond to heroin. These receptors are found on nerve cells in many areas of the brain and body, especially in brain areas involved in the perception of pain and pleasure.

- Prescription stimulants, such as Ritalin, have similar effects to cocaine, by causing a buildup of dopamine and norepinephrine.

- Prescription depressants make a person feel calm and relaxed in the same manner as the club drugs GHB and rohypnol.

What Are The Other Effects Of Prescription Drugs?

Prescription drugs can cause dangerous short- and long-term health problems when they are not used as directed or when they are taken by someone other than the person they were prescribed for.

- Abusing opioids like oxycodone and codeine can cause you to feel sleepy, sick to your stomach, and constipated. At higher doses, opioids can make it hard to breathe properly and can cause overdose and death.

- Abusing stimulants like Adderall or Ritalin can make you feel paranoid (feeling like someone is going to harm you even though they aren't). It also can cause your body temperature to get dangerously high and make your heart beat too fast. This is especially likely if stimulants are taken in large doses or in ways other than swallowing a pill.

- Abusing depressants like barbiturates can cause slurred speech, shallow breathing, sleepiness, disorientation, and lack of coordination. People who abuse depressants regularly and then stop suddenly may experience seizures. At higher doses depressants can also cause overdose and death, especially when combined with alcohol.

In addition, abusing over-the-counter drugs that contain DXM can also produce very dangerous effects.

Abuse of any of these types of medications can lead to addiction. And, abusing any type of drug that causes changes in your mood, perceptions, and behavior can affect judgment and willingness to take risks—putting you at greater risk for HIV and other sexually transmitted diseases (STDs).

Prescription drugs can increase risk for health problems when combined with other prescription medications, over-the-counter medicines, illicit drugs, or alcohol. For example, combining opioids (painkillers) with alcohol can make breathing problems worse and can lead to death.

Can You Get Addicted To Prescription Drugs?

Yes, prescription drugs that affect the brain, including opioid painkillers, stimulants, and depressants, may cause physical dependence that can turn into addiction.

Dependence happens because the brain and body adapt to having drugs in the system for a while. A person may need larger doses of the drug to get the same initial effects. This is known as "tolerance." When drug use is stopped, withdrawal symptoms can occur. Dependence is not the same as addiction, but it can contribute to a person developing an addiction. It is one of the many reasons why a person should only take (and stop taking) prescription drugs under a doctor's care.

Carefully following the doctor's instructions for taking a medication can make it less likely that someone will develop dependence or addiction, because the medication is prescribed in amounts and forms that are considered appropriate for that person. However, dependence and addiction are still potential risks when taking certain types of prescription drugs. These risks should be carefully weighed against the benefits of the medication and patients should communicate any issues or concerns to their doctor as soon as they arise.

Medications that affect the brain can change the way it works—especially when they are taken over an extended period of time or with escalating doses. They can change the reward system, making it harder for a person to feel good without the drug and possibly leading to intense cravings, which make it hard to stop using. This is no different from what can happen when someone takes illicit drugs—addiction is a real possibility. When a person is addicted to a drug, finding and using that drug can begin to feel like the most important thing—more important than family, friends, school, sports, or health.

Other kinds of medications that do not act in the brain, such as antibiotics used to treat infections, are not addictive.

Can You Die If You Abuse Prescription Drugs?

Yes. More than half of the drug overdose deaths in the United States each year are caused by prescription drug abuse. In the last decade, the number of deaths from abuse of prescription drugs has increased dramatically.

In 2001, 9,197 people died from a prescription drug overdose; that number jumped to 22,810 in 2011. The trend holds true for young people—765 young people died as a result of a prescription drug overdose in 2001. In contrast, more than 2.5 times that—1,950 young people—died from an overdose in 2011. Close to 17,000 (74%) of all deaths from abuse of prescription drugs involved opioid painkillers and more than 6,800 (30%) involved a class of depressants known as benzodiazepines (some deaths include more than one type of drug).

Mixing different types of prescription drugs can be particularly dangerous. For example, benzodiazepines interact with opioids and increase the risk of overdose.

Chapter 31

Trends In The Abuse Of Prescription And OTC Medications Among U.S. Teens

How Many People Abuse Prescription Drugs?

According to results from the 2010 National Survey on Drug Use and Health (NSDUH), an estimated 2.4 million Americans used prescription drugs nonmedically for the first time within the past year, which averages to approximately 6,600 initiates per day. More than one-half were females and about a third were aged 12 to 17. Although prescription drug abuse affects many Americans, certain populations, such as youth, older adults, and women, may be at particular risk.

Prescription and over-the-counter (OTC) drugs are the most commonly abused substances by high school seniors (after marijuana and alcohol). Some medications have psychoactive (mind-altering) properties and, because of that, are sometimes abused—taken for reasons or in ways not intended by a doctor, or taken by someone with no prescription.

About This Chapter: Information in this chapter is excerpted from "Trends In Prescription Drug Abuse," National Institute on Drug Abuse (NIDA), November 2014; information from "During National Drug Facts Week: The Truth About Prescription Drugs," NIDA for Teens, National Institute on Drug Abuse (NIDA), February 1, 2013; and information from "Drug Overdoses Kill More Than Cars, Guns, and Falling," NIDA for Teens, National Institute on Drug Abuse (NIDA), September 18, 2014.

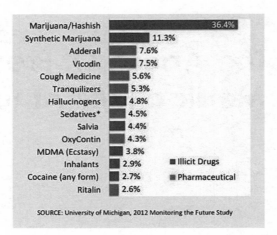

Marijuana/Hashish	36.4%
Synthetic Marijuana	11.3%
Adderall	7.6%
Vicodin	7.5%
Cough Medicine	5.6%
Tranquilizers	5.3%
Hallucinogens	4.8%
Sedatives+	4.5%
Salvia	4.4%
OxyContin	4.3%
MDMA (Ecstasy)	3.8%
Inhalants	2.9%
Cocaine (any form)	2.7%
Ritalin	2.6%

■ Illicit Drugs
■ Pharmaceutical

SOURCE: University of Michigan, 2012 Monitoring the Future Study

Figure 31.1. This figure shows results of 2012 *Monitoring the Future* survey, which looks at drug use among 8th, 10th, and 12th graders. Teens fill out the questionnaires themselves, privately, in their classrooms.

People often think that prescription and OTC drugs are safer than illicit drugs, but that's only true when they are taken exactly as prescribed and for the purpose intended. When abused, prescription and OTC drugs can be addictive and lead to other bad health effects, including overdose—especially when taken along with other drugs or alcohol.

Adolescents And Young Adults

Abuse of prescription drugs is highest among young adults aged 18 to 25, with 5.9 percent reporting nonmedical use in the past month (NSDUH, 2010). Among youth aged 12 to 17, 3.0 percent reported past-month nonmedical use of prescription medications.

According to the 2010 MTF, prescription and OTC drugs are among the most commonly abused drugs by 12th graders, after alcohol, marijuana, and tobacco. While past-year nonmedical use of sedatives and tranquilizers decreased among 12th graders over the last 5 years, this is not the case for the nonmedical use of amphetamines or opioid pain relievers.

When asked how prescription opioids were obtained for nonmedical use, more than half of the 12th graders surveyed said they were given the drugs or bought them from a friend or relative. Interestingly, the number of students who purchased opioids over the Internet was negligible.

Youth who abuse prescription medications are also more likely to report use of other drugs. Multiple studies have revealed associations between prescription drug abuse and higher rates of cigarette smoking; heavy episodic drinking; and marijuana, cocaine, and other illicit drug use among adolescents, young adults, and college students in the United States.

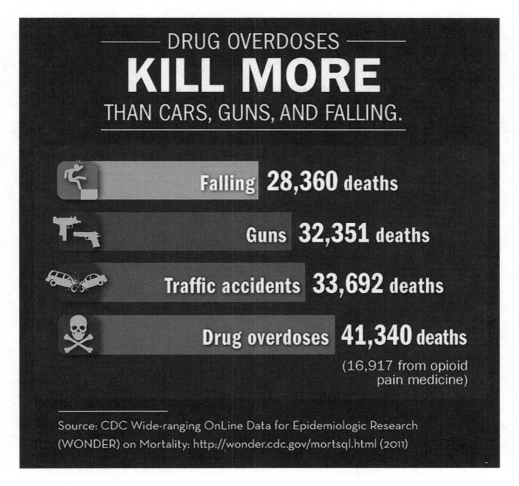

Figure 31.2. Drug Overdose Deaths (2011)

Chapter 32
Commonly Abused Pain Relievers

What Are Opioids?

Also known as: oxy, percs, happy pills, hillbilly heroin, OC, or vikes

Opioids, which usually come in pill form, are prescription medications used to reduce pain. Doctors prescribe them after surgery or to help patients with severe pain or pain that lasts a long time. When opioids are taken as prescribed by a medical professional, they are relatively safe and can reduce pain effectively. However, dependence and addiction are still potential risks when taking prescription opioids. These risks increase when these drugs are abused. Painkillers are one of the most commonly abused drugs by teens, after tobacco, alcohol, and marijuana. Examples include the illicit drug heroin and pharmaceutical drugs like OxyContin®, Vicodin®, codeine, morphine, methadone, and fentanyl.

How Are Opioids Abused?

People abuse opioids by taking them in a way that is not intended, such as:

- Taking someone else's prescription opioid medication.

  - Even if the person taking the opioid is doing so for the medication's intended purpose, such as to ease pain, it is considered abuse if the medication is not prescribed to you by a health care clinician.

  - Taking a prescription opioid medication in a way other than prescribed.

About This Chapter: Information in this chapter is from "Prescription Pain Medications (Opioids)," NIDA for Teens, National Institute on Drug Abuse (NIDA), October 26, 2015; and information from "The Connection Between Pain Medications and Heroin," NIDA for Teens, National Institute on Drug Abuse (NIDA), April 2, 2014.

- Taking more of the medication than prescribed, combining it with alcohol or other drugs, or crushing the pills into powder to snort or inject the drug is abuse. Taking opioids in this way increases risk for both addiction and overdose.

- Taking the opioid prescription to get high.

  - If the primary (most important) reason to take the medication is to get high, it is abuse.

Table 32.1. Common Opioids

Opioid Types

- Oxycodone (OxyContin, Percodan, Percocet)
- Hydrocodone (Vicodin, Lortab, Lorcet)
- Diphenoxylate (Lomotil)
- Morphine (Kadian, Avinza, MS Contin)
- Codeine
- Fentanyl (Duragesic)
- Propoxyphene (Darvon)
- Hydromorphone (Dilaudid)
- Meperidine (Demerol)
- Methadone

Conditions They Treat

- Severe pain, often after surgery
- Chronic (long-lasting) or acute (severe) pain
- Cough and diarrhea

The Connection Between Pain Medications And Heroin

More and more young people are using heroin these days, and sometimes they start using it because they've gotten addicted to prescription painkillers.

One study showed that people who abuse painkillers like OxyContin are 19 times more likely to start using heroin. The study also found that 8 out of 10 people who started using heroin abused painkillers first.

Heroin and painkillers belong to the same class of drugs: Opioids.

Opioids attach to specific molecules called opioid receptors, which are found on nerve cells in the brain, spinal cord, intestines, and other organs. When painkillers or heroin attach to these receptors, they can decrease the feeling of pain. Opioids can also cause a person to feel relaxed and happy, which can lead some people to abuse the drugs.

Opioids have many negative effects. Painkillers and heroin can cause sleepiness, constipation, and, depending on the amount taken, affect a person's ability to breathe properly. In fact, taking just one large dose of painkillers or heroin could cause a person's breathing to stop, sometimes killing them.

The Danger in Abusing Painkillers or Heroin

Not everyone who abuses painkillers starts using heroin, but even painkiller abuse alone can hurt you. Opioid drugs of all kinds can be very addictive. Addiction is a disease where you feel like you need to use a drug even if that drug is hurting you and messing up your life. Addiction is caused by chemical changes in the brain after drug use.

When someone is addicted to painkillers or heroin, it is very difficult for them to stop using the drug. People trying to stop using opioids after they are addicted may have withdrawal. Some of the effects of opioid withdrawal are restlessness, muscle and bone pain, trouble sleeping, diarrhea, vomiting, cold flashes with goosebumps, and uncontrollable leg movements.

How Do Opioids Affect The Brain?

Opioids attach to specific proteins, called opioid receptors, in the brain, spinal cord, gut, and other organs. When these drugs attach to their receptors, they block pain messages sent from the body through the spinal cord to the brain.

Opioids also can change the part of the brain that controls emotions and cause a person to feel relaxed and extremely happy (euphoric). Repeated abuse of opioids can lead to addiction.

What Are The Other Effects of Opioids?

Opioids can have effects on many parts of the brain and body beyond those that are involved in pain. Other effects of opioids include:

- Sleepiness

- Confusion

- Nausea (feeling sick to the stomach)

- Constipation

- Breathing problems. Taking just 1 large dose could cause serious breathing problems that lead to death.

These medications are not safe to use with alcohol or other medications that may slow breathing, such as depressants, because their combined effects also cause serious breathing problems that could lead to death.

A First Step to Heroin Use?

Prescription opioid pain medications such as OxyContin and Vicodin are made from opium, which comes from the poppy plant. Morphine and codeine are two natural products of opium. Morphine can be turned into heroin. Different opioids are very similar chemically which is why, when prescription opioids are abused, they can have effects that are similar to heroin. Some people who start out abusing opioids and get addicted to them may turn to heroin, which can be cheaper and easier to get on the street. Nearly half of young people who inject heroin surveyed in 3 recent studies reported abusing prescription opioids before starting to use heroin.

Many of these young people also report that crushing prescription opioid pills to snort or inject the powder introduced them to these addictive and dangerous methods of drug taking.

Can You Become Addicted To Prescription Opioids?

Yes. People who abuse prescription opioids are at greater risk than people who take them as prescribed, but the medication is addictive. People who are prescribed opioids by their doctor for a period of several weeks or more may develop a physical dependence to the drug and, in some cases, this may turn into addiction. Dependence is not the same as addiction. Dependence means that the body gets used to the presence of the drug. Addiction is when a person seeks out and uses the drug over and over even though they know it is damaging their health and their life. When someone is dependent on a drug and they stop using or abusing it, they may experience withdrawal symptoms.

Opioid withdrawal can cause:

- Restlessness

- Muscle and bone pain

- Sleep problems

- Diarrhea

- Vomiting (throwing up)

- Cold flashes with goosebumps

- Involuntary leg movements

Carefully following the doctor's instructions for taking a medication can make it less likely that someone will develop dependence or addiction, because the medication is prescribed in amounts and forms that are considered appropriate for that person. However, dependence and addiction are still potential risks when taking certain types of prescription drugs. These risks should be carefully weighed against the benefits of the medication and patients should communicate any issues or concerns to their doctor as soon as they arise. Fortunately, there are effective treatments available for people who abuse or are addicted to prescription opioid medications.

Can You Die If You Abuse Opioids?

Yes. In fact, taking just 1 large dose could cause serious breathing problems that lead to death. In 2011, opioid painkillers accounted for close to 17,000 deaths in the United States. This is more than 3 times the number of deaths from a decade ago (5,528 in 2001). Among young people, males are 3 times more likely to overdose from opioid abuse than are females.

The risk for overdose and death are increased when opioids are combined with alcohol or other drugs, especially depressants such as Benzodiazepines.

There is an "opioid antagonist" medication, Naloxone, which can reverse the effects of opioid overdose and prevent death if it is given in time. Doctors can prescribe Naloxone to people who abuse opioid drugs in the hopes that a friend or family could deliver the drug in the event of an overdose. Naloxone is also commonly carried by emergency responders including police officers and EMTs.

How Many Teens Abuse Opioids?

NIDA's *Monitoring the Future* study collects data on teen abuse of two types of prescription opioids—Vicodin and OxyContin:

Table 32.2. Trends in Prevalence of Various Drugs for 8th Graders, 10th Graders, and 12th Graders; 2014 (in percent)*

Drug	Time Period	8th Graders	10th Graders	12th Graders
Vicodin	Past Year	1	3.4	4.8
OxyContin	Past Year	[1.00]	3	3.3

* Data in brackets indicate statistically significant change from the previous year.

Chapter 33

Commonly Abused Depressant Medications

What Are Depressants?

Also known as: barbs, reds, red birds, phennies, tooies, yellows, or yellow jackets, candy, downers, sleeping pills, or tranks, A-minus, or zombie pills

Depressants, sometimes referred to as central nervous system (CNS) depressants or tranquilizers, slow down (or "depress") the normal activity that goes on in the brain and spinal cord. Doctors often prescribe them for people who are anxious or can't sleep. Taken as prescribed by a doctor, they can be relatively safe and helpful. However, dependence and addiction are still potential risks when taking prescription depressants. These risks increase when these drugs are abused. Taking someone else's prescription drugs or taking the drugs to get "high" can cause serious, and even dangerous, problems.

Depressants can be divided into three primary groups: barbiturates, benzodiazepines, and sleep medications (refer Table 35.1).

How Are Depressants Abused?

Depressants usually come in pill or capsule form. People abuse depressants by taking them in a way that is not intended, such as:

- Taking someone else's prescription depressant medication.

About This Chapter: Information in this chapter is excerpted from "Prescription Depressant Medications," NIDA for Teens, National Institute on Drug Abuse (NIDA), October 26, 2015.

- Taking a depressant medication in a way other than prescribed by their doctor.

- Taking a depressant for fun or to get high.

- Taking a depressant with other drugs or to counteract the effects of those drugs, such as stimulants.

Table 33.1. Depressants

Type	Conditions They Treat
Barbiturates	
• Mephobarbital (Mebaral)	• Seizure disorders
• Sodium pentobarbital (Nembutal)	• Anxiety and tension
Benzodiazepines	
• Diazepam (Valium)	• Acute stress reactions
• Alprazolam (Xanax)	• Panic attacks
• Estazolam (ProSom)	• Convulsions
• Clonazepam (Klonopin)	• Sleep disorders
• Lorazepam (Ativan)	
Sleep Medications	
• Zolpidem (Ambien)	• Sleep disorders
• Zaleplon (Sonata)	
• Eszopiclone (Lunesta)	

How Do Depressants Affect The Brain?

Most depressants affect the brain by increasing the activity of gamma-aminobutyric acid (GABA), a chemical in the brain that sends messages between cells. The increased GABA activity in turn slows down brain activity. This causes a relaxing effect that is helpful to people with anxiety or sleep problems. Too much GABA activity, though, can be harmful.

What Are The Other Effects Of Depressants?

As depressants slow down brain activity, they cause other effects:

- Slurred speech

- Shallow breathing, which can lead to overdose and even death

- Sleepiness

- Disorientation

- Lack of coordination

These effects can lead to serious accidents or injuries. Abuse of depressants can also lead to physical dependence, another reason they should only be used as prescribed.

Depressants should not be combined with any medicine or substance that causes sleepiness, like prescription pain medicines, certain over-the-counter cold and allergy medicines, or alcohol. If combined, they can slow both the heart rate and breathing increasing the risk of overdose and death.

Can You Get Addicted To Depressants?

Yes. Abuse of depressants can lead to physical dependence, which is when the body gets used to the drug and a person can't stop taking it without feeling discomfort or even worse symptoms (withdrawal). It can also lead to addiction, which is when a person compulsively seeks and takes the drug, to the point of damaging their life.

Depressants work by slowing the brain's activity. During the first few days of taking a depressant, a person usually feels sleepy and uncoordinated. With continuing use, the body becomes used to these effects and they lessen. This is known as tolerance, which means a person has to take more of the drug to get the same initial effects.

When someone who is physically dependent on a depressant stops abruptly, the brain reacts strongly, even violently sometimes, because it is missing the chemicals it's come to depend on through repeated drug use. In some cases, the brain activity races out of control to the point where it causes seizures. Just like with illegal drugs, quitting depressants is hard and can be dangerous. Someone who is either thinking about stopping use, or who has stopped and is suffering withdrawal, should get medical treatment.

Can You Die If You Abuse Depressants?

Yes, you can die if you abuse depressants. Of the 22,810 deaths related to prescription drug overdose in 2011, more than 6,800 (30%) involved benzodiazepines (such as Valium and Xanax). Among young people, males are almost 3 times more likely to overdose from depressants than are females. The risk for overdose and death are increased when depressants are combined with alcohol or other drugs.

How Many Teens Abuse Depressants?

NIDA's *Monitoring the Future* study collects data on teen abuse of depressants, referring to the drugs as tranquilizers:

Table 33.2. Trends In Prevalence Of Tranquilizers For 8th Graders, 10th Graders, And 12th Graders; 2014 (In Percent)*

Drug	Time Period	8th Graders	10th Graders	12th Graders
Tranquilizers	Lifetime	2.9	5.8	7.4
	Past Year	1.7	3.9	4.7
	Past Month	0.8	1.6	2.1

Chapter 34
Commonly Abused Prescription Stimulants

What Are Stimulants (Amphetamines)?

Also known as: skippy, the smart drug, vitamin R, bennies, black beauties, roses, hearts, speed, or uppers

Prescription stimulants increase—or "stimulate"—activities and processes in the body. This increased activity can boost alertness, attention, and energy. It also can raise a person's blood pressure and make their heart beat faster. When prescribed by a doctor for a specific health condition, they can be relatively safe and effective. However, dependence and addiction are still potential risks when taking prescription stimulants. These risks increase when these drugs are abused. Taking someone else's prescription drugs or taking the drugs to get "high" can have serious health risks.

There are two commonly abused types of stimulants: amphetamines and methylphenidate. In the past, stimulants were used to treat a variety of conditions, including asthma and other breathing problems, obesity, and health problems that affect your nervous system. Now, because the risk for abuse and addiction is better understood, doctors prescribe them less often and only for a few health conditions, including attention deficit hyperactivity disorder (ADHD), narcolepsy (a sleep disorder), and, in some instances, depression that has not responded to other treatments.

About This Chapter: Information in this chapter is excerpted from "Prescription Stimulant Medications (Amphetamines)," NIDA for Teens, National Institute on Drug Abuse (NIDA), October 23, 2015; and information from "5 Myths About ADHD Drugs," NIDA for Teens, National Institute on Drug Abuse (NIDA), December 12, 2013.

Table 34.1. Stimulants

Type
- Amphetamines (Adderall and Dexedrine)
- Methylphenidate (Ritalin and Concerta)

Conditions They Treat
- ADHD
- Narcolepsy (sleep disorder)
- Depression

How Are Stimulants Abused?

Prescription stimulants are normally taken in pill form, but some people who abuse them crush the tablets and snort or inject them, which can cause additional problems because ingredients in the tablets can block small blood vessels which can cause damage to the heart and other organs.

People abuse stimulants by taking them in a way that is not intended, such as:

- Taking someone else's prescription stimulant medication.

- Taking a prescription stimulant medication in a way other than prescribed.

- Taking the prescription stimulant to get high.

Stimulants have been abused as an "academic performance enhancement" (such as to stay up all night cramming for an exam). However, studies have found that stimulants do not increase learning or thinking ability when taken by people who have not been diagnosed with ADHD.

How Do Prescription Stimulants Affect The Brain?

The brain is made up of nerve cells that send messages to each other by releasing chemicals called neurotransmitters. Common stimulants, such as amphetamines (e.g., Adderall) and methylphenidate (e.g., Ritalin), have chemical structures that are similar to certain key brain neurotransmitters including dopamine and norepinephrine. Stimulants boost the effects of these chemicals in the brain and body.

When doctors prescribe stimulants, they start with low doses and increase them slowly until they find the appropriate dose for the patient to treat the condition for which they are prescribed. However, when taken in doses and in ways other than those prescribed, like snorting or injecting, stimulants can increase the dopamine in the brain very quickly. This changes the normal communication between brain cells, producing a 'high' while also increasing the risk for dangerous side effects and, over time, for addiction.

What Are The Other Effects Of Stimulant Abuse?

Stimulant abuse can be extremely dangerous. Taking high doses of a stimulant can cause:

- Increased blood pressure

- Irregular heartbeat

- Dangerously high body temperatures

- Decreased sleep

- Lack of interest in eating, which can lead to poor nutrition

- Intense anger or paranoia (feeling like someone is going to harm you even though they aren't)

- Risk for seizures and stroke at high doses

Stimulants should not be mixed with medicines used to treat depression or over-the-counter cold medicines that contain decongestants. These mixtures increase the risk for developing dangerously high blood pressure and irregular heartbeat.

Can You Get Addicted To Stimulants?

Yes, abusing stimulants can lead to addiction. Addiction is when a person continues to seek out and takes the drug even though they know it is damaging their health and their life.

When a person who regularly abuses stimulants stops taking them, they may experience withdrawal symptoms. Stimulant withdrawal can cause:

- An inability to feel pleasure

- Thoughts of suicide

- Anxiety and irritability

- Feeling very tired, lack of energy, and changes in sleep patterns

- Intense drug cravings

Treatment of mood symptoms may help lessen these effects.

5 Myths About ADHD Drugs

Prescription stimulants—like Adderall and Ritalin—have been in the news a lot recently because some high school and college students say they take these drugs to help them study better or party longer. Prescription stimulants are usually prescribed to treat attention deficit hyperactivity disorder (ADHD), and misusing them can lead to serious health problems.

Let's look at 5 myths about prescription stimulants.

Myth #1: Drugs like Ritalin and Adderall can make you smarter.

Fact: While these drugs may help you focus, they don't help you learn better, and they won't improve your grades.

Being "smart" is about improving your ability to master new skills, concepts, and ideas. Like a muscle, the brain gets stronger through exercise. Learning strengthens brain connections through repetition and practice to enhance cognition—"smartness"—over a lifetime. Short-cuts, like abusing prescription stimulants, do not "exercise" the brain.

Research has shown that students who abuse prescription stimulants actually have lower GPAs in high school and college than those who don't.

Myth #2: Prescription stimulants are just "brain vitamins."

Fact: Unlike vitamins, these drugs contain ingredients that can change brain chemistry and may have serious side effects.

Also, unlike vitamins, they require a doctor's prescription. If you take these drugs more often than directed, in too high a dose, or in some way other than by mouth, you are abusing the drug, which can lead to addiction.

Myth #3: These drugs can't hurt you.

Fact: Prescription stimulants like Adderall or Ritalin are safe and effective when prescribed for people with ADHD and used properly. But the same drugs, when used by someone without ADHD, can be dangerous.

Stimulants taken without a medical reason can disrupt brain communication. When used improperly or in excess, they can cause mood swings and loss of sleep, and can increase your blood pressure, heart rate, and body temperature.

Myth #4: Taking someone else's prescription—just once in a while—is okay.

Fact: Doctors prescribe medicine based on your weight, symptoms, and body chemistry. Doctors may adjust how much you take or change to a different medication to better treat symptoms or respond to side effects.

When you take a stimulant prescribed for a friend or family member, you haven't been looked at by a doctor. The possible side effects can make you sick. Side effects include elevated heart rate, dizziness, and fainting—or, even worse, heart attacks and stroke. Side effects may also include depression and exhaustion.

Myth #5: If your doctor prescribed the drug, it doesn't matter how you take it.

> **Fact:** If you are diagnosed with ADHD, stimulants the doctor prescribes for you can help. But always be sure to take the medication exactly as directed—no more, no less.
>
> Also, be sure to tell your doctor everything that's going on at home and at school. Combining prescription stimulants with other drugs or alcohol can be dangerous.
>
> And don't help your friends or family members abuse prescription drugs by sharing your pills with them.

Can You Die If You Abuse Stimulants?

Yes, it is possible to die from stimulant abuse. Taking high doses of a stimulant can raise a person's body temperature and blood pressure to dangerous levels and make the heart beat irregularly. This can lead to seizures, heart failure, and death.

How Many Teens Abuse Stimulants?

NIDA's *Monitoring the Future* study collects data on teen abuse of amphetamines in general, as well as Adderall and Ritalin:

Table 34.2. Trends In Prevalence Of Various Drugs For 8th Graders, 10th Graders, And 12th Graders; 2014 (In Percent)

Drug	Time Period	8th Graders	10th Graders	12th Graders
Amphetamine	Lifetime	6.7	10.6	12.1
	Past Year	4.3	7.6	8.1
	Past Month	2.1	3.7	3.8
Adderall	Past Year	1.3	4.6	6.8
Ritalin	Past Year	0.9	1.8	1.8

Chapter 35

The Abuse Of Cold And Cough Medicines

What Are Cough And Cold Medicines?

Also known as: robotripping, robo, tussin, triple c, dex, skittles, candy, velvet, and drank

Millions of Americans take cough and cold medicines each year to help with symptoms of colds, and when taken as instructed, these medicines can be safe and effective. However, several cough and cold medicines contain ingredients that are psychoactive (mind-altering) when taken in higher-than-recommended dosages, and some people may abuse them. These products also contain other ingredients that can add to the risks.

Two commonly abused cough and cold medicines are:

1. **Cough syrups and capsules containing dextromethorphan (DXM).** These over-the-counter (OTC)—meaning they can be bought without a prescription—cough medicines are safe for stopping coughs during a cold if you take them as directed. Taking more than the recommended amount can produce euphoria (a relaxed pleasurable feeling) and dissociative effects (like you are detached from your body).

2. **Promethazine-codeine cough syrup.** These prescription medications contain an opioid drug called codeine, which stops coughs, but when taken in higher doses produces euphoria.

About This Chapter: Information in this chapter is excerpted from "Cough and Cold Medicine (DXM and Codeine Syrup)," NIDA for Teens, National Institute on Drug Abuse (NIDA), October 23, 2015; information from "Sizzurp: It's Not Cool," NIDA for Teens, National Institute on Drug Abuse (NIDA), June 13, 2013; and information from "Commonly Abused Drugs Charts," National Institute on Drug Abuse (NIDA), October 2015.

Facts About Sizzurp

First, it is not cool. In fact, it's quite dangerous.

Sizzurp, also known as "Lean" and "Purple Drank," is a mixture of cough medicine—often prescription strength, containing an opioid called codeine—and soft drinks and candy for flavor.

Abuse of cough medicines, especially ones that contain opioids, can cause an overdose leading to coma or even death. Less grave (but still serious) symptoms include nausea, dizziness, impaired vision, memory loss, hallucinations, and seizures.

Teens may think that just because something is available from the pharmacy, it won't harm them—but that's not true. When not used as directed on the label, cough and cold medicines (even over-the-counter ones) can be dangerous.

How Are Cough And Cold Medicines Abused?

Cough and cold medicines are usually sold in liquid syrup, capsule, or pill form. They may also come in a powder. Young people are more likely to abuse cough and cold medicines containing DXM because these medicines can be purchased without a prescription. Some people mix promethazine-codeine cough syrup with soda or alcohol and flavor the mixture by adding hard candies.

How Do Cough and Cold Medicines Affect The Brain?

When cough and cold medicines are taken as directed, they safely treat symptoms caused by colds and flu. But when taken in higher quantities or when such symptoms aren't present, they may affect the brain in ways very similar to illegal drugs.

DXM acts on the same brain cell receptors as drugs like ketamine or PCP. A single high dose of DXM can cause hallucinations (imagined experiences that seem real). Ketamine and PCP are called "dissociative" drugs, which means they make you feel separated from your body or your environment, and they twist the way you think or feel about something or someone.

Codeine attaches to the same cell receptors as opioids like heroin. High doses of promethazine-codeine cough syrup can produce euphoria similar to that produced by other opioid drugs. Also, both codeine and promethazine depress activities in the central nervous system (brain and spinal cord), which produces calming effects.

Both codeine and DXM cause an increase in the amount of dopamine in the brain's reward pathway. Extra amounts of dopamine increase the feeling of pleasure and at the same time cause important messages to get lost, causing a range of effects from lack of motivation to serious health problems. Repeatedly seeking to experience that feeling can lead to addiction.

What Are The Other Effects Of Cough And Cold Medicines?

DXM abuse can cause:

- Loss of coordination

- Numbness

- Feeling sick to the stomach

- Increased blood pressure

- Faster heart beat

- In rare instances, lack of oxygen to the brain, creating lasting brain damage, when DXM is taken with decongestants

Promethazine-codeine cough syrup can cause:

- Slowed heart rate

- Slowed breathing (high doses can lead to overdose and death)

Also, cough and cold medicines are even more dangerous when taken with alcohol or other drugs.

Table 35.1. Effects Of Cough And Cold Medicines

Possible Health Effects

Short-term	Euphoria; slurred speech; increased heart rate, blood pressure, temperature; numbness; dizziness; nausea; vomiting; confusion; paranoia; altered visual perceptions; problems with movement; buildup of excess acid in body fluids.
Long-term	Unknown.
Other Health-related Issues	Breathing problems, seizures, and increased heart rate may occur from other ingredients in cough/cold medicines.
In Combination with Alcohol	Increased risk of adverse effects.
Withdrawal Symptoms	Unknown.

Treatment Options

Medications	There are no FDA-approved medications to treat addiction to over-the-counter cough/cold medicines.
Behavioral Therapies	More research is needed to find out if behavioral therapies can be used to treat addiction to over-the-counter cough/cold medicines.

Can You Get Addicted To Cough and Cold Medicines?

Yes, high doses and repeated abuse of cough and cold medicines can lead to addiction. That's when a person seeks out and takes the drug over and over even though they know that it is causing problems with their health and their life.

Can You Die If You Abuse Cough And Cold Medicines?

Yes. Abuse of promethazine-codeine cough syrup slows down the central nervous system, which can slow or stop the heart and lungs. Mixing it with alcohol greatly increases this risk. Promethazine-codeine cough syrup has been linked to the overdose deaths of a few prominent musicians.

How Many Teens Abuse Cough And Cold Medicines?

NIDA's *Monitoring the Future* study collects data on teen abuse of cough medicines:

Table 35.2. Trends In Prevalence Of Cough Medicine (Non-Prescription) For 8Th Graders, 10Th Graders, And 12th Graders; 2014 (In Percent)*

Drug	Time Period	8th Graders	10th Graders	12th Graders
Cough Medicine (non-prescription)	2013	[2.00]	3.7	4.1

* Data in brackets indicate statistically significant change from the previous year.

Chapter 36

Anabolic Steroids And Sports Supplements

What Are Anabolic Steroids?

Also known as: Anabolic-androgenic steroids, "roids," or "juice"

Common brand names: Androsterone, Oxandrin, Dianabol, Winstrol, Deca-durabolin, and Equipoise

Anabolic steroids are manmade substances related to testosterone (male sex hormone). Doctors use anabolic steroids to treat hormone problems in men, delayed puberty, and muscle loss from some diseases.

Bodybuilders and athletes may use anabolic steroids to build muscles and improve athletic performance, often taking doses much higher than would be prescribed for a medical condition. Using them this way is not legal—or safe.

Anabolic steroids are only one type of steroid. Other types of steroids include cortisol, estrogen, and progesterone. These are different chemicals and do not have the same effects.

Do Anabolic Steroids Really Make the Body Stronger?

You may have heard that some athletes use anabolic steroids to gain size and strength. Maybe you've even seen an anabolic steroid user develop bigger muscles over time.

About This Chapter: Information in this chapter is excerpted from "Anabolic Steroids," NIDA for Teens, National Institute on Drug Abuse (NIDA), October 23, 2015; information from "Do Anabolic Steroids Really Make the Body Stronger?" NIDA for Teens, National Institute on Drug Abuse (NIDA), October 23, 2015; information from "Anabolic Steroids Can Confuse the Brain and Body," NIDA for Teens, National Institute on Drug Abuse (NIDA), October 23, 2015; and information from "Sports Supplements: Not a Safe "Quick Fix"," NIDA for Teens, National Institute on Drug Abuse (NIDA), September 24, 2013.

But while anabolic steroids can make some people look stronger on the outside, they may create weaknesses on the inside. For example, anabolic steroids are bad for the heart—they can increase fat deposits in blood vessels, which can cause heart attacks and strokes. They may also damage the liver. Steroids can halt bone growth—which means that a teenage steroid user may not grow to his/her full adult height.

How Are Anabolic Steroids Abused?

Anabolic steroids affect a part of the brain called the limbic system, which controls mood. Long-term steroid abuse can lead to aggressive behavior and extreme mood swings. This is sometimes referred to as "roid rage."

Steroids can also lead to feeling paranoid (like someone or something is out to get you), jealousy, delusions (belief in something that is not true), and feeling invincible (like nothing can hurt you).

How Do Anabolic Steroids Affect The Brain?

Anabolic steroids affect a part of the brain called the limbic system, which controls mood. Long-term steroid abuse can lead to aggressive behavior and extreme mood swings. This is sometimes referred to as "roid rage."

Steroids can also lead to feeling paranoid (like someone or something is out to get you), jealousy, delusions (belief in something that is not true), and feeling invincible (like nothing can hurt you).

Anabolic Steroids Can Confuse The Brain And Body

Your body's testosterone production is controlled by a group of nerve cells at the base of the brain, called the hypothalamus. The hypothalamus also does a lot of other things. It helps control appetite, blood pressure, moods, and reproductive ability.

Anabolic steroids can change the messages the hypothalamus sends to the body. This can disrupt normal hormone function.

In guys, anabolic steroids can interfere with the normal production of testosterone. They can also act directly on the testes and cause them to shrink. This can result in a lower sperm count. They can also cause an irreversible loss of scalp hair.

In girls, anabolic steroids can cause a loss of the monthly period by acting on both the hypothalamus and reproductive organs. They can also cause loss of scalp hair, growth of body and facial hair, and deepening of the voice. These changes can also be irreversible.

What Are The Other Effects Of Anabolic Steroids?

Abuse of anabolic steroids has been linked with serious health problems. They include:

- High blood pressure
- Changes in blood cholesterol (increases in "bad" cholesterol or LDL, decreases in "good" cholesterol or HDL)
- Enlarged heart
- Heart attack or stroke (even in young people)
- Liver disease, including cancer
- Kidney problems or failure
- Severe acne

Males

- Breast growth and shrinking of testicles
- Low sperm count/infertility (unable to have children)
- Increased risk for prostate cancer

Females

- Voice deepening
- Growth of facial hair
- Male-pattern baldness
- Changes in or end of menstrual cycle/getting your period
- Enlargement of clitoris

In addition, if teens abuse anabolic steroids, they may never achieve their full height because anabolic steroids can stop growth in the middle of puberty.

Can You Get Addicted To Anabolic Steroids?

Yes. Addiction to steroids is different compared to other drugs of abuse, because users don't become high when using. People who do become addicted keep using steroids despite bad effects on their bodies and lives. Also, people who abuse steroids typically spend large amount of time and money obtaining the drugs, which is another sign they may be addicted.

When they stop using steroids, people can experience withdrawal symptoms such as feeling depressed, mood swings, feeling tired or restless, loss of appetite, being unable to sleep (insomnia), and the desire to take more steroids. Depression can be very dangerous, because it sometimes leads people to think of or attempt suicide (killing themselves). If not treated, some symptoms of depression that are linked with anabolic steroid withdrawal have lasted for a year or more after the person stops taking the drugs.

NIDA has two education programs for players on high school sports teams. In the ATLAS (for guys) and ATHENA (for girls) programs, coaches and sports team leaders talk about how steroids and other illegal drugs can affect sports performance, and they teach how to say no to offers of drugs. They also discuss how strength training and eating healthy foods can help teens build their bodies without the use of steroids. Later, special trainers teach the players proper weightlifting skills.

If you see or hear about someone abusing steroids, talk to a coach, teacher, or other trusted adult. Hear a neuroscientist talk about the teen brain and drug use.

Can You Die If You Abuse Anabolic Steroids?

Yes. Although it is rare, there are a few ways steroid abuse can cause death.

- **Heart attacks and strokes.** Steroid use can lead to a condition called atherosclerosis, in which fat builds up inside arteries and makes it hard for blood to flow. When blood flow to the heart is blocked, a heart attack can occur. If blood flow to the brain is blocked, a stroke can occur.

- **HIV.** People who inject anabolic steroids using needles may share dirty drug injection equipment that can spread serious viral infections such as HIV/AIDS or hepatitis (a liver disease).

How Many Teens Abuse Anabolic Steroids?

See the most recent statistics on teen drug use from NIDA's *Monitoring the Future* study below:

Table 36.1. Trends in Prevalence of Steroids for 8th Graders, 10th Graders, and 12th Graders; 2014 (in percent)*

Drug	Time Period	8th Graders	10th Graders	12th Graders
Steroids	Lifetime	1	1.4	1.9
	Past Year	0.6	0.8	1.5
	Past Month	0.2	0.4	0.9

Sports Supplements

Sports Supplements: Not A Safe "Quick Fix"

When working out or playing sports, you may feel like you want to up your game. There are lots of sports products out there that claim to help you run faster, be stronger, or play longer—but be careful.

It's important to make sure any sports supplement or "vitamin" you want to take is safe. The ingredients in sports products are not required to meet the same high standards as medications. This means it's up to you to find out what's in any pills, drinks, or powders before you take them.

Know What You Put In Your Body

In July 2013, USPlabs, a maker of several sports products, destroyed $8 million worth of its sports supplements Jack3d and OxyElite Pro, after the government said the two products might be dangerous. These two products had the stimulant dimethylamylamine (DMAA), which the government warns can cause heart pro blems like shortness of breath and heart attacks. Stimulants are drugs that increase your energy and speed up your body.

Do Your Research

If you are thinking about taking a sports product, do more than just read the label. Look into the ingredients and all the effects they may have on your body. Ask your coach if he or she knows anything about the product. A healthy body is the best body, so make sure you know what you are taking and that it is right for you.

There's no magic pill that will make you a better athlete—only hard work can do that.

Chapter 37
Caffeine

The Buzz On Caffeine

Question: What's the most widely used drug?

It's not marijuana—and no, it's not tobacco or alcohol either. Nine out of 10 Americans take it in some form every day, and it's not limited to adults.

Hint: According to a recent study published by the American Academy of Pediatrics, nearly three-fourths (75%) of children, teens, and young adults use it daily too—in the form of soda, coffee, and energy drinks.

Answer: Caffeine!

That's right, caffeine is a drug—a stimulant drug, to be exact. It's even possible to be physically dependent on it—which means that a person who is used to drinking lots of caffeinated beverages can experience withdrawal symptoms if they quit.

Caffeine: Breaking Down The Buzz

Caffeine has a perk-up effect because it blocks a brain chemical, adenosine, which causes sleepiness. On its own, moderate amounts of caffeine rarely cause harmful long-term health effects, although it is definitely possible to take too much caffeine and get sick as a result.

Consuming too much caffeine can make you feel jittery or jumpy—your heart may race and your palms may sweat, kind of like a panic attack. It may also interfere with your sleep, which is especially important while your brain is still developing.

About This Chapter: Information in this chapter is excerpted from "The Buzz on Caffeine," NIDA for Teens, National Institute on Drug Abuse (NIDA), June 25, 2014.

Some caffeine drinks and foods will affect you more than others, because they contain very different amounts.

Table 37.1. Caffeine Source And Content

Caffeine Source	Caffeine Content
8 oz black tea	14–70 milligrams (mg)
12 oz cola	23–35 mg
8.4 oz Red Bull	75–80 mg
8 oz regular coffee	95–200 mg
1 cup semi-sweet chocolate chips	104 mg
2 oz 5-Hour Energy Shot	200–207 mg

But it's more than just how much caffeine a beverage has that can make it harmful. Even though energy drinks don't necessarily have more caffeine than other popular beverages (that is, unless you take 8 ounces of 5-Hour Energy Shot, which has 400 milligrams!), it's the way they are sometimes used that worries health experts.

In 2011, of the 20,783 emergency room visits because of energy drinks, 42% were because the user combined them with other drugs (e.g., prescription drugs, alcohol, or marijuana).

Caffeine + Alcohol = Danger

Mixing alcohol and caffeine is serious business. As a stimulant, caffeine sort of has the opposite effect on the brain as alcohol, which is a depressant. But don't think the effects of each are canceled out! In fact, drinking caffeine doesn't reduce the intoxication effect of alcohol (that is, how drunk you become) or reduce its cognitive impairments (that is, your ability to walk or drive or think clearly). But it does reduce alcohol's sedation effects, so you feel more awake and probably drink for longer periods of time, and you may think you are less drunk than you really are.

That can be super dangerous. People who consume alcohol mixed with energy drinks are 3 times more likely to binge drink than people who do not report mixing alcohol with energy drinks.

Stay Away From Caffeine?

Drinking a cup of coffee, or eating a bar of chocolate, is usually not a big deal. But there are alternatives to caffeine if you're looking for an energy burst but don't want to get that jittery feeling caffeine sometimes causes. Here are a few alternatives you can try to feel energized without overdoing the caffeine:

- **Sleep.** This may sound obvious, but getting enough sleep is important. Teens need 9 hours of sleep a night.

- **Eat regularly.** When you don't eat, your glucose (sugar) levels drop, making you feel drained. Some people find it helpful to eat four or five smaller meals throughout the day instead of fewer big meals.

- **Drink enough water.** Since our bodies are more than two-thirds water, we need at least 64 ounces of water a day.

- **Take a walk.** If you're feeling drained in the middle of the day, it helps to move around. Do sit-ups or jumping jacks. Go outside for a brisk walk or ride your bike.

Chapter 38
Inhalant Abuse

What Are Inhalants?

Also known as: "laughing gas" (nitrous oxide), "snappers" (amyl nitrite), "poppers" (amyl nitrite and butyl nitrite), "whippets" (fluorinated hydrocarbons), "bold" (nitrites), and "rush" (nitrites)

Inhalants are chemicals found in ordinary household or workplace products that people inhale on purpose to get "high." Because many inhalants can be found around the house, people often don't realize that inhaling their fumes, even just once, can be very harmful to the brain and body and can lead to death. In fact, the chemicals found in these products can change the way the brain works and cause other problems in the body.

Although different inhalants cause different effects, they generally fall into one of four categories.

Volatile solvents are liquids that become a gas at room temperature. They are found in:

- Paint thinner, nail polish remover, degreaser, dry-cleaning fluid, gasoline, and contact cement (an adhesive)

- Some art or office supplies, such as correction fluid, felt-tip marker fluid, and electronic contact cleaner

Aerosols are sprays that contain propellants and solvents. They include:

- Spray paint, hair spray, deodorant spray, vegetable oil sprays, and fabric protector spray

About This Chapter: Information in this chapter is excerpted from "Inhalants," NIDA for Teens, National Institute on Drug Abuse (NIDA), October 23, 2015; and information from "How Can Inhalant Abuse Be Recognized?" National Institute on Drug Abuse (NIDA), July 2012.

Gases may be in household or commercial products, or used in the medical field to provide pain relief. They are found in:

- Butane lighters, propane tanks, whipped cream dispensers, and refrigerant gases

- Anesthesia, including ether, chloroform, halothane, and nitrous oxide (commonly called "laughing gas")

Nitrites are a class of inhalants used mainly to enhance sexual experiences. Organic nitrites include amyl, butyl, and cyclohexyl nitrites and other related compounds. Amyl nitrite was used in the past by doctors to help with chest pain and is sometimes used today to diagnose heart problems. Nitrites now are prohibited by the Consumer Product Safety Commission but can still be found, sold in small bottles labeled as "video head cleaner," "room odorizer," "leather cleaner," or "liquid aroma."

How Are Inhalants Used?

People who use inhalants breathe in the fumes through their nose or mouth, usually by:

- "Sniffing" or "snorting" fumes from containers

- Spraying aerosols directly into the nose or mouth

- Sniffing or inhaling fumes from substances sprayed or placed into a plastic or paper bag ("bagging")

- "Huffing" from an inhalant-soaked rag stuffed in the mouth

- Inhaling from balloons filled with nitrous oxide

Because the "high" lasts only a few minutes, people who use inhalants often try to make the feeling last longer by inhaling repeatedly over several hours.

How Can Inhalant Abuse Be Recognized?

Early identification and intervention are the best ways to stop inhalant abuse before it causes serious health consequences. Parents, educators, family physicians, and other health care practitioners should be alert to the following signs:

1. Chemical odors on breath or clothing
2. Paint or other stains on face, hands, or clothes
3. Hidden empty spray paint or solvent containers, and chemical-soaked rags or clothing

4. Drunk or disoriented appearance
6. Slurred speech
7. Nausea or loss of appetite
8. Inattentiveness, lack of coordination, irritability, and depression

How Do Inhalants Affect The Brain?

The lungs absorb inhaled chemicals into the bloodstream very quickly, sending them throughout the brain and body. Nearly all inhalants (except nitrites) produce a pleasurable effect by slowing down brain activity. Nitrites, in contrast, expand and relax blood vessels.

Short-Term Effects

Within seconds, users feel intoxicated and experience effects similar to those of alcohol, such as slurred speech, lack of coordination, euphoria (a feeling of intense happiness), and dizziness. Some users also experience lightheadedness, hallucinations (seeing things that are not really there), and delusions (believing something that is not true). If enough of the chemical is inhaled, nearly all solvents and gases produce anesthesia—a loss of sensation—and can lead to unconsciousness.

The high usually lasts only a few minutes, causing people to continue the high by inhaling repeatedly, which is very dangerous. Repeated use in one session can cause a person to lose consciousness and possibly even die.

With repeated inhaling, many users feel less inhibited and less in control. Some may feel drowsy for several hours and have a headache that lasts a while.

Long-Term Effects

Inhalants often contain more than one chemical. Some chemicals leave the body quickly, but others stay for a long time and get absorbed by fatty tissues in the brain and central nervous system. Over the long term, the chemicals can cause serious problems:

- **Damage to nerve fibers.** Long-term inhalant use can break down the protective sheath around certain nerve fibers in the brain and elsewhere in the body. When this happens, nerve cells are not able to send messages as well, which can cause muscle spasms and tremors or even permanent trouble with basic actions like walking, bending, and talking. These effects are similar to what happens to people with multiple sclerosis.

- **Damage to brain cells.** Inhalants also can damage brain cells by preventing them from getting enough oxygen. The effects of this condition, also known as brain hypoxia, depend on the area of the brain affected. The hippocampus, for example, is responsible for memory, so someone who repeatedly uses inhalants may be unable to learn new things or may have a hard time carrying on simple conversations. If the cerebral cortex is affected, the ability to solve complex problems and plan ahead will be compromised. And, if the cerebellum is affected, it can cause a person to move slowly or be clumsy.

What Are The Other Effects Of Inhalants?

Regular use of inhalants can cause serious harm to vital organs and systems besides the brain. Inhalants can cause:

- Heart damage
- Liver failure
- Muscle weakness
- Aplastic anemia—the body produces fewer blood cells
- Nerve damage, which can lead to chronic pain

Damage to these organs is not reversible even when the person stops abusing inhalants.

Effects Of Specific Chemicals

Depending on the type of inhalant used, the harmful health effects will differ. The table below lists some of the harmful effects of inhalants.

Table 38.1. Inhalants And Their Effects

Inhalant	Examples	Effects
Amyl nitrite, butyl nitrite	Poppers, video head cleaner	• Sudden sniffing death • Weakened immune system • Damage to red blood cells (interfering with oxygen supply to vital tissues)
Benzene	Gasoline	• Bone marrow damage • Weakened immune system • Increased risk of leukemia (a form of cancer) • Reproductive system complications

Table 38.1. Continued

Inhalant	Examples	Effects
Butane, propane	Lighter fluid, hair and pain strays	• Sudden sniffing death from heart effects • Serious burn injuries
Freon (difluoroethane substitutes)	Refrigerant and aerosol propellant	• Sudden sniffing death • Breathing problems and death (from sudden cooling of airways) • Liver damage
Methylene chloride	Paint thinners and removers, degreasers	• Reduced ability of blood to carry oxygen to the brain and body • Changes to heart muscle and heartbeat
Nitrous oxide, hexane	"Laughing gas"	• Death from lack of oxygen to the brain • Altered perception and motor coordination • Loss of sensation • Spasms • Blackouts caused by blood pressure changes • Depression of heart muscle functioning
Toluene	Gasoline, paint thinners and removers, correction fluid	• Brain damage (loss of brain tissue, impaired thinking, loss of coordination, limb spasms, hearing and vision loss) • Liver and kidney damage
Tricholoroethylene	Spot removers, degreasers	• Sudden sniffing death • Liver disease • Reproductive problems • Hearing and vision loss

Signs Of Inhalant Use

Sometimes you can see signs that tell you a person is abusing inhalants, such as:

- Chemical odors on breath or clothing
- Paint or other stains on the face, hands, or clothing
- Hidden empty spray paint or solvent containers, or rags or clothing soaked with chemicals
- Drunk or disoriented actions
- Slurred speech
- Nausea (feeling sick) or loss of appetite and weight loss
- Confusion, inattentiveness, lack of coordination, irritability, and depression

Can You Get Addicted To Inhalants?

It isn't common, but addiction can happen. Some people, particularly those who use inhalants a lot and for a long time, report a strong need to continue using inhalants. Using inhalants over and over again can cause mild withdrawal when stopped. In fact, research in animal models shows that toluene can affect the brain in a way that is similar to other drugs of use (e.g., amphetamines). Toluene increases dopamine activity in reward areas of the brain, and the long-term disruption of the dopamine system is one of the key factors leading to addiction.

Can You Die If You Use Inhalants?

Yes, using inhalants can cause death, even after just one use, by:

- Sudden sniffing death—heart beats quickly and irregularly, and then suddenly stops (cardiac arrest)

- Asphyxiation—toxic fumes replace oxygen in the lungs so that a person stops breathing

- Suffocation—air is blocked from entering the lungs when inhaling fumes from a plastic bag placed over the head

- Convulsions or seizures—abnormal electrical discharges in the brain

- Coma—the brain shuts down all but the most vital functions

- Choking—inhaling vomit after inhalant use

- Injuries—accidents, including driving, while intoxicated

How Many Teens Use Inhalants?

Inhalants are often among the first drugs that young adolescents use. In fact, they are one of the few classes of drugs that are used more by younger adolescents than older ones. Inhalant use can become chronic and continue into adulthood.

Part Six
Abuse Of Illegal Substances

Chapter 39
Club Drugs

What Are Date Rape Drugs And How Do You Avoid Them?

You may have been warned that sometimes people secretly slip drugs into other people's drinks to take advantage of them sexually. These drugs are called "date rape drugs."

Date rape, also known as "drug-facilitated sexual assault," is any type of sexual activity that a person does not agree to. It may come from someone you know, may have just met, and/or thought you could trust.

Date rape drugs can make people become physically weak or pass out. This is why people who want to rape someone use them, because they leave individuals unable to protect themselves.

Many of these drugs have no color, smell, or taste, and people often do not know that they've taken anything. Many times people (usually girls or women, but not always) who have been drugged are unable to remember what happened to them.

What Are Club Drugs?

Club drugs are a pharmacologically heterogeneous group of psychoactive compounds that tend to be abused by teens and young adults at a nightclub, bar, rave, or trance scene.

About This Chapter: Information in this chapter is excerpted from "What Are Date Rape Drugs and How Do You Avoid Them? NIDA for Teens, National Institute on Drug Abuse (NIDA), March 16, 2015; information from "Drugs of Abuse," Drug Enforcement Administration (DEA), 2015; information from "Commonly Abused Drugs Charts," National Institute on Drug Abuse (NIDA), October 2015; information from "Club Drugs (GHB, Ketamine, and Rohypnol)," U.S. Department of Veterans Affairs (VA), July 2013; and information from "DrugFacts: Hallucinogens - LSD, Peyote, Psilocybin, and PCP," National Institute on Drug Abuse (NIDA), December 2014.

How Are Club Drugs Abused?

Raves and trance events are generally night-long dances, often held in warehouses. Many who attend raves and trances do not use club drugs, but those who do may be attracted to their generally low cost and the intoxicating highs that are said to deepen the rave or trance experience.

- Rohypnol is usually taken orally, although there are reports that it can be ground up and snorted.

- GHB and Rohypnol have both been used to facilitate date rape (also known as "drug rape," "acquaintance rape," or "drug-assisted" assault). They can be colorless, tasteless, and odorless, and can be added to beverages and ingested unbeknownst to the victim.

  When mixed with alcohol, Rohypnol can incapacitate victims and prevent them from resisting sexual assault.

- GHB also has anabolic effects (it stimulates protein synthesis) and has been sought by bodybuilders to aid in fat reduction and muscle building.

- Ketamine is usually snorted or injected intramuscularly.

MDMA (Ecstasy/Molly)

What Is Ecstasy/MDMA?

MDMA acts as both a stimulant and psychedelic, producing an energizing effect, distortions in time and perception, and enhanced enjoyment of tactile experiences.

Adolescents and young adults use it to reduce inhibitions and to promote:

- Euphoria, feelings of closeness, empathy, and sexuality

Although MDMA is known among users as Ecstasy, researchers have determined that many Ecstasy tablets contain not only MDMA but also a number of other drugs or drug combinations that can be harmful, such as:

- Methamphetamine, ketamine, cocaine, the over-the-counter cough suppressant dextromethorphan (DXM), the diet drug ephedrine, and caffeine.

In addition, other drugs similar to MDMA, such as MDA or PMA, are often sold as Ecstasy, which can lead to overdose and death when the user takes additional doses to obtain the desired effect.

What Is Its Origin?

MDMA is a synthetic chemical made in labs. Seized MDMA across our borders from, clandestine laboratories in Canada and, to a lesser extent, the Netherlands. A small number of MDMA clandestine laboratories have also been identified operating in the United States.

What Are Common Street Names?

Common street names include:

- Adam
- Beans
- Clarity
- Disco Biscuit
- E
- Ecstasy
- Eve
- Go
- Hug Drug
- Lover's Speed
- MDMA
- PMeace
- STP
- X
- XTC

What Does It Look Like?

MDMA is mainly distributed in tablet form. MDMA tablets are sold with logos, creating brand names for users to seek out. The colorful pills are often hidden among colorful candies. MDMA is also distributed in capsules, powder, and liquid forms.

How Is It Abused?

MDMA use mainly involves swallowing tablets (50–150 mg), which are sometimes crushed and snorted, occasionally smoked but rarely injected. MDMA is also available as a powder.

MDMA abusers usually take MDMA by "stacking" (taking three or more tablets at once) or by "piggy-backing" (taking a series of tablets over a short period of time). One trend among young adults is "candy flipping," which is the co-abuse of MDMA and LSD.

MDMA is considered a "party drug." As with many other drugs of abuse, MDMA is rarely used alone. It is common for users to mix MDMA with other substances, such as alcohol and marijuana.

What Is Its Effect On The Mind?

MDMA mainly affects brain cells that use the chemical serotonin to communicate with each other. Serotonin helps to regulate mood, aggression, sexual activity, sleep, and sensitivity to pain. Clinical studies suggest that MDMA may increase the risk of long-term, perhaps permanent, problems with memory and learning.

MDMA causes changes in perception, including euphoria and increased sensitivity to touch, energy, sensual and sexual arousal, need to be touched, and need for stimulation.

Some unwanted psychological effects include:

• Confusion, anxiety, depression, paranoia, sleep problems, and drug craving

All these effects usually occur within 30 to 45 minutes of swallowing the drug and usually last 4 to 6 hours, but they may occur or last weeks after ingestion.

What Is Its Effect On The Body?

Users of MDMA experience many of the same effects and face many of the same risks as users of other stimulants such as cocaine and amphetamines. These include increased motor activity, alertness, heart rate, and blood pressure.

Some unwanted physical effects include:

• Muscle tension, tremors, involuntary teeth clenching, muscle cramps, nausea, faintness, chills, sweating, and blurred vision

High doses of MDMA can interfere with the ability to regulate body temperature, resulting in a sharp increase in body temperature (hyperthermia), leading to liver, kidney and cardiovascular failure.

Severe dehydration can result from the combination of the drug's effects and the crowded and hot conditions in which the drug is often taken.

Studies suggest chronic use of MDMA can produce damage to the serotonin system. It is ironic that a drug that is taken to increase pleasure may cause damage that reduces a person's ability to feel pleasure.

What Are Its Overdose Effects?

In high doses, MDMA can interfere with the body's ability to regulate temperature. On occasions, this can lead to a sharp increase in body temperature (hyperthermia), resulting in liver, kidney, and cardiovascular system failure, and death. Because MDMA can interfere with

Table 39.1. Possible Health Effects And Treatment Options Of MDMA

Possible Health Effects

Short-Term	Lowered inhibition; enhanced sensory perception; confusion; depression; sleep problems; anxiety; increased heart rate and blood pressure; muscle tension; teeth clenching; nausea; blurred vision; faintness; chills or sweating; sharp rise in body temperature leading to liver, kidney, or heart failure and death.
Long-Term	Long-lasting confusion, depression, problems with attention, memory, and sleep; increased anxiety, impulsiveness, aggression; loss of appetite; less interest in sex.
Other Health-Related Issues	Unknown.
In Combination With Alcohol	May increase the risk of cell and organ damage.
Withdrawal Symptoms	Fatigue, loss of appetite, depression, trouble concentrating.
Treatment Options	
Medications	There is conflicting evidence about whether MDMA is addictive. There are no FDA-approved medications to treat MDMA addiction.
Behavioral Therapies	More research is needed to find out if behavioral therapies can be used to treat MDMA addiction.

its own metabolism (that is, its break down within the body), potentially harmful levels can be reached by repeated drug use within short intervals.

Which Drugs Cause Similar Effects?

No other drug is quite like MDMA, but MDMA produces both amphetamine-like stimulation and mild mescaline-like hallucinations.

What Is Its Legal Status In The United States?

MDMA is a Schedule I drug under the Controlled Substances Act, meaning it has a high potential for abuse, no currently accepted medical use in treatment in the United States, and a lack of accepted safety for use under medical supervision.

GHB

What Is GHB?

Gamma-Hydroxybutyric acid (GHB) is another name for the generic drug sodium oxybate. Xyrem® (which is sodiumoxybate) is the trade name of the U.S. Food and Drug Administration (FDA)-approved prescription medication.

Analogues that are often substituted for GHB include GBL (gamma butyrolactone) and 1,4 BD (also called just "BD"), which is 1,4-butanediol. These analogues are available legally as industrial solvents used to produce polyurethane, pesticides, elastic fibers, pharmaceuticals, coatings on metal or plastic, and other products. They are also are sold illicitly as supplements for bodybuilding, fat loss, reversal of baldness, improved eyesight, and to combat aging, depression, drug addiction, and insomnia.

GBL and BD are sold as "fish tank cleaner," "ink stain remover," "ink cartridge cleaner," and "nail enamel remover" for approximately $100 per bottle—much more expensive than comparable products. Attempts to identify the abuse of GHB analogues are hampered by the fact that routine toxicological screens do not detect the presence of these analogues.

What Is Its Origin?

GHB is produced illegally in both domestic and foreign clandestine laboratories. The major source of GHB on the street is through clandestine synthesis by local operators. At bars or "rave" parties, GHB is typically sold in liquid form by the capful or "swig" for $5 to $25 per cap. Xyrem® has the potential for diversion and abuse like any other pharmaceutical containing a controlled substance. GHB has been encountered in nearly every region of the country.

What Are Common Street Names?

Common street names include:

- Easy Lay
- G
- Georgia Home Boy
- GHB
- Goop

- Grievous Bodily Harm
- Liquid Ecstasy
- Liquid X
- Scoop

What Does It Look Like?

GHB is usually sold as a liquid or as a white powder that is dissolved in a liquid, such as water, juice, or alcohol, GHB. dissolved in liquid has been packaged in small vials or small water bottles. In liquid form, GHB is clear and colorless and slightly salty in taste.

How Is It Abused?

GHB and its analogues are abused for their euphoric and calming effects and because some people believe they build muscles and cause weight loss.

GHB and its analogues are also misused for their ability to increase libido, suggestibility, passivity, and to cause amnesia (no memory of events while under the influence of the substance) — traits that make users vulnerable to sexual . assault and other criminal acts.

GHB abuse became popular among teens and young adults at dance clubs and "raves" in the 1990s and gained notoriety as a date rape drug. GHB is taken alone or in combination with other drugs, such as alcohol (primarily), other depressants, stimulants, hallucinogens, and marijuana.

The average dose ranges from 1 to 5 grams (depending on the purity of the compound, this can be 1 to 2 teaspoons mixed in a beverage). However, the concentrations of these "homebrews" have varied so much that users are usually unaware of the actual dose they are drinking.

What Is Its Effect On The Mind?

GHB occurs naturally in the central nervous system in very small amounts. Use of GHB produces Central Nervous System (CNS) depressant effects including:

- Euphoria, drowsiness, decreased anxiety, confusion, and memory impairment

GHB can also produce both visual hallucinations and —paradoxically — excited and aggressive behavior. GHB greatly increases the CNS depressant effects of alcohol and other depressants.

What Is Its Effect On The Body?

GHB takes effect in 15 to 30 minutes, and the effects last 3 to 6 hours. Low doses of GHB produce nausea.

At high doses, GHB overdose can result in:

- Unconsciousness, seizures, slowed heart rate, greatly slowed breathing, lower body temperature, vomiting, nausea, coma, and death

Regular use of GHB can lead to addiction and withdrawal that includes:

- Insomnia, anxiety, tremors, increased heart rate and blood pressure, and occasional psychotic thoughts

Currently, there is no antidote available for GHB intoxication.GHB analogues are known to produce side effects such as:

- Topical irritation to the skin and eyes, nausea, vomiting, incontinence, loss of consciousness, seizures, liver damage, kidney failure, respiratory depression, and death.

Table 39.2. Possible Health Effects And Treatment Options Of GHB

Possible Health Effects

Short-Term	Euphoria, drowsiness, decreased anxiety, confusion, memory loss, hallucinations, excited and aggressive behavior, nausea, vomiting, unconsciousness, seizures, slowed heart rate and breathing, lower body temperature, coma, death.
Long-Term	Unknown.
Other Health-Related Issues	Sometimes used as a date rape drug.
In Combination With Alcohol	Nausea, problems with breathing, greatly increased depressant effects.
Withdrawal Symptoms	Insomnia, anxiety, tremors, sweating, increased heart rate and blood pressure, psychotic thoughts.

Treatment Options

Medications	Benzodiazepines.
Behavioral Therapies	More research is needed to find out if behavioral therapies can be used to treat GHB addiction.

What Are Its Overdose Effects?

GHB overdose can cause death.

Which Drugs Cause Similar Effects?

GHB analogues are often abused in place of GHB. Both GBL and BD metabolize to GHB when taken and produce effects similar to GHB. CNS depressants such as barbiturates and methaqualone also produce effects similar to GHB.

What Is Its Legal Status In The United States?

GHB is a Schedule I controlled substance, meaning that it has a high potential for abuse, no currently accepted medical use in treatment in the United States, and a lack of accepted safety for use under medical supervision. GHB products are Schedule III substances under the Controlled Substances Act. In addition, GBL is a List I chemical.

It was placed on Schedule I of the Controlled Substances Act in March 2000. However, when sold as GHB products (such as Xyrem®), it is considered Schedule III, one of several drugs that are listed in multiple schedules.

Rohypnol®

What Is Rohypnol®?

Rohypnol® is a trade name for flunitrazepam, a central nervous system (CNS) depressant that belongs to a class of drugs known as benzodiazepines. Flunitrazepam is also marketed as generic preparations and other trade name products outside of the United States.

Like other benzodiazepines, Rohypnol® produces sedative-hypnotic, anti-anxiety, and muscle relaxant effects. This drug has never been approved for medical use in the United States by the Food and Drug Administration. Outside the United States, Rohypnol is commonly prescribed to treat insomnia.

Rohypnol is also referred to as a "date rape" drug.

What Is Its Origin?

Rohypnol is smuggled into the United States from other countries, such as Mexico.

What Are Common Street Names?

Common street names include:

- Circles
- Forget Pill
- Forget-Me-Pill
- La Rocha
- Lunch Money Drug
- Mexican Valium
- Pingus
- R2
- Reynolds
- Roach
- Roach 2
- Roaches
- Roachies
- Roapies
- Robutal
- Rochas Dos
- Rohypnol
- Roofies
- Rophies
- Ropies
- Roples
- Row-Shay
- Ruffies
- Wolfies

What Does It Look Like?

Prior to 1997, Rohypnol® was manufactured as a white tablet (0.5-2 milligrams per tablet), and when mixed in drinks, was colorless, tasteless, and odorless. In 1997, the manu-

203

facturer responded to concerns about the drug's role in sexual assaults by reformulating the drug.

Rohypnol® is now manufactured as an oblong olive green tablet with a speckled blue core that when dissolved in light-colored drinks will dye the liquid blue. However, generic versions of the drug may not contain the blue dye.

How Is It Abused?

The tablet can be swallowed whole, crushed and snorted, or dissolved in liquid. Adolescents may abuse Rohypnol® to produce a euphoric effect often described as a "high." While high, they experience reduced inhibitions and impaired judgment.

Rohypnol® is also abused in combination with alcohol to produce an exaggerated intoxication.

In addition, abuse of Rohypnol® may be associated with multiple-substance abuse. For example, cocaine addicts may use benzodiazepines such as Rohypnol® to relieve the side effects (e.g., irritability and agitation) associated with cocaine binges.

Rohypnol® is also misused to physically and psychologically incapacitate women targeted for sexual assault. The drug is usually placed in the alcoholic drink of an unsuspecting victim to incapacitate them and prevent resistance to sexual assault. The drug leaves the victim unaware of what has happened to them.

What Is Its Effect On The Mind?

Like other benzodiazepines, Rohypnol® slows down the functioning of the CNS producing:

- Drowsiness (sedation), sleep (pharmacological hypnosis), decreased anxiety, and amnesia (no memory of events while under the influence of the substance)

Rohypnol® can also cause:

- Increased or decreased reaction time, impaired mental functioning and judgment, confusion, aggression, and excitability

What Is Its Effect On The Body?

Rohypnol® causes muscle relaxation. Adverse physical effects include:

- Slurred speech, loss of motor coordination, weakness, headache, and respiratory depression

Rohypnol also can produce physical dependence when taken regularly over a period of time.

What Are Its Overdose Effects?

High doses of Rohypnol®, particularly when combined with CNS depressant drugs such as alcohol and heroin, can cause severe sedation, unconsciousness, slow heart rate, and suppression of respiration that may be sufficient to result in death.

Which Drugs Cause Similar Effects?

Drugs that cause similar effects include GHB (gamma hydroxybutyrate) and other benzodiazepines such as alprazolam (e.g., Xanax®), clonazepam (e.g., Klonopin®), and diazepam (e.g., Valium®).

What Is Its Legal Status In The United States?

Rohypnol® is a Schedule IV substance under the Controlled Substance Act. Rohypnol® is not approved for manufacture, sale, use or importation to the United States. It is legally manu-

Table 39.3. Possible Health Effects And Treatment Options Of Rohypnol© (Flunitrazepam)

Possible Health Effects

Short-Term	Drowsiness, sedation, sleep; amnesia, blackout; decreased anxiety; muscle relaxation, impaired reaction time and motor coordination; impaired mental functioning and judgment; confusion; aggression; excitability; slurred speech; headache; slowed breathing and heart rate.
Long-Term	Unknown.
Other Health-Related Issues	Unknown.
In Combination With Alcohol	Severe sedation, unconsciousness, and slowed heart rate and breathing, which can lead to death.
Withdrawal Symptoms	Headache; muscle pain; extreme anxiety, tension, restlessness, confusion, irritability; numbness and tingling of hands or feet; hallucinations, delirium, convulsions, seizures, or shock.

Treatment Options

Medications	There are no FDA-approved medications to treat addiction to Rohypnol® or other prescription sedatives.
Behavioral Therapies	More research is needed to find out if behavioral therapies can be used to treat addiction to Rohypnol® or other prescription sedatives.

factured and marketed in many countries. Penalties for possession, trafficking, and distribution involving one gram or more are the same as those of a Schedule I drug.

Ketamine

What Is Its Effect On The Body?

A couple of minutes after taking the drug, the user may experience an increase in heart rate and blood pressure that gradually decreases over the next 10 to 20 minutes. Ketamine can make users unresponsive to stimuli.

When in this state, users experience:

- Involuntarily rapid eye movement, dilated pupils, salivation, tear secretions, and stiffening of the muscles

This drug can also cause nausea.

All Drugs Lower Your Defenses

It's important to remember that all drugs affect how well your mind and body operate. In fact, alcohol is linked to far more date rapes than the drugs we've mentioned here. And nearly all drugs of abuse make people vulnerable to being taken advantage of by impairing judgment, reducing reaction time, and clouding a person's thinking.

And as disgusting as it is, when you don't have your wits about you, someone may take that as an opportunity to push themselves on you.

Table 39.4. Possible Health Effects And Treatment Options Of Ketamine

Possible Health Effects

Short-Term	Problems with attention, learning, and memory; dreamlike states, hallucinations; sedation; confusion and problems speaking; loss of memory; problems moving, to the point of being immobile; raised blood pressure; unconsciousness; slowed breathing that can lead to death.
Long-Term	Ulcers and pain in the bladder; kidney problems; stomach pain; depression; poor memory.
Other Health-Related Issues	Sometimes used as a date rape drug.
	Risk of HIV, hepatitis, and other infectious diseases from shared needles.
In Combination With Alcohol	Increased risk of adverse effects.

Table 39.4. Continued

Possible Health Effects

Withdrawal Symptoms	Unknown.

Treatment Options

Medications	There are no FDA-approved medications to treat addiction to ketamine or other dissociative drugs.
Behavioral Therapies	More research is needed to find out if behavioral therapies can be used to treat addiction to dissociative drugs.

How You Can Avoid Date Rape Drugs

If you are at a party where people are drinking alcohol, you should be aware that there could be predators hoping to make you drunk or vulnerable. No matter what you are drinking, even if it's sodas or juice, people can slip drugs in your drinks—so pour all drinks yourself and never leave them unattended (even if you have to take them into the bathroom with you).

Also, be sure to stick with your friends—there's safety in numbers.

But even if you leave your drink or leave your friends behind, know this for certain: if you are drugged and taken advantage of, it's not your fault.

Bottom line
People who date rape other people are committing a crime.

Chapter 40

Hallucinogens

Hallucinogenic compounds found in some plants and mushrooms (or their extracts) have been used—mostly during religious rituals—for centuries. Almost all hallucinogens contain nitrogen and are classified as alkaloids. Many hallucinogens have chemical structures similar to those of natural neurotransmitters (e.g., acetylcholine-, serotonin-, or catecholamine-like). While the exact mechanisms by which hallucinogens exert their effects remain unclear, research suggests that these drugs work, at least partially, by temporarily interfering with neurotransmitter action or by binding to their receptor sites. This Section will discuss four common types of hallucinogens:

1. LSD (d-lysergic acid diethylamide) is one of the most potent mood-changing chemicals. It was discovered in 1938 and is manufactured from lysergic acid, which is found in ergot, a fungus that grows on rye and other grains.

2. Peyote is a small, spineless cactus in which the principal active ingredient is mescaline. This plant has been used by natives in northern Mexico and the southwestern United States as a part of religious ceremonies. Mescaline can also be produced through chemical synthesis.

3. Psilocybin (4-phosphoryloxy-N,N-dimethyltryptamine) is obtained from certain types of mushrooms that are indigenous to tropical and subtropical regions of South America, Mexico, and the United States. These mushrooms typically contain less

About This Chapter: Information in this chapter is excerpted from "DrugFacts: Hallucinogens – LSD, Peyote, Psilocybin, and PCP," National Institute on Drug Abuse (NIDA), December 2014; and information from "Salvia," NIDA for Teens, National Institute on Drug Abuse (NIDA), October 23, 2015.

than 0.5 percent psilocybin plus trace amounts of psilocin, another hallucinogenic substance.

4. PCP (phencyclidine) was developed in the 1950s as an intravenous anesthetic. Its use has since been discontinued due to serious adverse effects.

How Are Hallucinogens Abused?

The very same characteristics that led to the incorporation of hallucinogens into ritualistic or spiritual traditions have also led to their propagation as drugs of abuse. Importantly, and unlike most other drugs, the effects of hallucinogens are highly variable and unreliable, producing different effects in different people at different times. This is mainly due to the significant variations in amount and composition of active compounds, particularly in the hallucinogens derived from plants and mushrooms. Because of their unpredictable nature, the use of hallucinogens can be particularly dangerous.

LSD: LSD is sold in tablets, capsules, and, occasionally, liquid form; thus, it is usually taken orally. LSD is often added to absorbent paper, which is then divided into decorated pieces, each equivalent to one dose. The experiences, often referred to as "trips," are long; typically, they end after about 12 hours.

Peyote: The top of the peyote cactus, also referred to as the crown, consists of disc-shaped buttons that are cut from the roots and dried. These buttons are generally chewed or soaked in water to produce an intoxicating liquid. The hallucinogenic dose of mescaline is about 0.3 to 0.5 grams, and its effects last about 12 hours. Because the extract is so bitter, some individuals prefer to prepare a tea by boiling the cacti for several hours.

Psilocybin: Mushrooms containing psilocybin are available fresh or dried and are typically taken orally. Psilocybin (4-phosphoryloxy-N,N-dimethyltryptamine) and its biologically active form, psilocin (4-hydroxy-N,N-dimethyltryptamine), cannot be inactivated by cooking or freezing preparations. Thus, they may also be brewed as a tea or added to other foods to mask their bitter flavor. The effects of psilocybin, which appear within 20 minutes of ingestion, last approximately 6 hours.

PCP: PCP is a white crystalline powder that is readily soluble in water or alcohol. It has a distinctive bitter chemical taste. PCP can be mixed easily with dyes and is often sold on the illicit drug market in a variety of tablet, capsule, and colored powder forms that are normally snorted, smoked, or orally ingested. For smoking, PCP is often applied to a leafy material such as mint, parsley, oregano, or marijuana. Depending upon how much and by what route PCP is taken, its effects can last approximately 4–6 hours.

How Do Hallucinogens Affect the Brain?

LSD, peyote, psilocybin, and PCP are drugs that cause hallucinations, which are profound distortions in a person's perception of reality. Under the influence of hallucinogens, people see images, hear sounds, and feel sensations that seem real but are not. Some hallucinogens also produce rapid, intense emotional swings. LSD, peyote, and psilocybin cause their effects by initially disrupting the interaction of nerve cells and the neurotransmitter serotonin. Distributed throughout the brain and spinal cord, the serotonin system is involved in the control of behavioral, perceptual, and regulatory systems, including mood, hunger, body temperature, sexual behavior, muscle control, and sensory perception. On the other hand, PCP acts mainly through a type of glutamate receptor in the brain that is important for the perception of pain, responses to the environment, and learning and memory.

LSD: LSD binds to and activates a specific receptor for the neurotransmitter serotonin. Normally, serotonin binds to and activates its receptors and then is taken back up into the neuron that released it. In contrast, LSD binds very tightly to the serotonin receptor, causing a greater than normal activation of the receptor. Because serotonin has a role in many of the brain's functions, activation of its receptors by LSD produces widespread effects, including rapid emotional swings, and altered perceptions, and if taken in a large enough dose, delusions and visual hallucinations.

Peyote: The long-term residual psychological and cognitive effects of mescaline, peyote's principal active ingredient, remain poorly understood. Peyote abusers may also experience flashbacks.

Psilocybin: The active compounds in psilocybin-containing "magic" mushrooms have LSD-like properties and produce alterations of autonomic function, motor reflexes, behavior, and perception. The psychological consequences of psilocybin use include hallucinations, an altered perception of time, and an inability to discern fantasy from reality. Panic reactions and psychosis also may occur, particularly if a user ingests a large dose. Long-term effects such as flashbacks, risk of psychiatric illness, impaired memory, and tolerance have been described in case reports.

PCP: PCP, which is not a true hallucinogen, can affect many neurotransmitter systems. It interferes with the functioning of the neurotransmitter glutamate, which is found in neurons throughout the brain. Like many other drugs, it also causes dopamine to be released from neurons into the synapse. At low to moderate doses, PCP causes altered perception of body image, but rarely produces visual hallucinations. PCP can also cause effects that mimic the primary symptoms of schizophrenia, such as delusions and mental turmoil. People who use PCP for long periods of time have memory loss and speech difficulties.

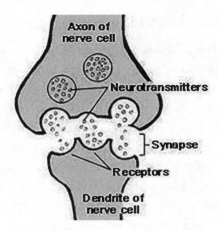

Figure 40.1. Hallucinogens And Neurotransmitters

How Hallucinogens Affect Your Senses

Your brain controls all of your perceptions—the way you see, hear, smell, taste, and feel. How does your brain communicate with the rest of your body? Chemical messengers transmit information from nerve cell to nerve cell in the body and the brain. Messages are constantly being sent back and forth with amazing speed.

Your nerve cells are called neurons, and their chemical messengers are called neurotransmitters. When neurotransmitters attach to special places on nerve cells (called receptors), they cause changes in the nerve cells.

This communication system can be disrupted by chemicals like hallucinogens, and the results are changes in the way you sense the world around you.

What Other Adverse Effects Do Hallucinogens Have on Health?

Unpleasant adverse effects as a result of the use of hallucinogens are not uncommon. These may be due to the large number of psychoactive ingredients in any single source of hallucinogen.

LSD: The effects of LSD depend largely on the amount taken. LSD causes dilated pupils; can raise body temperature and increase heart rate and blood pressure; and can cause profuse sweating, loss of appetite, sleeplessness, dry mouth, and tremors.

Peyote: Its effects can be similar to those of LSD, including increased body temperature and heart rate, uncoordinated movements (ataxia), profound sweating, and flushing. The active ingredient mescaline has also been associated, in at least one report, to fetal abnormalities.

Psilocybin: It can produce muscle relaxation or weakness, ataxia, excessive pupil dilation, nausea, vomiting, and drowsiness. Individuals who abuse psilocybin mushrooms also risk poisoning if one of many existing varieties of poisonous mushrooms is incorrectly identified as a psilocybin mushroom.

PCP: At low-to-moderate doses, physiological effects of PCP include a slight increase in breathing rate and a pronounced rise in blood pressure and pulse rate. Breathing becomes shallow; flushing and profuse sweating, generalized numbness of the extremities, and loss of muscular coordination may occur.

At high doses, blood pressure, pulse rate, and respiration drop. This may be accompanied by nausea, vomiting, blurred vision, flicking up and down of the eyes, drooling, loss of balance, and dizziness. PCP abusers are often brought to emergency rooms because of overdose or because of the drug's severe untoward psychological effects. While intoxicated, PCP abusers may become violent or suicidal and are therefore dangerous to themselves and others. High doses of PCP can also cause seizures, coma, and death (though death more often results from accidental injury or suicide during PCP intoxication). Because PCP can also have sedative effects, interactions with other central nervous system depressants, such as alcohol and benzo-diazepines, can also lead to coma.

Salvia (*Salvia divinorum*)

What Is Salvia?

Also known as: "shepherdess's herb," "diviner's sage," "seer's sage," "Maria pastora," "magic mint," and or "Sally-D"

Salvia (*Salvia divinorum*) is an herb in the mint family found in southern Mexico. The main active ingredient in salvia, salvinorin A, changes the chemistry in the brain, causing hallucinations (seeing something that seems real but isn't). The effects are short lived, but may be very intense and frightening.

Although salvia is not illegal according to federal law, several states and countries have passed laws to regulate its use. The Drug Enforcement Administration (DEA) lists salvia as a drug of concern that poses risk to people who use it.

How Is Salvia Used?

Usually, people chew fresh salvia leaves or drink their extracted juices. The dried leaves of salvia also can be smoked in rolled cigarettes, inhaled through water pipes (hookahs), or vaporized and inhaled.

How Does Salvia Affect The Brain?

Researchers are studying salvia to learn exactly how it acts in the brain to produce its effects. What is currently known is that salvinorin A, the main active ingredient in salvia, attaches to parts of nerve cells called kappa opioid receptors.

The effects of salvinorin A are described as intense but short lived, generally lasting for less than 30 minutes. People who use salvia generally have hallucinations—they see or feel things that aren't really there. They also have changes in vision, mood and body sensations, emotional swings, and feelings of detachment (disconnected from their environment). There are reports of people losing contact with reality—being unable to tell the difference between what's real and what's not. Many of these effects raise concern about the dangers of driving under the influence of salvia.

What Are The Other Effects Of Salvia?

Physical and other effects of saliva use have not been fully studied. There have been reports that the drug causes loss of coordination, dizziness, and slurred speech.

In addition, we also don't know the long-term effects of using the drug. However, recent studies with animals showed that salvia harms learning and memory.

Can You Get Addicted To Salvia?

It's not clear if using salvia leads to addiction. More studies are needed to learn whether it has addictive properties.

Can You Die If You Use Salvia?

It is not clear whether there have been any deaths associated with salvia. However, because we do not know all of salvia's effects, it is a drug that authorities are watching carefully.

Chapter 41
Stimulants: An Overview

What Are Stimulants?

Stimulants speed up the body's systems. this class of drugs includes:

- Prescription drugs such as amphetamines [Adderall® and dexedrine®], methylphenidate [Concerta® and Ritalin®], diet aids [such as didrex®, Bontril®, Preludin®, Fastin®, Adipex P®, ionomin®, and Meridia®] and illicitly produced drugs such as methamphetamine, cocaine, and methcathinone.

What Is Their Origin?

Stimulants are diverted from legitimate channels and clandestinely manufactured exclusively for the illicit market.

What Are Common Street Names?

Common street names for Oxycodone include:

- Bennies
- Black Beauties
- Cat
- Coke
- Crank

- Crystal
- Flake
- Ice
- Pellets
- R-Ball

About This Chapter: Information in this chapter is excerpted from "Drugs of Abuse," Drug Enforcement Administration (DEA), 2015.

- Skippy
- Snow
- Speed
- Uppers
- Vitamin R

What Do They Look Like?

Stimulants come in the form of:

- Pills, powder, rocks, and injectable liquids

How Are They Abused?

Stimulants can be pills or capsules that are swallowed. Smoking, snorting, or injecting stimulants produces a sudden sensation known as a "rush" or a "flash."

Abuse is often associated with a pattern of binge use—sporadically consuming large doses of stimulants over a short period of time. Heavy users may inject themselves every few hours, continuing until they have depleted their drug supply or reached a point of delirium, psychosis, and physical exhaustion. During heavy use, all other interests become secondary to recreating the initial euphoric rush.

What Is Their Effect On The Mind?

When used as drugs of abuse and not under a doctor's supervision, stimulants are frequently taken to:

- Produce a sense of exhilaration, enhance self-esteem, improve mental and physical performance, increase activity, reduce appetite, extend wakefulness for prolonged period, and "get high".

Chronic, high-dose use is frequently associated with agitation, hostility, panic, aggression, and suicidal or homicidal tendencies.

Paranoia, sometimes accompanied by both auditory and visual hallucinations, may also occur.

Tolerance, in which more and more drug is needed to produce the usual effects, can develop rapidly, and psychological dependence occurs. In fact, the strongest psychological dependence observed occurs with the more potent stimulants, such as amphetamine, methylphenidate, methamphetamine, cocaine and methcathinone.

Abrupt cessation is commonly followed by depression, anxiety, drug craving, and extreme fatigue, known as a "crash."

What Is Their Effect On The Body?

Stimulants are sometimes referred to as uppers and reverse the effects of fatigue on both mental and physical tasks. Therapeutic levels of stimulants can produce exhilaration, extended wakefulness, and loss of appetite. These effects are greatly intensified when large doses of stimulants are taken.

Taking too large a dose at one time or taking large doses over an extended period of time may cause such physical side effects as:

- Dizziness, tremors, headache, flushed skin, chest pain with palpitations, excessive sweating, vomiting, and abdominal cramps.

What Are Their Overdose Effects?

In overdose, unless there is medical intervention, high fever, convulsions, and cardiovascular collapse may precede death. Because accidental death is partially due to the effects of stimulants on the body's cardiovascular and temperature-regulating systems, physical exertion increases the hazards of stimulant use.

Which Drugs Cause Similar Effects?

Some hallucinogenic substances, such as Ecstasy, have a stimulant component to their activity.

What Is Their Legal Status In The United States?

A number of stimulants have no medical use in the United States but have a high potential for abuse. These stimulants are controlled in Schedule I. Some prescription stimulants are not controlled, and some stimulants like tobacco and caffeine don't require a prescription—though society's recognition of their adverse effects has resulted in a proliferation of caffeine-free products and efforts to discourage cigarette smoking. Stimulant chemicals in over-the-counter products, such as ephedrine and pseudoephedrine can be found in allergy and cold medicine.

As required by The Combat Methamphetamine Epidemic Act of 2005, a retail outlet must store these products out of reach of customers, either behind the counter or in a locked cabinet. Regulated sellers are required to maintain a written or electronic form of a logbook to record sales of these products. In order to purchase these products, customers must now show a photo identification issued by a state or federal government. They are also required to write or enter into the logbook: their name, signature, address, date, and time of sale. In addition to the above, there are daily and monthly sales limits set for customers.

Chapter 42
Bath Salts

What Are Bath Salts?

Also known as: "Bloom," "Cloud Nine," "Vanilla Sky," "White Lightning," and "Scarface"

"Bath salts" is the name given to a family of drugs that have one or more manmade chemicals related to cathinone. Cathinone is an amphetamine-like stimulant found naturally in the khat plant. Chemically, they are similar to other amphetamines such as methamphetamine and to MDMA (Ecstasy or Molly). Common manmade cathinones found in bath salts include 3,4-methylenedioxypyrovalerone (MDPV), mephedrone ("Drone," "Meph," or "Meow Meow"), and methylone, but there are many others.

Bath salts are usually white or brown crystal-like powder and are sold in small plastic or foil packages labeled "Not for Human Consumption." Sometimes labeled as "plant food"—or, more recently, as "jewelry cleaner" or "phone screen cleaner"—they are sold online and in drug product stores. These names or descriptions have nothing to do with the product. It's a way for the drug makers to avoid detection by the Drug Enforcement Administration or local police.

The manmade cathinone products sold as "bath salts" should not be confused with Epsom salts (the original bath salts), which are made of a mineral mixture of magnesium and sulfate and are added to bathwater to help ease stress and relax muscles.

Use of bath salts sometimes causes severe intoxication (a person seems very drunk or "out of it") and dangerous health effects. There are also reports of people becoming psychotic (losing touch with reality) and violent. Although it is rare, there have been several cases where bath salts have been the direct cause of death.

About This Chapter: Information in this chapter is excerpted from "Bath Salts," NIDA for Teens, National Institute on Drug Abuse (NIDA), October 23, 2015.

In addition, people who believe they are taking drugs such as MDMA (Molly or Ecstasy) may be getting bath salts instead. Methylone, a common chemical in bath salts, has been substituted for MDMA in capsules sold as Molly in some areas.

Banning Bath Salts

At the end of the last decade, bath salts began to be gain in popularity in the United States and Europe as "legal highs." In October 2011, the Drug Enforcement Administration (DEA) put an emergency ban on three common manmade cathinones until officials knew more about them. In July 2012, President Barack Obama signed legislation permanently making two of them—mephedrone and MDPV—illegal, along with several other manmade drugs often sold as marijuana substitutes (like Spice).

Although the law also bans chemically similar "analogues" of the named drugs, manufacturers have responded by making new drugs different enough from the banned substances to get around the law.

How Are Bath Salts Used?

Bath salts can be swallowed, snorted through the nose, inhaled, or injected with a needle. Snorting or injecting is the most harmful.

How Do Bath Salts Affect The Brain?

The manmade cathinones in bath salts can produce feelings of joy and increased social interaction and sex drive. These chemicals can also cause people to feel paranoid and nervous and to have hallucinations (see or hear things that are not real). There is a lot we still don't know about how the different chemicals in bath salts affect the brain.

The energizing and often agitating effects reported in people who have taken bath salts are similar to the effects of other drugs like amphetamines and cocaine. These drugs raise the level of dopamine in brain paths that control reward and movement. Dopamine is the main neurotransmitter (a substance that passes messages between nerve cells) that makes people feel good when they do something they enjoy. A rush of dopamine causes feelings of joy and increased activity and can also raise heart rate and blood pressure.

A study in animals found that MDPV raises brain dopamine in the same way as cocaine but is at least 10 times stronger. If this is also true in people, it may account for the reason that MDPV is the most common manmade cathinone found in the blood and urine of patients admitted to emergency rooms after taking bath salts.

Additionally, the hallucinations often reported by users of bath salts are similar to the effects caused by other drugs such as MDMA or LSD. These drugs raise levels of the neurotransmitter serotonin.

What Are The Other Effects Of Bath Salts?

In 2011, bath salts were reported in nearly 23,000 emergency room (ER) visits. Reports show bath salts users have needed help for heart problems (such as racing heart, high blood pressure, and chest pains) and symptoms like paranoia, hallucinations, and panic attacks.

Patients with the syndrome known as "excited delirium" from taking bath salts also may have dehydration, breakdown of muscle tissue attached to bones, and kidney failure. Intoxication from several manmade cathinones including MDPV, mephedrone, methedrone, and butylone has caused death among some users.

Another danger of bath salts is that these products may contain other ingredients that may cause their own harmful effects. There is no way to know what is in a dose of bath salts other than testing it in a lab.

Can You Get Addicted To Bath Salts?

Yes. Research shows and bath salts users have reported that the drugs cause an intense urge to use the drug again and that they are highly addictive. Frequent use may cause tolerance (a person needs to take more to feel the same effects), dependence, and strong withdrawal symptoms when not taking the drug.

Can You Die If You Use Bath Salts?

Yes. Intoxication from several manmade cathinones, including MDPV, mephedrone, methedrone, and butylone, has caused death among some users.

How Many Teens Use Bath Salts?

Bath salts have been involved in thousands of visits to the emergency room. In 2011, there were 22,904 reports of bath salts use during emergency room visits. About two thirds of those visits involved bath salts in combination with other drugs.

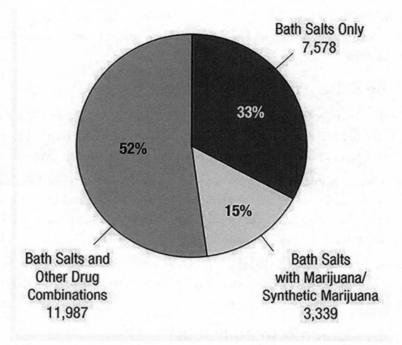

Figure 42.1. Emergency Visits Involving Bath Salts, By Drug Combination (2011)

Chapter 43

Cocaine And Khat

Cocaine

What Is Cocaine?

Also known as: "coke," "Coca," "C," "snow," "flake," "blow," "bump," "candy," "Charlie," "rock," and "toot"

Cocaine is a powerfully addictive stimulant drug made from the leaves of the coca plant native to South America. Cocaine comes in two forms:

1 **Powder cocaine** is a white powder (which scientists call a hydrochloride salt). Street dealers often mix cocaine with other substances like cornstarch, talcum powder, or sugar. They also mix cocaine with active drugs like procaine, a chemical that produces local anesthesia (a local anesthetic that causes you not to feel pain in a specific area of the body) and with other stimulants like amphetamines.

2 **Crack** is a form of cocaine that has been processed to make a rock crystal that people smoke. The term "crack" refers to the cracking sound the rocks make when they are heated. To make crack, the powder cocaine is mixed with ammonia or baking soda and water and then heated to produce the crystal.

About This Chapter: Information in this chapter is excerpted from "Cocaine," NIDA for Teens, National Institute on Drug Abuse (NIDA), October 23, 2015; information from "Drug Facts Chat Day: Cocaine," NIDA for Teens, National Institute on Drug Abuse (NIDA), November 10, 2015; information from "Real Teens Ask About Speedballs," NIDA for Teens, National Institute on Drug Abuse (NIDA), June 26, 2013; information from "Let's Talk About Khat," NIDA for Teens, National Institute on Drug Abuse (NIDA), April 23, 2014; and information from "Drugs of Abuse," U.S. Drug Enforcement Administration (DEA), 2015.

How Is Cocaine Used?

Powder cocaine can be snorted up the nose or mixed with water and injected with a needle. Sometimes, powder cocaine is rubbed onto gums or other tissues in the body. Crack is smoked in a small glass pipe. The crystal is heated to produce vapors that are absorbed into the blood through the lungs.

In order to keep the "high" going, people may take the drug repeatedly within a short period of time, at increasingly higher doses.

How Does Cocaine Affect The Brain?

Stimulants like cocaine change the way the brain works by changing the way nerve cells communicate. Nerve cells, called neurons, send messages to each other by releasing chemicals called neurotransmitters. These neurotransmitters attach to molecules on neurons called receptors.

There are many neurotransmitters, but dopamine is the main one that makes people feel good when they do something they enjoy, like eating a piece of chocolate cake or playing a video game. It is then recycled back into the cell that released it, thus shutting off the signal. Cocaine prevents the dopamine from being recycled, causing a buildup of the neurotransmitter in the brain. It is this flood of dopamine that causes cocaine's high. The drug can cause a feeling of intense pleasure and increased energy.

With repeated use, stimulants can disrupt how the brain's dopamine system works, reducing a person's ability to feel any pleasure at all. People may try to make up for it by taking more and more of the drug to feel the same pleasure.

After the "high" of the cocaine wears off, many people experience a "crash" and feel tired or sad for days. They also experience a strong craving to take cocaine again to try to feel better.

How Does Cocaine Make You Feel?

Cocaine belongs to a class of drugs called "stimulants," because they usually make you feel euphoric, energetic, hyperstimulated, and mentally alert. The high from snorting may last 15 to 20 minutes, while smoking may last 5 to 10 minutes. Cocaine can also make you feel hypersensitive to touch, sights, and sounds. Some cocaine abusers report feelings of restlessness, irritability and anxiety. Some of the immediate effects after using cocaine include constricted blood vessels, dilated pupils, increased heart rate and blood pressure. Heavy doses can lead to violent behavior and users may experience tremors, vertigo, muscle twitches, and paranoia. As a user begins to increase the dose and/or the frequency of drug taking the duration and intensity of the high may lessen, and once it is over, users can feel very tired and depressed. Cocaine is a powerfully addictive drug, and while it can make you feel high when you first use it, addiction is a very real albeit unpredictable possibility. Naturally, the wisest move is never to start.

What Are The Other Effects Of Cocaine?

The surge of dopamine in the brain affects the body in a variety of ways:

- Constricted blood vessels and dilated pupils
- Higher body temperature
- Higher blood pressure and faster heartbeat
- Feeling sick to the stomach
- Restlessness
- Decreased appetite and, over time, a loss of weight
- Inability to sleep
- Increased risk of heart attack or stroke due to high blood pressure
- Increased risk of HIV because of impaired judgment leading to risky sexual behavior
- Strange, unpredictable behavior, panic attacks, or paranoid psychosis (losing touch with reality)

How cocaine is used leads to different physical problems. For example, regularly snorting cocaine can lead to a hoarse voice, loss of the sense of smell, nosebleeds, and a constant runny nose. Cocaine taken by mouth can reduce blood flow in your intestines, leading to bowel problems. Injecting cocaine can increase a person's risk of getting HIV, hepatitis C (a liver disease), and other diseases transmitted by blood contact.

Can You Get Addicted To Cocaine?

Yes, repeated use can lead to addiction, a devastating brain disease where people can't stop using drugs even when they really want to and even after it causes terrible consequences to their health and other parts of their lives. Using cocaine over and over can cause tolerance to the drug. This means that it takes more of the drug for the user to get the same high felt when first using it.

Because a cocaine high usually doesn't last very long, people take it again and again to try to keep feeling good. Once addicted, people who are trying to quit taking cocaine might:

- Act nervous and restless

- Feel very sad and tired

- Have bad dreams

- Not trust people and things around them

- Feel a strong need to take cocaine

The right treatment, however, can help an addicted person control their cravings and stop using cocaine.

How Many Teens Use Cocaine?

For recent statistics on cocaine use among teens, see the results below from NIDA's *Monitoring the Future* study.

Can You Die If You Use Cocaine?

Yes. In 2011, more than 4,600 people died from a cocaine overdose. Males are nearly three times more likely to die from a cocaine overdose than females.

Cocaine can be deadly when taken in large doses or when mixed with other drugs or alcohol. Cocaine-related deaths are often a result of the heart stopping (cardiac arrest) fol-

Table 43.1. Trends In Prevalence Of Various Drugs For 8th Graders, 10th Graders, And 12th Graders; 2014 (In Percent)

Drug	Time Period	8th Graders	10th Graders	12th Graders
Cocaine	Lifetime	1.8	2.6	4.6
	Past Year	1	1.5	2.6
	Past Month	0.5	0.6	1
Crack Cocaine	Lifetime	1.2	[1.00]	1.8
	Past Year	0.7	[0.50]	1.1
	Past Month	0.3	0.3	0.7

Data in brackets indicate statistically significant change from the previous year.

lowed by stopped breathing. Abusing cocaine with alcohol or other drugs increases these dangers, including the risk of overdose. For example, combining cocaine and heroin (known as a "speedball") puts a person at higher risk of death from an overdose.

In rare instances, sudden death can occur on the first use of cocaine or soon after.

Speedball

A speedball is a combination of heroin and cocaine. Cocaine acts as a stimulant and heroin acts as a depressant, so taking them together creates a sort of "push-pull" reaction in the body and brain.

People use cocaine and heroin at the same time to get an intense rush with a high that is supposed to combine the effects of both drugs, while hoping to reduce the negative effects. However, the combination of cocaine and heroin can have fatal consequences. Negative effects of stimulants include anxiety, high blood pressure, and strong or irregular heartbeat, while the negative effects of depressants include drowsiness and suppression of breathing.

Taking stimulants with depressants can cause negative side effects typically associated with the abuse of either one individually, such as a state of general confusion, incoherence, blurred vision, stupor, drowsiness, paranoia, and mental impairment because of lack of sleep. The combination can also result in uncontrolled and uncoordinated motor skills, and also the risk of death from stroke, heart attack, aneurysm, or respiratory failure.

Respiratory failure is particularly likely with speedballs because the effects of cocaine wear off far more quickly than the effects of heroin. Fatal slowing of the breathing can occur when the stimulating cocaine wears off and the full effects of the heroin are felt on their own.

Khat

What Is Khat?

Khat is a flowering evergreen shrub that is abused for its stimulant-like effect. Khat has two active ingredients: cathine and cathinone.

What Is Its Origin?

Khat is native to East Africa and the Arabian Peninsula, where the use of it is an established cultural tradition for many social situations

What Are Common Street Names?

Common street names for Khat include:

- Abyssinian Tea
- Catha
- Kat
- African Salad
- Chat
- Oat

What Does It Look Like?

Khat is a flowering evergreen shrub. Khat that is sold and abused is usually just the leaves, twigs, and shoots of the Khat shrub.

Who Uses Khat?

People in Africa and the Arabian Peninsula—and people who have emigrated from those areas elsewhere—are the main users of khat. People in those regions have used khat for centuries as part of their cultural traditions and social interactions, and demand for khat has increased in the United States as people from those areas have moved here.

How Is It Abused?

Khat is typically chewed like tobacco, then retained in the cheek and chewed intermittently to release the active drug, which produces a stimulant-like effect. Dried Khat leaves can be made into tea or a chewable paste, and Khat can also be smoked and even sprinkled on food.

What Is Its Effect On The Mind?

Khat can induce manic behavior with:

Grandiose delusions, paranoia, nightmares, hallucinations, and hyperactivity

Chronic Khat abuse can result in violence and suicidal depression.

What Is Its Effect On The Body?

Khat causes an immediate increase in blood pressure and heart rate. Khat can also cause a brown staining of the teeth, insomnia, and gastric disorders. Chronic abuse of Khat can cause physical exhaustion.

What Are Its Overdose Effects?

The dose needed to constitute an overdose is not known, however it has historically been associated with those who have been long-term chewers of the leaves.

Symptoms of toxicity include:

Delusions, loss of appetite, difficulty with breathing, and increases in both blood pressure and heart rate

Additionally, there are reports of liver damage (chemical hepatitis) and of cardiac complications, specifically myocardial infarctions. This mostly occurs among long-term chewers of khat or those who have chewed too large a dose.

Which Drugs Cause Similar Effects?

Khat's effects are similar to other stimulants, such as cocaine and methamphetamine.

What Is Its Legal Status In The United States?

The chemicals found in khat are controlled under the Controlled Substances Act. Cathine is a Schedule IV stimulant, and cathinone is a Schedule I stimulant under the Controlled Substances Act, meaning that it has a high potential for abuse, no currently accepted medical use in treatment in the United States, and a lack of accepted safety for use under medical supervision.

Chapter 44
Methamphetamine

What Is Methamphetamine?

Methamphetamine (meth) is a stimulant. The FDA-approved brand-name medication is Desoxyn®.

What Is Its Origin?

Mexican drug trafficking organizations have become the primary manufacturers and distributors of methamphetamine to cities throughout the United States, including in Hawaii. Domestic clandestine laboratory operators also produce and distribute meth but usually on a smaller scale. The methods used depend on the availability of precursor chemicals. Currently, this domestic clandestinely produced meth is mainly made with diverted products that contain pseudoephedrine. Mexican methamphetamine is made with different precursor chemicals. The Combat Methamphetamine Epidemic Act of 2005 requires retailers of non-prescription products containing pseudoephedrine, ephedrine, or phenylpropanolamine to place these products behind the counter or in a locked cabinet. Consumers must show identification and sign a logbook for each purchase.

About This Chapter: Information in this chapter is excerpted from "Drugs of Abuse," Drug Enforcement Administration (DEA), 2015; and information from "Meth Use Is Down, But We Still Have Work To Do," NIDA for Teens, National Institute on Drug Abuse (NIDA), December 3, 2013.

What Are Common Street Names?

Common street names include:

- Batu
- Bikers Coffee
- Black Beauties
- Chalk
- Chicken Feed
- Crank
- Crystal
- Glass
- Go-Fast
- Hiropon
- Ice
- Meth
- Methlies Quick

- Poor Man's Cocaine
- Shabu
- Shards
- Speed
- Stove Top
- Tina
- Trash
- Tweak
- Uppers
- Ventana
- Vidrio
- Yaba
- Yellow Bam

What Does It Look Like?

Regular meth is a pill or powder. Crystal meth resembles glass fragments or shiny blue-white "rocks" of various sizes.

How Is It Abused?

Meth is swallowed, snorted, injected, or smoked. To intensify the effects, users may take higher doses of the drug, take it more frequently, or change their method of intake.

What Is Its Effect On The Mind?

Meth is a highly addictive drug with potent central nervous system (CNS) stimulant properties. Those who smoke or inject it report a brief, intense sensation, or rush. Oral ingestion or snorting produces a long-lasting high instead of a rush, which reportedly can continue for as long as half a day. Both the rush and the high are believed to result from the release of very high levels of the neurotransmitter dopamine into areas of the brain that regulate feelings of pleasure.

Long-term meth use results in many damaging effects, including addiction. Chronic meth abusers can exhibit violent behavior, anxiety, confusion, insomnia, and psychotic features including paranoia, aggression, visual and auditory hallucinations, mood disturbances, and delusions — such as the sensation of insects creeping on or under the skin. Such paranoia can result in homicidal or suicidal thoughts.

Researchers have reported that as much as 50% of the dopamine-producing cells in the brain can be damaged after prolonged exposure to relatively low levels of meth. Researchers also have found that serotonin-containing nerve cells may be damaged even more extensively.

What Is Its Effect On The Body?

Taking even small amounts of meth can result in: Increased wakefulness, increased physical activity, decreased appetite, rapid breathing and heart rate, irregular heartbeat, increased blood pressure, and hyperthermia (overheating).

High doses can elevate body temperature to dangerous, sometimes lethal, levels, and cause convulsions and even cardiovascular collapse and death. Meth abuse may also cause extreme anorexia, memory loss, and severe dental problems.

Methamphetamine

Methamphetamine, or meth, is a manmade stimulant that is sometimes made in basement labs from the cold medicine pseudoephedrine and various toxic chemicals like drain cleaner, battery acid, and antifreeze.

Meth makes a person more awake and physically active, causes rapid heart rate, and increases blood pressure and body temperature. Repeated use causes your teeth to fall out and makes you pick at your skin until you have open sores.

Meth is a nasty stuff, and teens get that. Only 1% of teens (8th, 10th, and 12th graders) used meth in 2012—reflecting a steady decline since 1999. The number of adults using meth dropped too: About 133,000 people tried meth in 2012, down more than 50% from 2002 to 2004.

This is all good news, but we still have work to do to prevent meth use. Meth is becoming more available, more pure (making it more dangerous), and less expensive to buy. The U.S. Department of Justice considers meth use a threat to this country because of how destructive it is.

233

Which Drugs Cause Similar Effects?

Cocaine and potent stimulant pharmaceuticals, such as amphetamines and methylphenidate, produce similar effects.

What Is Its Legal Status In The United States?

Methamphetamine is a Schedule II stimulant under the Controlled Substances Act, which means that it has a high potential for abuse and limited medical use. It is available only through a prescription that cannot be refilled. At present, there is only one legal meth product, Desoxyn®. It is currently marketed in 5-milligram tablets and has very limited use in the treatment of obesity and attention deficit hyperactivity disorder (ADHD).

Chapter 45

Opiates: Heroin, Methadone, And Buprenorphine

Heroin

What Is Heroin?

Also known as: "Smack," "Junk," "H," "Black tar," "Ska," and "Horse"

Heroin is a type of opioid drug that is partly manmade and partly natural. It is made from morphine, a psychoactive (mind-altering) substance that occurs naturally in the resin of the opium poppy plant. Heroin's color and look depend on how it is made and what else it may be mixed with. It can be white or brown powder or a black, sticky substance called "black tar heroin."

Heroin is becoming an increasing concern in areas where lots of people abuse prescription opioid painkillers, like OxyContin and Vicodin. They may turn to heroin since it produces a similar high but is cheaper and easier to obtain. Nearly half of young people who inject heroin surveyed in recent studies reported abusing prescription opioids before starting to use heroin.

How Is Heroin Used?

Heroin is mixed with water and injected with a needle. It can also be smoked or snorted.

About This Chapter: Information in this chapter is excerpted from "Heroin," NIDA for Teens, National Institute on Drug Abuse (NIDA), October 23, 2015; information from "Drug of Abuse," U.S. Drug Enforcement Administration (DEA), 2015; information from "Buprenorphine," Substance Abuse and Mental Health Services Administration (SAMHSA), September 25, 2015; and information from "Heroin," National Institute on Drug Abuse (NIDA), November 2014.

How Does Heroin Affect The Brain?

When heroin enters the brain, it is converted back into morphine. It then binds to molecules on cells known as opioid receptors. These receptors are located in many areas of the brain and body, especially areas involved in the perception of pain and pleasure.

Short-term effects of heroin include a rush of good feelings and clouded thinking. For the first several hours after taking heroin, people want to sleep, and their heart rate and breathing slow down. When the drug wears off, people may feel a strong urge to take more.

Regular heroin use changes the functioning of the brain. Using heroin repeatedly can result in:

- Tolerance—more of the drug is needed to achieve the same "high"

- Dependence—the need to continue use of the drug to avoid withdrawal symptoms

- Addiction—a devastating brain disease where, without proper treatment, people can't stop using drugs even when they really want to and even after it causes terrible consequences to their health and other parts of their lives

What Are The Other Effects Of Heroin?

The changes that take place in the brain from heroin use have effects on the rest of the body. Some of these effects are quite serious. In 2011, more than 250,000 visits to a hospital emergency department involved heroin.

Heroin use can cause:

- Feeling sick to the stomach and throwing up

- Severe itching

- Slowed (or even stopped) breathing

- Increased risk of HIV and hepatitis (a liver disease) through shared needles

- Coma—a deep state of unconsciousness

In addition to the effects of the drug itself, heroin bought on the street often contains a mix of substances, some of which can be toxic and can clog the blood vessels leading to the lungs, liver, kidney, or brain. This can cause permanent damage to those organs.

What Are The Immediate (Short-Term) Effects Of Heroin Use?

Once heroin enters the brain, it is converted to morphine and binds rapidly to opioid receptors. Abusers typically report feeling a surge of pleasurable sensation—a "rush." The intensity of the rush is a function of how much drug is taken and how rapidly the drug enters the brain and binds to the opioid receptors. With heroin, the rush is usually accompanied by a warm flushing of the skin, dry mouth, and a heavy feeling in the extremities, which may be accompanied by nausea, vomiting, and severe itching. After the initial effects, users usually will be drowsy for several hours; mental function is clouded; heart function slows; and breathing is also severely slowed, sometimes enough to be life-threatening. Slowed breathing can also lead to coma and permanent brain damage.

What Are The Long-Term Effects Of Heroin Use?

Repeated heroin use changes the physical structure and physiology of the brain, creating long-term imbalances in neuronal and hormonal systems that are not easily reversed. Studies have shown some deterioration of the brain's white matter due to heroin use, which may affect decision-making abilities, the ability to regulate behavior, and responses to stressful situations. Heroin also produces profound degrees of tolerance and physical dependence. Tolerance occurs when more and more of the drug is required to achieve the same effects. With physical dependence, the body adapts to the presence of the drug and withdrawal symptoms occur if use is reduced abruptly.

Withdrawal may occur within a few hours after the last time the drug is taken. Symptoms of withdrawal include restlessness, muscle and bone pain, insomnia, diarrhea, vomiting, cold flashes with goose bumps ("cold turkey"), and leg movements. Major withdrawal symptoms peak between 24–48 hours after the last dose of heroin and subside after about a week. However, some people have shown persistent withdrawal signs for many months.

Finally, repeated heroin use often results in addiction—a chronic relapsing disease that goes beyond physical dependence and is characterized by uncontrollable drug-seeking no matter the consequences. Heroin is extremely addictive no matter how it is administered, although routes of administration that allow it to reach the brain the fastest (i.e., injection and smoking) increase the risk of addiction. Once a person becomes addicted to heroin, seeking and using the drug becomes their primary purpose in life.

Can You Get Addicted To Heroin?

Yes, heroin is very addictive. It enters the brain quickly, causing a fast, intense high. Because users can develop a tolerance, people who use heroin need to take more and more of it to get the same effect, and eventually they may need to keep taking the drug just to feel normal. It is estimated that about 23 percent of individuals who use heroin become addicted. For those who use heroin repeatedly (over and over again), addiction is very likely. Once a person becomes addicted to heroin, seeking and using the drug becomes their main goal in life.

The number of people addicted to heroin doubled from 214,000 in 2002 to 517,000 in 2013.

When someone is addicted to heroin and stops using it, he or she may experience:

- Muscle and bone pain
- Cold flashes with chills
- Throwing up
- Inability to sleep
- Restlessness
- Kicking movements
- Strong craving for the drug

Fortunately, treatment can help an addicted person stop using and stay off heroin. Medicines can help with cravings that occur after quitting, helping a person to take control of their health and their lives.

Can You Die If You Use Heroin?

Yes, heroin slows, and sometimes stops, breathing, and this can kill a person. Dying in this way is known as overdosing. Deaths from drug overdoses have been increasing since the early 1990s—fueled most recently by a surge in heroin use. In 2011, 4,397 people died in the United States from a heroin overdose, an increase of almost 2.5 times compared to the 1,784 people who died from a heroin overdose in 2001. For young people (ages 15 to 24), the increase in the past 10 years has been about 4 times greater, with 809 young people dying from heroin overdose in 2011 compared with 212 in 2001.

Signs of a heroin overdose are slow breathing, blue lips and fingernails, cold damp skin, and shaking. People who might be overdosing should be taken to the emergency room right away.

How Many Teens Use Heroin?

For the most recent statistics on heroin use among teens, see the results below from NIDA's *Monitoring the Future* study.

Table 45.1. Trends In Prevalence Of Heroin for 8th Graders, 10th Graders, And 12th Graders; 2014 (In Percent)

Drug	Time Period	8th Graders	10th Graders	12th Graders
Heroin	Lifetime	0.9	0.9	1
	Past Year	0.5	0.5	0.6
	Past Month	0.3	0.4	0.4

Methadone

What Is Methadone?

Methadone is a synthetic (man-made) narcotic.

What Are Common Street Names?

Common street names include:

- Amidone
- Chocolate Chip Cookies
- Fizzies
- Maria
- Pastora
- Salvia
- Street Methadone
- Wafer

What Does It Look Like?

Methadone is available as a tablet, disc, oral solution, or injectable liquid.

How Is It abused?

Methodone can be swallowed or injected.

What Is Its Effect On The Mind?

Abuse of methadone can lead to psychological dependence.

What Is Its Effect On The Body?

When an individual uses methadone, he/she may experience physical symptoms like sweating, itchy skin, or sleepiness.

Individuals who abuse methadone risk becoming tolerant of and physically dependent on the drug.

When use is stopped, individuals may experience withdrawal symptoms including:

- Anxiety, muscle tremors, nausea, diarrhea, vomiting, and abdominal cramps

What Are Its Overdose Effects?

The effects of a methadone overdose are:

- Slow and shallow breathing, blue fingernails and lips, stomach spasms, clammy skin, convulsions, weak pulse, coma, and possible death

Which Drugs Cause Similar Effects?

Although chemically unlike morphine or heroin, methadone produces many of the same effects.

What Is Its Legal Status In The United States?

Methadone is a Schedule II drug under the Controlled Substances Act. While it may legally be used under a doctor's supervision, its non-medical use is illegal.

Buprenorphine

What Is Buprenorphine?

Buprenorphine is used in medication-assisted treatment (MAT) to help people reduce or quit their use of heroin or other opiates, such as pain relievers like morphine.

How Buprenorphine Works

Buprenorphine has unique pharmacological properties that help:

- Lower the potential for misuse

- Diminish the effects of physical dependency to opioids, such as withdrawal symptoms and cravings

- Increase safety in cases of overdose

Buprenorphine is an opioid partial agonist. This means that, like opioids, it produces effects such as euphoria or respiratory depression. With buprenorphine, however, these effects are weaker than those of full drugs such as heroin and methadone.

Buprenorphine's opioid effects increase with each dose until at moderate doses they level off, even with further dose increases. This "ceiling effect" lowers the risk of misuse, dependency, and side effects. Also, because of buprenorphine's long-acting agent, many patients may not have to take it every day.

What Are The Side Effects Of Buprenorphine?

Buprenorphine's side effects are similar to those of opioids and can include:

- Nausea, throwing up (vomiting), and constipation

- Muscle aches and cramps

- Cravings
- Inability to sleep
- Distress and irritability
- Fever

Part Seven
Other Drug-Related Health Concerns

Chapter 46
The Medical Consequences Of Drug Abuse

What Are The Medical Consequences Of Drug Addiction?

People who suffer from addiction often have one or more accompanying medical issues, which may include lung or cardiovascular disease, stroke, cancer, and mental disorders. Imaging scans, chest X-rays, and blood tests show the damaging effects of long-term drug abuse throughout the body. For example, research has shown that tobacco smoke causes cancer of the mouth, throat, larynx, blood, lungs, stomach, pancreas, kidney, bladder, and cervix. In addition, some drugs of abuse, such as inhalants, are toxic to nerve cells and may damage or destroy them either in the brain or the peripheral nervous system.

The Impact Of Addiction Can Be Far-Reaching

- Cardiovascular disease
- Stroke
- Cancer
- HIV/AIDS
- Hepatitis B and C
- Lung disease
- Mental disorders

About This Chapter: Information in this chapter is excerpted from "Drugs, Brains, and Behavior—The Science of Addiction," National Institute on Drug Abuse (NIDA), NIH Publication No. 14-5605, July 2014.

Does Drug Abuse Cause Mental Disorders, Or Vice Versa?

Drug abuse and mental illness often co-exist. In some cases, mental disorders such as anxiety, depression, or schizophrenia may precede addiction; in other cases, drug abuse may trigger or exacerbate those mental disorders, particularly in people with specific vulnerabilities.

How Can Addiction Harm Other People?

Beyond the harmful consequences for the person with the addiction, drug abuse can cause serious health problems for others. Three of the more devastating and troubling consequences of addiction are:

1   Negative effects of prenatal drug exposure on infants and children

A mother's abuse of heroin or prescription opioids during pregnancy can cause a withdrawal syndrome (called neonatal abstinence syndrome, or NAS) in her infant. It is also likely that some drugexposed children will need educational support in the classroom to help them overcome what may be subtle deficits in developmental areas such as behavior, attention, and thinking. Ongoing research is investigating whether the effects of prenatal drug exposure on the brain and behavior extend into adolescence to cause developmental problems during that time period.

2   Negative effects of secondhand smoke

Secondhand tobacco smoke, also called environmental tobacco smoke (ETS), is a significant source of exposure to a large number of substances known to be hazardous to human health, particularly to children. According to the Surgeon General's 2006 Report, *The Health Consequences of Involuntary Exposure to Tobacco Smoke*, involuntary exposure to secondhand smoke increases the risks of heart disease and lung cancer in people who have never smoked by 25–30 percent and 20– 30 percent, respectively.

3   Increased spread of infectious diseases

Injection of drugs such as heroin, cocaine, and methamphetamine currently accounts for about 12 percent of new AIDS cases.

Injection drug use is also a major factor in the spread of hepatitis C, a serious, potentially fatal liver disease. Injection drug use is not the only way that drug abuse contributes to the spread of infectious diseases. All drugs of abuse cause some form of intoxication, which interferes with judgment and increases the likelihood of risky sexual behaviors. This, in turn, contributes to the spread of HIV/AIDS, hepatitis B and C, and other sexually transmitted diseases.

What Are Some Effects Of Specific Abused Substances?

- **Nicotine** is an addictive stimulant found in cigarettes and other forms of tobacco. Tobacco smoke increases a user's risk of cancer, emphysema, bronchial disorders, and cardiovascular disease. The mortality rate associated with tobacco addiction is staggering. Tobacco use killed approximately 100 million people during the 20th century, and, if current smoking trends continue, the cumulative death toll for this century has been projected to reach 1 billion.

- **Alcohol** consumption can damage the brain and most body organs. Areas of the brain that are especially vulnerable to alcohol-related damage are the cerebral cortex (largely responsible for our higher brain functions, including problem solving and decision making), the hippocampus (important for memory and learning), and the cerebellum (important for movement coordination).

- **Marijuana** is the most commonly abused illegal substance. This drug impairs short-term memory and learning, the ability to focus attention, and coordination. It also increases heart rate, can harm the lungs, and can increase the risk of psychosis in those with an underlying vulnerability.

- **Prescription medications**, including opioid pain relievers (such as OxyContin® and Vicodin®), anti-anxiety sedatives (such as Valium® and Xanax®), and ADHD stimulants (such as Adderall ® and Ritalin®), are commonly misused to self-treat for medical problems or abused for purposes of getting high or (especially with stimulants) improving performance. However, misuse or abuse of these drugs (that is, taking them other than exactly as instructed by a doctor and for the purposes prescribed) can lead to addiction and even, in some cases, death. Unfortunately, there is a common misperception that because medications are prescribed by physicians, they are safe even when used illegally or by another person than they were prescribed for.

- **Inhalants** are volatile substances found in many household products, such as oven cleaners, gasoline, spray paints, and other aerosols, that induce mind-altering effects; they are frequently the first drugs tried by children or young teens. Inhalants are extremely toxic and can damage the heart, kidneys, lungs, and brain. Even a healthy person can suffer heart failure and death within minutes of a single session of prolonged sniffing of an inhalant.

- **Cocaine** is a short-acting stimulant, which can lead users to take the drug many times in a single session (known as a "binge"). Cocaine use can lead to severe medical consequences related to the heart and the respiratory, nervous, and digestive systems.

- **Amphetamines**, including methamphetamine, are powerful stimulants that can produce feelings of euphoria and alertness. Methamphetamine's effects are particularly long-lasting and harmful to the brain. Amphetamines can cause high body temperature and can lead to serious heart problems and seizures.

- **MDMA (Ecstasy or "Molly")** produces both stimulant and mindaltering effects. It can increase body temperature, heart rate, blood pressure, and heart-wall stress. MDMA may also be toxic to nerve cells.

- **LSD** is one of the most potent hallucinogenic, or perception-altering, drugs. Its effects are unpredictable, and abusers may see vivid colors and images, hear sounds, and feel sensations that seem real but do not exist. Users may also have traumatic experiences and emotions that can last for many hours.

- **Heroin** is a powerful opioid drug that produces euphoria and feelings of relaxation. It slows respiration, and its use is linked to an increased risk of serious infectious diseases, especially when taken intravenously. People who become addicted to opioid pain relievers sometimes switch to heroin instead, because it produces similar effects and may be cheaper or easier to obtain.

- **Steroids**, which can also be prescribed for certain medical conditions, are abused to increase muscle mass and to improve athletic performance or physical appearance. Serious consequences of abuse can include severe acne, heart disease, liver problems, stroke, infectious diseases, depression, and suicide.

- **Drug combinations**. A particularly dangerous and common practice is the combining of two or more drugs. The practice ranges from the co-administration of legal drugs, like alcohol and nicotine, to the dangerous mixing of prescription drugs, to the deadly combination of heroin or cocaine with fentanyl (an opioid pain medication). Whatever the context, it is critical to realize that because of drug-drug interactions, such practices often pose significantly higher risks than the already harmful individual drugs.

Treatment And Recovery

Can Addiction Be Treated Successfully?

Yes. Addiction is a treatable disease. Research in the science of addiction and the treatment of substance use disorders has led to the development of evidence-based interventions that help people stop abusing drugs and resume productive lives.

Can Addiction Be Cured?

Not always—but like other chronic diseases, addiction can be managed successfully. Treatment enables people to counteract addiction's powerful disruptive effects on their brain and behavior and regain control of their lives.

Chapter 47

Substance Abuse And Mental Illness

Mental and Substance Use Disorders – Overview

Mental and substance use disorders affect people from all walks of life and all age groups. These illnesses are common, recurrent, and often serious, but they are treatable and many people do recover. Learning about some of the most common mental and substance use disorders can help people recognize their signs and to seek help.

According to SAMHSA's 2014 National Survey on Drug Use and Health (NSDUH) an estimated 43.6 million (18.1%) Americans ages 18 and up experienced some form of mental illness. In the past year, 20.2 million adults (8.4%) had a substance use disorder. Of these, 7.9 million people had both a mental disorder and substance use disorder, also known as co-occurring mental and substance use disorders.

Various mental and substance use disorders have prevalence rates that differ by gender, age, race, and ethnicity.

Mental Disorders

Mental disorders involve changes in thinking, mood, and/or behavior. These disorders can affect how we relate to others and make choices. Mental disorders take many different forms, with some rooted in deep levels of anxiety, extreme changes in mood, or reduced ability to focus or behave appropriately. Others involve unwanted, intrusive thoughts and some may

---

About This Chapter: Information in this chapter is excerpted from "Mental and Substance Use Disorders," Substance Abuse and Mental Health Services Administration (SAMHSA), October 29, 2015; and information from "Prevention of Substance Abuse and Mental Illness," Substance Abuse and Mental Health Services Administration (SAMHSA), October 30, 2015.

result in auditory and visual hallucinations or false beliefs about basic aspects of reality. Reaching a level that can be formally diagnosed often depends on a reduction in a person's ability to function as a result of the disorder.

Anxiety disorders are the most common type of mental disorders, followed by depressive disorders. Different mental disorders are more likely to begin and occur at different stages in life and are thus more prevalent in certain age groups. Lifetime anxiety disorders generally have the earliest age of first onset, most commonly around age 6. Other disorders emerge in childhood, approximately 11% of children 4 to 17 years of age (6.4 million) have been diagnosed with attention deficit hyperactivity disorder (ADHD) as of 2011. Schizophrenia spectrum and psychotic disorders emerge later in life, usually in early adulthood. Not all mental health issues first experienced during childhood or adolescence continue into adulthood, and not all mental health issues are first experienced before adulthood. Mental disorders can occur once, reoccur intermittently, or be more chronic in nature. Mental disorders frequently co-occur with each other and with substance use disorders. Because of this and because of variation in symptoms even within one type of disorder, individual situations and symptoms are extremely varied.

Serious Emotional Disturbance

The term serious emotional disturbance (SED) is used to refer to children and youth who have had a diagnosable mental, behavioral, or emotional disorder in the past year, which resulted in functional impairment that substantially interferes with or limits the child's role or functioning in family, school, or community activities. A Centers for Disease Control and Prevention (CDC) review of population-level information found that estimates of the number of children with a mental disorder range from 13 to 20%, but current national surveys do not have an indicator of SED.

Substance Use Disorders

Substance use disorders occur when the recurrent use of alcohol and/or drugs causes clinically significant impairment, including health problems, disability, and failure to meet major responsibilities at work, school, or home.

In 2014, about 21.5 million Americans ages 12 and older (8.1%) were classified with a substance use disorder in the past year. Of those, 2.6 million had problems with both alcohol and drugs, 4.5 million had problems with drugs but not alcohol, and 14.4 million had problems with alcohol only.

Co-Occurring Mental and Substance Use Disorders

The coexistence of both a mental illness and a substance use condition is referred to as co-occurring mental and substance use disorders. There are no specific combinations of substance use disorders and mental disorders that are defined uniquely as co-occurring disorders. Co-occurring disorders may include any combination of two or more substance use disorders and mental disorders identified in the *Diagnostic and Statistical Manual of Mental Disorders, Fifth Edition (DSM-5)*. They are also referred to as having a dual diagnosis.

People with a mental health issue are more likely to experience an alcohol or substance use disorder than those not affected by a mental illness. Approximately 7.9 million adults had co-occurring disorders in 2014.

Co-occurring disorders can be difficult to diagnose due to the complexity of symptoms. Both disorders may be severe or mild, or one may be more severe than the other. In many cases, one disorder is addressed while the other disorder remains untreated. Both substance use disorders and mental disorders have biological, psychological, and social components.

There are many consequences of undiagnosed, untreated, or undertreated co-occurring disorders including higher likelihood of experiencing homelessness, incarceration, medical illnesses, suicide, and early death.

Chapter 48
Substance Abuse And Suicide Risks

Suicide is a serious public health problem that causes immeasurable pain, suffering, and loss to individuals, families, and communities nationwide. The causes of suicide are complex and determined by multiple combinations of factors, such as mental illness, substance abuse, painful losses, exposure to violence, and social isolation. Suicide prevention efforts seek to:

- Reduce factors that increase the risk for suicidal thoughts and behaviors

- Increase the factors that help strengthen, support, and protect individuals from suicide

Ideally, these efforts address individual, relationship, community, and societal factors while promoting hope, easing access into effective treatment, encouraging connectedness, and supporting recovery.

"Prevent Suicide By Preventing Substance Abuse"

When we prevent or successfully treat substance abuse, we prevent suicides. There is a powerful connection between the missions of the substance abuse prevention and treatment communities and the suicide prevention community – and much to be gained when these groups come together around their common goals.

Warning Signs Of Suicidal Behavior

These signs may mean that someone is at risk for suicide. Risk is greater if the behavior is new, or has increased, and if it seems related to a painful event, loss, or change:

- Talking about wanting to die or kill oneself

- Looking for a way to kill oneself

About This Chapter: Information in this chapter is excerpted from "Suicide Prevention," Substance Abuse and Mental Health Services Administration (SAMHSA), October 29, 2015; and information from "Substance Abuse Prevention is Suicide Prevention," WhiteHouse.gov, September 10, 2013.

- Talking about feeling hopeless or having no reason to live

- Talking about feeling trapped or being in unbearable pain

- Talking about being a burden to others

- Increasing the use of alcohol or drugs

- Acting anxious or agitated; behaving recklessly

- Sleeping too little or too much

- Withdrawing or feeling isolated

- Showing rage or talking about seeking revenge

- Displaying extreme mood swings

What You Can Do

If you believe someone may be thinking about suicide:

- Ask them if they are thinking about killing themselves. (This will not put the idea into their head or make it more likely that they will attempt suicide.)

- Listen without judging and show you care.

- Stay with the person (or make sure the person is in a private, secure place with another caring person) until you can get further help.

- Remove any objects that could be used in a suicide attempt.

- Call SAMHSA's National Suicide Prevention Lifeline at 1-800-273-TALK (8255) and follow their guidance.

- If danger for self-harm seems imminent, call 911.

Everyone has a role to play in preventing suicide. For instance, faith communities can work to prevent suicide simply by fostering cultures and norms that are life-preserving, providing perspective and social support to community members, and helping people navigate the struggles of life to find a sustainable sense of hope, meaning, and purpose.

Schools And Campus Suicide Prevention

SAMHSA's Garrett Lee Smith Campus Suicide Prevention Program provides funding to institutions of higher education to identify students who are at risk for suicide and suicide attempts, increase protective factors that promote mental health, reduce risk factors for suicide, and reduce suicides and suicide attempts.

Many of SAMHSA's Garrett Lee Smith Youth Suicide Prevention and Early Intervention grantees focus efforts on middle and high schools. SAMHSA also funded the development of Preventing Suicide: A Toolkit for High Schools – 2012 to help high schools, school districts, and their partners design and implement strategies to prevent suicide and promote behavioral health among their students.

Loss Survivors

Losing a loved one to suicide can be profoundly painful for family members and friends. SAMHSA's Suicide Prevention Resource Center helps loss survivors find local and national organizations, websites, and other resources that provide support, healing, and a sense of community

Chapter 49

Drug Use And Infectious Diseases

HIV, Hepatitis, And Other Infectious Diseases

Drug abuse not only weakens the immune system but is also linked to risky behaviors like needle sharing and unsafe sex. The combination greatly increases the likelihood of acquiring HIV/AIDS, hepatitis and many other infectious diseases.

> ### Drugs That Can Lead To HIV, Hepatitis, And Other Infectious Diseases:
> - Heroin
> - Cocaine
> - Steroids
> - Methamphetamine

Heroin

Why Does Heroin Use Create Special Risk For Contracting HIV/ AIDS And Hepatitis B And C?

Heroin use increases the risk of being exposed to HIV, viral hepatitis, and other infectious agents through contact with infected blood or body fluids (e.g., semen, saliva) that results from the sharing of syringes and injection paraphernalia that have been used by infected individuals or

About This Chapter: Information in this chapter is excerpted from "Medical Consequences of Drug Abuse," National Institute on Drug Abuse (NIDA), December 2012; information from "Heroin," National Institute on Drug Abuse (NIDA), November 2014; and information from "Methamphetamine," National Institute on Drug Abuse (NIDA), September 2013.

through unprotected sexual contact with an infected person. Snorting or smoking does not eliminate the risk of infectious disease like hepatitis and HIV/AIDS because people under the influence of drugs still engage in risky sexual and other behaviors that can expose them to these diseases.

Injection drug users (IDUs) are the highest-risk group for acquiring hepatitis C (HCV) infection and continue to drive the escalating HCV epidemic. Each IDU infected with HCV is likely to infect 20 other people. Of the 17,000 new HCV infections occurring in the United States in 2010, over half (53 percent) were among IDUs. Hepatitis B (HBV) infection in IDUs was reported to be as high as 20 percent in the United States in 2010, which is particularly disheartening since an effective vaccine that protects against HBV infection is available. Drug use, viral hepatitis and other infectious diseases, mental illnesses, social dysfunctions, and stigma are often co-occuring conditions that affect one another, creating more complex health challenges that require comprehensive treatment plans tailored to meet all of a patient's needs. For example, NIDA-funded research has found that drug abuse treatment along with HIV prevention and community-based outreach programs can help people who use drugs change the behaviors that put them at risk for contracting HIV and other infectious diseases. They can reduce drug use and drug-related risk behaviors such as needle sharing and unsafe sexual practices and, in turn, reduce the risk of exposure to HIV/AIDS and other infectious diseases. Only through coordinated utilization of effective antiviral therapies coupled with treatment for drug abuse and mental illness can the health of those suffering from these conditions be restored.

Drug Use And HIV/AIDS

What Is HIV/AIDS?

HIV/AIDS has been a global epidemic for more than 30 years. People born after 1980 have never known a world without it. The Centers for Disease Control and Prevention (CDC) estimates that more than 1 million people are infected with HIV.

HIV (human immunodeficiency virus) is the virus that causes AIDS (acquired immune deficiency syndrome). AIDS is a disease of the immune system that can be treated, but not cured. Most people say "HIV/AIDS" when talking about either the virus (HIV) or the syndrome it causes (AIDS).

HIV destroys certain cells, called CD4+ cells, in the immune system—the body's disease-fighting system. HIV converts the CD4+ T cells into "factories" that produce more HIV virus to infect other healthy cells. Without these cells, a person with HIV can't fight off germs and becomes more prone to illness and common infections. AIDS is diagnosed when a person has one or more of these infections and a low number of CD4+ cells in their body.

A person can have HIV for many years, and the virus may or may not progress to the disease of AIDS. This is why a person may appear healthy or uninfected when, in fact, they carry the HIV virus. A medical test is the only way to know if a person has HIV.

From the efforts of medical science, HIV is no longer necessarily fatal. A big part of this success is the treatment called HAART (highly active antiretroviral therapy). HAART is a combination of three or more medications that can hold back the virus and prevent or decrease symptoms of illness.

What Is The Link Between Drug Use And HIV/AIDS?

Drug use and HIV/AIDS are connected in a few different ways.

Injection drug use. Lots of people know that injection drug use and needle sharing contribute to the risk of spreading HIV/AIDS. Injection drug use is when a drug is injected into a tissue or vein with a needle. When people share "equipment"—such as needles, syringes, and other drug injection tools—HIV can be passed between users because the bodily fluid (for example, blood) from the infected person can remain on the equipment. Other infections—such as hepatitis C—can also be spread this way. Hepatitis C can cause liver disease and permanent liver damage.

Poor judgment and risky behavior. Drugs and alcohol affect the way a person makes choices and can lead to unsafe sexual practices, which put them at risk for getting HIV or giving it to someone else.

Biological effects of drugs. Drug use and addiction can make HIV and its consequences worse, especially in the brain. For example, research has shown that HIV causes more harm to nerve cells in the brain and greater cognitive (thinking) damage among people who use methamphetamine than among people with HIV who do not use drugs.

How Is HIV Spread?

HIV can spread when blood or other bodily fluids of someone who is infected comes in contact with the blood, broken skin, or mucous membranes (e.g., the genital area) of an uninfected person. The two main ways HIV is spread are: 1) through unprotected sex; and 2) by sharing needles or other equipment used for injection drug use.

How Many Teens Have HIV?

Among people ages 13 to 19, more than 2,300 were newly diagnosed with HIV in 2011. However, this does not represent the number of youth that were already diagnosed or those that have not (yet) been diagnosed. In fact, CDC estimates 60 percent of youth with HIV in the United States do not know they are infected.

In youth, as in adults, some populations are more affected than others. For example, among adolescents, most (more than 75 percent) of HIV infection diagnoses are among males. In addition, blacks/African Americans age 13 to 19 represent only 15 percent of the U.S. teenage population, but they accounted for nearly 70 percent of the HIV infections among people age 13 to 19 in 2010. The reasons for this gap aren't completely understood; in fact, black/African American youth have lower rates of drug use than whites and Hispanics.

In general, middle and late adolescence is a time when young people take risks that may put them in danger of getting HIV. Regardless of whether a young person takes drugs, unsafe sex increases a person's risk of getting HIV. But drugs and alcohol can increase the chances of unsafe behavior by affecting how a person makes decisions.

What Can Be Done To Prevent The Spread Of HIV?

Because of the strong link between drug use and the spread of HIV, drug use treatment can be an effective way to prevent HIV. When people who have a drug problem enter treatment, they stop or reduce their drug use and related risk behaviors, including drug use with needles and unsafe sex. Drug treatment programs also play an important role in getting out good information about HIV/AIDS and related diseases, providing counseling and testing services, and offering referrals for medical and social services.

In addition, NIDA's research has shown that tailoring prevention intervention programs for specific populations can reduce HIV risk behaviors. For example, research shows that school- and community-based prevention programs designed for inner-city African American boys can be effective in reducing high-risk behaviors, including drug use and risky sexual practices that can lead to HIV infection.

Methamphetamine

Are People Who Abuse Methamphetamine At Risk For Contracting HIV/AIDS And Hepatitis B And C?

Methamphetamine abuse raises the risk of contracting or transmitting HIV and hepatitis B and C—not only for individuals who inject the drug but also for noninjecting methamphetamine abusers. Among injecting drug users, HIV and other infectious diseases are spread primarily through the re-use or sharing of contaminated syringes, needles, or related paraphernalia. But regardless of how methamphetamine is taken, its intoxicating effects can alter judgment and inhibition and lead people to engage in unsafe behaviors like unprotected sex.

The combination of injection practices and sexual risk-taking may result in HIV becoming a greater problem among methamphetamine abusers than among other drug abusers, and some epidemiologic reports are already showing this trend. For example, while the link between HIV infection and methamphetamine abuse has not yet been established for heterosexuals, data show an association between methamphetamine abuse and the spread of HIV among men who have sex with men.

Methamphetamine abuse may also worsen the progression of HIV disease and its consequences. Clinical studies in humans suggest that current methamphetamine users taking highly active antiretroviral therapy (HAART) to treat HIV may be at greater risk of developing AIDS than non-users, possibly as a result of poor medication adherence. Methamphetamine abusers with HIV also have shown greater neuronal injury and cognitive impairment due to HIV, compared with those who do not abuse the drug.

NIDA-funded research has found that, through drug abuse treatment, prevention, and community-based outreach programs, drug abusers can change their HIV risk behaviors. Drug abuse and drug-related risk behaviors, such as needle sharing and unsafe sexual practices, can be reduced significantly, thus decreasing the risk of exposure to HIV and other infectious diseases. Therefore, drug abuse treatment is HIV prevention.

Chapter 50

Drug Use And Pregnancy

Using Drugs When Pregnant Harms The Baby

Did you know that using alcohol, cigarettes, and illegal drugs during pregnancy can harm the mother and her baby? Everything a pregnant woman eats, drinks, or takes affects the baby. Using drugs can hurt the baby's growth or even cause the baby to get sick.

About 1 in 6 pregnant teen girls (ages 15 to 17) used illegal drugs between 2008 and 2009. Below are just a few of the problems a baby can face if the mother drinks alcohol or uses drugs while she is pregnant.

Cigarettes: Pregnant women who smoke expose their babies to nicotine and the dangerous chemicals in cigarettes. If the mother smokes, her baby may:

- Be born early (a preemie)

- Develop an addiction to nicotine

- Have breathing and behavioral problems

- Die before it is born or in the first year of life

Secondhand smoke can also be harmful to a baby. The baby is more likely to develop problems breathing, ear infections, and cavities.

Alcohol: Drinking alcohol while pregnant can cause babies to be born with illnesses. These children may:

- Have problems seeing and hearing

About This Chapter: Information in this chapter is excerpted from "Using Drugs When Pregnant Harms The Baby," NIDA For Teens, National Institute on Drug Abuse (NIDA), September 26, 2013; and information from "How Does Heroin Use Affect Pregnant Women?" National Institute on Drug Abuse (NIDA), November 2014.

- Be born too small

- Struggle with eating and sleeping

- Have problems in school with learning and paying attention

Illegal drugs: Pregnant women who use illegal drugs like marijuana, cocaine, Ecstasy, meth, or heroin can cause lifelong harm to their babies. Drug use can cause babies to:

- Be born early

- Grow slowly

- Have withdrawal symptoms, including fever, vomiting, poor sleep, and shaking

- Have heart problems or a stroke

- Suffer lifelong disabilities

If you have been using drugs and think you might be pregnant, stop using the drug and talk to a doctor as soon as possible. (Exception: If you use heroin and you are pregnant, you will need to see a doctor to help you gradually get off the drug—if you stop too suddenly, it can harm the baby.) There are programs that can help teen moms stop using drugs and get healthy for their babies.

How Does Heroin Use Affect Pregnant Women?

Heroin use during pregnancy can result in neonatal abstinence syndrome (NAS). NAS occurs when heroin passes through the placenta to the fetus during pregnancy, causing the baby to become dependent along with the mother. Symptoms include excessive crying, fever, irritability, seizures, slow weight gain, tremors, diarrhea, vomiting, and possibly death. NAS requires hospitalization and treatment with medication (often morphine) to relieve symptoms; the medication is gradually tapered off until the baby adjusts to being opioid-free.

Methadone maintenance combined with prenatal care and a comprehensive drug treatment program can improve many of the outcomes associated with untreated heroin use for both the infant and mother, although infants exposed to methadone during pregnancy typically require treatment for NAS as well.

A recent NIDA-supported clinical trial demonstrated that buprenorphine treatment of opioid-dependent mothers is safe for both the unborn child and the mother. Once born, these infants require less morphine and shorter hospital stays as compared to infants born of mothers on methadone maintenance treatment. Research also indicates that buprenorphine combined with naloxone (compared to a morphine taper) is equally safe for treating babies born with NAS, further reducing side effects experienced by infants born to opioid-dependent mothers.

Chapter 51
Substance Abuse In The Military

Members of the armed forces are not immune to the substance use problems that affect the rest of society. Although illicit drug use is lower among U.S. military personnel than among civilians, heavy alcohol and tobacco use, and especially prescription drug abuse, are much more prevalent and are on the rise.

The stresses of deployment during wartime and the unique culture of the military account for some of these differences. Zero-tolerance policies and stigma pose difficulties in identifying and treating substance use problems in military personnel, as does lack of confidentiality that deters many who need treatment from seeking it.

Those with multiple deployments and combat exposure are at greatest risk of developing substance use problems. They are more apt to engage in new-onset heavy weekly drinking and binge drinking, to suffer alcohol- and other drug-related problems, and to have greater prescribed use of behavioral health medications. They are also more likely to start smoking or relapse to smoking.

Illicit And Prescription Drugs

According to the 2008 Department of Defense (DoD) *Survey of Health Related Behaviors among Active Duty Military Personnel*, just 2.3 percent of military personnel were past-month users of an illicit drug, compared with 12 percent of civilians. Among those age 18–25 (who are most likely to use drugs), the rate among military personnel was 3.9 percent, compared with 17.2 percent among civilians.

About This Chapter: Information in this chapter is excerpted from "DrugFacts: Substance Abuse in the Military," National Institute on Drug Abuse (NIDA), March 2013.

A policy of zero tolerance for drug use among DoD personnel is likely one reason why illicit drug use has remained at a low level in the military for 2 decades. The policy was instituted in 1982 and is currently enforced by frequent random drug testing; service members face dishonorable discharge and even criminal prosecution for a positive drug test.

However, in spite of the low level of illicit drug use, abuse of prescription drugs is higher among service members than among civilians and is on the increase. In 2008, 11 percent of service members reported misusing prescription drugs, up from 2 percent in 2002 and 4 percent in 2005. Most of the prescription drugs misused by service members are opioid pain medications.

Mental Health Problems In Returning Veterans

Service members may carry the psychological and physical wounds of their military experience with them into subsequent civilian life. In one study, one in four veterans returning from Iraq and Afghanistan reported symptoms of a mental or cognitive disorder; one in six reported symptoms of post-traumatic stress disorder (PTSD). These disorders are strongly associated with substance abuse and dependence, as are other problems experienced by returning military personnel, including sleep disturbances, traumatic brain injury, and violence in relationships.

Young adult veterans are particularly likely to have substance use or other mental health problems. According to a report of veterans in 2004-2006, a quarter of 18- to 25-year-old veterans met criteria for a past-year substance use disorder, which is more than double the rate of veterans aged 26-54 and five times the rate of veterans 55 or older.

The greater availability of these medications and increases in prescriptions for them may contribute to their growing misuse by service members. Pain reliever prescriptions written by military physicians quadrupled between 2001 and 2009—to almost 3.8 million. Combat-related injuries and the strains from carrying heavy equipment during multiple deployments likely play a role in this trend.

Drinking And Smoking

Alcohol use is also higher among men and women in military service than among civilians. Almost half of active duty service members (47 percent) reported binge drinking in 2008—up from 35 percent in 1998. In 2008, 20 percent of military personnel reported binge drinking every week in the past month; the rate was considerably higher—27 percent—among those with high combat exposure.

In 2008, 30 percent of all service members were current cigarette smokers—comparable to the rate for civilians (29 percent). However, as with alcohol use, smoking rates are significantly higher among personnel who have been exposed to combat.

Suicides And Substance Use

Suicide rates in the military were traditionally lower than among civilians in the same age range, but in 2004 the suicide rate in the U.S. Army began to climb, surpassing the civilian rate in 2008. Substance use is involved in many of these suicides. The 2010 report of the Army Suicide Prevention Task Force found that 29 percent of active duty Army suicides from fiscal year (FY) 2005 to FY 2009 involved alcohol or drug use; and in 2009, prescription drugs were involved in almost one third of them.

Addressing The Problem

A 2012 report prepared for the DoD by the Institute of Medicine (IOM Report) recommended ways of addressing the problem of substance use in the military, including increasing the use of evidence-based prevention and treatment interventions and expanding access to care. The report recommends broadening insurance coverage to include effective outpatient treatments and better equipping healthcare providers to recognize and screen for substance use problems so they can refer patients to appropriate, evidence-based treatment when needed. It also recommends measures like limiting access to alcohol on bases.

The IOM Report also notes that addressing substance use in the military will require increasing confidentiality and shifting a cultural climate in which drug problems are stigmatized and evoke fear in people suffering from them.

Branches of the military have already taken steps to curb prescription drug abuse. The Army, for example, has implemented changes that include limiting the duration of prescriptions for opioid pain relievers to 6 months and having a pharmacist monitor a soldier's medications when multiple prescriptions are being used.

NIDA and other government agencies are currently funding research to better understand the causes of drug abuse and other mental health problems among military personnel, veterans, and their families and how best to prevent and treat them.

Chapter 52
Drug Use And Violence

Drug Use And Violence: An Unhappy Relationship

Most of us have been in an argument. How far it goes and whether it escalates and turns violent depends on a lot of different factors—what the argument is about, the personalities of the people involved, where the fight takes place, and whether or not one or both people are under the influence of drugs and alcohol.

A NIDA-funded study looked at youth who were treated in an urban emergency department because of a violence-related injury. It turns out that not all drug use leads to the same kinds of violence. This study looked specifically at whether the violence was "dating violence" or "non-dating violence" and what impact, if any, the type of drug used made.

> Dating violence is controlling, abusive, and aggressive behavior in a romantic relationship. It can happen in straight or gay relationships. It can include verbal, emotional, physical, or sexual abuse, or a combination.

The researchers found that teens treated in the emergency department for an injury related to dating violence were more likely to be girls than boys. There were also differences in the types of drugs used before a dating violence incident versus. non-dating violence incidents.

For example, some youth tended to use alcohol alone or in combination with marijuana just before a non-dating violence incident occurred and tended to abuse prescription sedatives

About This Chapter: Information in this chapter is excerpted from "Drug Use and Violence: An Unhappy Relationship," NIDA for Teens, National Institute on Drug Abuse (NIDA), November 4, 2015; and information from "Drug Addiction Treatment in the Criminal Justice System," National Institute on Drug Abuse (NIDA), April 2014.

(Xanax or Valium) and/or opioids (like Vicodin and OxyContin) before a dating violence incident occurred.

This study tells us that the drug of choice may be different for boys and girls, and that girls are more likely than boys to experience dating violence. The drugs used may also be different depending on the situation (for example, being at home versus being at a bar or club). But more research is needed to learn how different drugs may make us more or less aggressive or more likely to be the victim of someone else who is using drugs or alcohol. Understanding more about this, and how gender and substance use factor into dating violence (and non-dating violence), will help public health educators develop programs to help teens who may end up in violent situations.

Drug Use, Crime, And Incarceration

The connection between drug use and crime is well known. Drug use is implicated in at least five types of drug-related offenses:

- Offenses related to drug possession or sales

- Offenses directly related to obtaining drugs (e.g., stealing to get money for drugs)

- Offenses related to a lifestyle that includes association with other offenders or with illicit markets

- Offenses related to abusive and violent behaviors, including domestic violence and sexual assault

- Offenses related to driving while intoxicated or under the influence, which can include property damage, accidents, injuries, and fatalities.

Incarceration

Drug use and intoxication can impair judgment, resulting in criminal behavior, poor anger management, and violent behavior. Sometimes drug users steal money or property to be able to buy drugs. Often they will commit crimes while "high" on drugs, and many drug users are sent to jail or prison. In 2012, nearly 7 million adults were involved with the criminal justice system (state or federal prisons, local jails), including nearly 5 million who were under probation or parole supervision. A 2004 survey by the U.S. Department of Justice (DOJ) estimated that about 70 percent of state and 64 percent of federal prisoners regularly used drugs prior to incarceration. The study also showed that 1 in 4 violent offenders in state prisons committed their offenses under the influence of drugs.

Most prisoners serving time for drug-related crimes were not arrested for simple possession. Among sentenced prisoners under state jurisdiction in 2008, 18 percent were sentenced for drug offenses and only 6 percent were incarcerated for drug possession alone. Just over 4 percent (4.4%) were drug offenders with no prior sentences. In 2009 about half (51 percent) of federal prisoners, who represent 13 percent of the total prison population, had a drug offense as the most serious offense. Federal data show that the vast majority (99.8 percent) of federal prisoners sentenced for drug offenses were incarcerated for drug trafficking.

Simple possession is even less of a factor with crimes related to marijuana. Only one-tenth of 1 percent (0.1 percent) of state prisoners were marijuana possession offenders with no prior sentences.

Drug Abuse Treatment

Treatment offers the best alternative for interrupting the drug use/criminal justice cycle for offenders with drug problems. Jail or prison should be a place where people can get the help they need, and offenders should ask if treatment is available. Untreated substance using offenders are more likely to relapse into drug use and criminal behavior, jeopardizing public health and safety and taxing criminal justice system resources. Additionally, treatment consistently has been shown to reduce the costs associated with lost productivity, crime, and incarceration caused by drug use.

Why Family Support Is Critical

Drug use often leads to violence; separation of parents and children; loss of jobs; feelings of hopelessness; serious money problems; single parenthood and worry over childcare needs; harmful relationships; emotional and behavioral difficulties in children; and dangerous driving that can result in the death of the drug user, family members, or innocent travelers on the road.

Effective treatment decreases future drug use and drug-related criminal behavior, and can improve a person's relationship with his or her family. In addition, the family needs tools and support to help deal with the offender's incarceration, rehabilitation, and loss of income.

Chapter 53
Drugged/Drunk Driving

Use of illegal drugs or misuse of prescription drugs can make driving a car unsafe—just like driving after drinking alcohol. Drugged driving puts not only the driver but also passengers and others who share the road at risk.

Why Is Drugged Driving Dangerous?

The effects of specific drugs differ depending on how they act in the brain. For example, marijuana can slow reaction time, impair judgment of time and distance, and decrease motor coordination. Drivers who have used cocaine or methamphetamine can be aggressive and reckless when driving. Certain kinds of sedatives, called benzodiazepines, can cause dizziness and drowsiness, which can lead to accidents.

Research studies have shown negative effects of marijuana on drivers, including an increase in lane weaving and poor reaction time and attention to the road. Use of alcohol with marijuana made drivers more impaired, causing even more lane weaving.

Scientists need to conduct more research to know how much of a drug impairs a person's driving ability. But even small amounts of some drugs can have a measurable effect. Some states have zero-tolerance laws for drugged driving. This means a person can face charges for driving under the influence (DUI) if there is *any* amount of drug in the blood or urine. It is important to note that many states are waiting for research to better define blood levels that indicate impairment, such as those they use with alcohol.

About This Chapter: Information in this chapter is excerpted from "DrugFacts: Drugged Driving," National Institute on Drug Abuse (NIDA), May 2015; and information from "Designated Drivers—You Are Not Alone," NIDA for Teens, National Institute on Drug Abuse (NIDA), January 8, 2015.

How Many People Take Drugs And Drive?

According to the 2013 National Survey on Drug Use and Health (NSDUH), an estimated 9.9 million people aged 12 or older (or 3.8 percent of teens and adults) reported driving under the influence of illicit* drugs during the year prior to being surveyed. This was lower than the rate in 2012 (3.9 percent). By comparison, in 2013, an estimated 28.7 million people (10.9 percent) reported driving under the influence of alcohol at least once in the past year.

The National Highway Traffic Safety Administration's (NHTSA) 2013-2014 National Roadside Survey found that more than 22 percent of drivers tested positive for illegal, prescription, or over-the-counter drugs. This was true for both weekday daytime and weekend nighttime drivers. But illegal drug use increased from daytime to nighttime while use of prescription drugs decreased. By comparison, 1.1 percent of drivers tested positive for alcohol during the daytime on weekdays, but 8.3 percent of drivers on weekend nights tested positive.

NSDUH data also show that men are more likely than women to drive under the influence of drugs or alcohol. And a higher percentage of young adults aged 18 to 25 drive after taking drugs or drinking than adults 26 or older.

"Illicit" refers to use of illegal drugs, including marijuana according to federal law, and misuse of prescription drugs.

How Often Does Drugged Driving Cause Accidents?

It is hard to measure how many accidents drugged driving causes. This is because:

- a good roadside test for drug levels in the body does not yet exist

- people are not usually tested for drugs if they are above the legal limit for alcohol because there is already enough evidence for a DUI charge

- many drivers who cause accidents are found to have both drugs and alcohol or more than one drug in their system, making it hard to know which substance had the greater effect

One NHTSA study found that in 2009, 18 percent of drivers killed in an accident tested positive for at least one drug—an increase from 13 percent in 2005. A 2010 study showed that 11.4 percent of fatal crashes involved a drugged driver.

Which Drugs Are Linked To Drugged Driving?

After alcohol, marijuana is the drug most often linked to drugged driving. Tests for detecting marijuana in drivers measure the level of delta-9-tetrahydrocannabinol (THC), marijuana's active ingredient, in the blood. In the 2013-2014 National Roadside Survey, 12.6 percent of drivers on weekend nights tested positive for THC. This was significantly higher than the 8.6 percent who tested positive in 2007.

A study of more than 3,000 fatally injured drivers in Australia showed that drivers with THC in their blood were much more likely to be at fault for an accident than drivers without drugs or alcohol in their system. This likelihood increased as the level of THC in the blood increased.

A 2010 nationwide study of fatal crashes found that 46.5 percent of drivers who tested positive for drugs had used a prescription drug, 36.9 percent had used marijuana, and 9.8 percent had used cocaine. The most common prescription drugs found were:

- alprazolam (Xanax®)—12.1 percent

- hydrocodone (Vicodin®)—11.1 percent

- oxycodone (OxyContin®)—10.2 percent

- diazepam (Valium®)—8.4 percent

Note that the study did not distinguish between legal and illicit use of the drugs.

In a small study of driver deaths in six states, 28.3 percent of drivers tested positive for drugs in 2010—12.2 percent for marijuana and 5.4 percent for opioids. These numbers were significantly higher than in 1999 when 16.6 percent of drivers tested positive—4.2 percent for marijuana and 1.8 percent for opioids.

Designated Drivers—You Are Not Alone

A new survey from Mothers Against Drunk Driving (MADD) and Nationwide Insurance found that 3 out of 4 people use designated drivers (DD). The DD is the person who does not drink, use drugs, or even take medication that might impair their driving. By the way, the DD is Not the least drunk person in the group—they are the ones who don't use any drug or alcohol at all at a party or event, even a little bit.

Why do they choose DDs?

Because they want to get home in one piece!

The MADD survey reveals that 75% of the people who volunteer to be the DD do so because they want to get home safely, and 85% ride with a sober driver for the same reason. Another reason for being or using a DD was not wanting to get in trouble with the law.

Problem solved, right?

Not quite. It's awesome that so many people understand the dangers of drunk driving and chose to use a DD. But there are still many who do not. While drunk driving deaths decreased by 2.5 percent from 2012 to 2013, they still account for 31 percent of overall traffic deaths, according to the National Highway Traffic Safety Administration (NHTSA). That's too many, considering drunk driving deaths are 100 percent preventable, 100 percent of the time. That's 32,719 deaths that could have been prevented in 2013.

What about drugged driving?

Driving after using other drugs is a real problem as well. An estimated 9.9 million people—or 3.8 percent of adolescents and adults—reported driving under the influence of illicit drugs during the year prior to being surveyed. The good news is that number has decreased a little.

Drugged driving, like drunk driving, causes traffic deaths. One NHTSA study found that in 2009, 18 percent of drivers killed in accidents tested positive for at least one drug.

What if I need a DD?

Drinking alcohol and using drugs is a bad idea. But don't make things worse by driving or getting into a car with someone who has been using. The best thing to do is to choose a DD *before* the group goes out.

If you didn't plan ahead, or your DD flakes out and uses drugs or alcohol, then here are a few alternative ways to get home:

- Call a cab. Google it on your phone or call 411 to get the number. And always bring along a little extra cash just in case you need it.
- Contact your local safe ride program. SafeRide America is a great place to start (they even have an app!).
- Find out (in advance) what your community offers. Many have their own "safe driver" programs.
- Request a ride from Uber, Lyft, or other car service.
- Use public transportation if you are traveling in a group of two or more (safety in numbers). If you have a smart phone, Google Maps will help you navigate using buses and rail.
- Call mom, dad, or a trusted adult. *Who knows? They might be less mad because you did the responsible thing.*
- Stay put. If you're at a friend's house, or near a friend's house, sleep it off and drive home in the morning.

Why Is Drugged Driving A Problem In Teens And Young Adults?

Motor vehicle crashes are the leading cause of death among young people aged 16 to 19. Teens are more likely than older drivers to underestimate or not recognize dangerous situations. They are also more likely to speed and allow less distance between vehicles. When lack of driving experience is combined with drug use, the results can be tragic.

Data from a 2011 survey of middle and high school students showed that in the 2 weeks before the survey, the number of 12th-grade students who had driven after using:

- marijuana was 12.4 percent

- other illicit drugs was 2.4 percent

- alcohol was 8.7 percent

A study of college students with access to a car found that 1 in 6 (about 17 percent) had driven under the influence of a drug other than alcohol at least once in the past year. Of those students, 57 to 67 percent did so at least three times and 27 to 37 percent at least 10 times. Marijuana was the most common drug used, followed by cocaine and prescription opioids.

Because drugged driving puts people at an increased risk for accidents, public health experts urge drug and alcohol users to develop social strategies to prevent them from getting behind the wheel of a car while impaired. Steps people can take include:

- offering to be a designated driver

- appointing a designated driver to take all car keys

- avoiding driving to parties where drugs and alcohol are present

- discussing the risks of drugged driving with friends in advanceDrugs That Can Lead To HIV, Hepatitis, And Other Infectious Diseases:

- Heroin
- Cocaine
- Steroids
  - Methamphetamine

Part Eight
Treatment For Addiction

Chapter 54
Dealing With Addiction

How Do I Know If I Have A Drug Abuse Problem?

Addiction can happen at any age, but it usually starts when a person is young. If you continue to use drugs despite harmful consequences, you could be addicted. It is important to talk to a medical professional about it—your health and future could be at stake.

Have friends or family told you that you are behaving differently for no apparent reason—such as acting withdrawn, frequently tired or depressed, or hostile? You should listen and ask yourself if they are right—and be honest with yourself. These changes could be a sign you are developing a drug-related problem. Parents sometimes overlook such signs, believing them to be a normal part of the teen years. Only you know for sure if you are developing a problem because of your drug use. Here are some other signs:

- Hanging out with different friends
- Not caring about your appearance
- getting worse grades
- Missing classes or skipping school
- Losing interest in your favorite activities
- Getting in trouble in school or with the law
- Having different eating or sleeping habits
- Having more problems with family members and friends

There is no special type of person who becomes addicted. It can happen to anyone.

About This Chapter: Information in this chapter is excerpted from "What to Do If You Have a Problem with Drugs: For Teens and Young Adults," National Institute on Drug Abuse (NIDA), October 2015.

Thanks to science, we know more than ever before about how drugs work in the brain, and we also know that addiction can be successfully treated to help young people stop using drugs and lead productive lives. Asking for help early, when you first suspect you have a problem, is important; don't wait to become addicted before you seek help. If you think you are addicted, there is treatment that can work. Don't wait another minute to ask for help.

Why Can't I Stop Using Drugs On My Own?

Repeated drug use changes the brain. Brain-imaging studies of drug-addicted people show changes in areas of the brain that are needed to learn and remember, make good decisions, and control yourself. Quitting is difficult, even for those who feel ready. If you aren't sure you are addicted, it would be helpful for you to look at this brief video. It helps explains why your inability to stop using drugs does not mean you're a bad person, just that you have an illness that needs to be treated.

If I Want To Ask For Help, Where Do I Start?

Asking for help is the first important step. If you have a good relationship with your parents, you should start there. If you do not have a good relationship with your parents (or if they are having some problems of their own and might need help), find an adult you trust and ask them for help.

The next step is to go to your doctor. You might want to ask your parents to call your doctor in advance to see if he or she is comfortable discussing drug use. Believe it or not, sometimes doctors are as uncomfortable discussing it as teens are! You will want to find a doctor who has experience with these issues.

Together with your parents and doctor, you can decide if you should enter a treatment program. If you do not have a good relationship with your parents, ask another adult you trust to help you.

It takes a lot of courage to seek help for a possible drug problem, because there is a lot of hard work ahead and it might get in the way of school and social activities. But treatment works, and you can recover. It just takes time, patience and hard work. It is important, because you will not be ready to go out into the world on your own until you take care of this issue. Treatment will help you counteract addiction's powerful hold on your brain and behavior so you can regain control of your life.

I'll Talk To A Doctor, But I Am Afraid They Will Tell My Parents Everything. Can I Prevent That?

There are privacy laws that prevent your doctor from telling your parents everything. They can't even tell law enforcement about your drug use, in case that worries you. But your parents might ask you to sign a permission form, so your doctor can discuss your issues with them. If you feel your parents are truly trying to help you, you should consider signing the form, because having accurate information will help them find the right care and treatment for you.

There is one exception to this rule: Doctors can speak to parents and some officials if they think you are in danger of hurting yourself or others.

If you feel you are being abused by your parents or caretakers, you should discuss with your doctor or contact a school counselor. If you are being abused, you can call the National Child Abuse Hotline for help at 1-800-4-A-CHILD (1-800-422-4453).

What Will The Doctor Ask Me?

The doctor will ask you a series of questions about your use of alcohol and drugs and other risky behaviors like driving under the influence or riding with other people who have been using drugs or alcohol. Your doctor can help you the best if you tell the truth. The doctor might also do a urine and/or blood test. This will provide important information about your drug use and how it is affecting your health.

If your goal is to truly get better and get your old life back, you should cooperate with your doctor. If you think problems at home are only making it harder to stay clean, share that information with your doctor. If they recommend counseling or treatment, you should give it a try. There is a whole network of trained adults out there who want to help you.

What Is Treatment Like?

Treatment for drug problems is tailored to each patient's unique drug abuse patterns and other medical, psychiatric, and social problems.

Some treatment centers offer outpatient treatment programs, which would allow you to stay in school, at least part time. Some teens and young adults, though, do better in inpatient (residential) treatment, where you stay overnight for a period of time. An addiction specialist can advise you about your best options.

I Don't Feel Well When I Stop Using Drugs. Do Treatment Centers Force People To Stop Taking Drugs Immediately?

Treatment is always based on the person's needs. However, if you are still using a drug when you are admitted to a treatment program, one of the first things they need to do is help you safely remove drugs from your system (called "detox"). This is important, because drugs impair the mental abilities you need to make treatment work for you.

When people first stop using drugs, they can experience different physical and emotional withdrawal symptoms, including depression, anxiety, and other mood disorders, as well as restlessness and sleeplessness. Remember that treatment centers are very experienced in helping you get through this process and keeping you safe and comfortable during it. Depending on your situation, you might also be given medications to reduce your withdrawal symptoms, making it easier to stop using.

Who Will Be Helping Me In Treatment?

Different kinds of addiction specialists will likely be involved in your care—including doctors, nurses, therapists, social workers, and others. They will work as a team.

Are There Medications That Can Help Me Stop Using?

There are medications that help treat addiction to alcohol, nicotine, and opioids (heroin and pain relievers). These are usually prescribed for adults, but sometimes doctors may prescribe them for younger patients. When medication is available, it can be combined with behavioral therapy for added benefit.

Medications are also sometimes prescribed to help with drug withdrawal and to treat possible mental health conditions (like depression) that might be contributing to your drug problem.

Your treatment provider will let you know what medications are available for your particular situation. You should be aware that some treatment centers don't believe a drug addiction should be treated with other drugs, so they may not want to prescribe medications. But scientific research shows that medication does help in many, many cases.

I Tried Rehab Once And It Didn't Work—Why Should I Try It Again?

If you have already been in rehab, it means you have already learned many of the skills needed to recover from addiction, and you should try it again. Relapsing (going back to using drugs after getting off them temporarily) does not mean the first treatment failed. People with all kinds of diseases relapse; people with other chronic diseases like high blood pressure, diabetes, and asthma relapse about as much as people who have addictions.

Treatment of all chronic diseases, including addiction, involves making tough changes in how you live and act, so setbacks are to be expected along the way. A return to drug use means treatment needs to be started again or adjusted, or that you might need a different treatment this time.

What Kind Of Counseling Should I Get?

Behavioral treatments ("talk therapy") help teens and young adults increase healthy life skills and learn how to be happy without drugs. They can give you some coping skills and will keep you motivated to recover from your drug problem.

Treatment can be one-on-one with a doctor, but some of the most effective treatments for teens are ones that involve one or more of your parents or other family members.

I Have Heard Of Support Groups. What Are Those Like?

These groups—called peer support groups—aren't the same thing as treatment, but they can help you a lot as you go through treatment and afterward. Self-help groups and other support services offer you an added layer of social support, to help you stick with your healthy choices over the course of a lifetime. If you are in treatment, ask your treatment provider about good support groups.

The most well-known self-help groups are those affiliated with Alcoholics Anonymous (AA), Narcotics Anonymous (NA), Cocaine Anonymous (CA), and Teen-Anon, all of which are based on the "12-step"approach. You can check the Internet sites of any of these groups for information about teen programs or meetings in your area.

There are other kinds of groups that can provide a lot of support, depending on where you live. To find support groups in your area, contact local hospitals, treatment centers, or faith-based organizations.

Other services available for teens include recovery high schools (in which teens attend school with other students who are also recovering) and peer recovery support services.

I Don't Like Lying To My Parents But They Don't Understand Me And My Problems. If We Talk About Drugs, They Will Just Yell At Me. How Can I Avoid A Fight?

First of all, remember that your parents were teens once, and they understand teen life more than you think. Second, when you first tell them about your problem, they might get angry out of fear and worry. They might raise their voices because they are very, very worried about you and your future. Try to stay calm and simply ask for help. Repeat over and over again that you need their help.

Parents do get angry when they find out their kids have been lying to them. You'd do the same! Be honest with them. Let them know you want to change and need their help.

I Am Also Afraid My Parents Will Take Away The Car Keys—What Can I Do About That?

The single most responsible thing you can do is stop driving until you get help for your drug use. This might be inconvenient, but if you do drugs and drive you could end up not only killing yourself but killing others as well. That could lead to a lifetime in prison. This is no different than drinking and driving.

If you tell your parents that you are willing to give up your driving privileges, they will know you are serious about getting help.

Taking Drugs Helps Me Feel Less Depressed—What's Wrong With That?

The relief you feel is only temporary and can cause more problems down the road, as your brain and body start to crave more and more drugs just to feel normal. It is very possible you need to find treatment for your depression as well as for your drug use. This is very common. It is called "comorbidity" or "co-ocurrence" when you have more than one health problem at the same time.

Be certain to tell your doctor about your depression (or other mental health problems) as well as your drug use. There are many non-addictive medicines that can help with depression or other mental health issues. Sometimes doctors do not talk to each other as much as they should, so you need to be your own best friend and advocate—and make sure all of your health care providers know about all of the health issues that concern you. You should be treated for all of them at the same time.

If you ever feel so depressed that you think about hurting yourself, there is a hotline you can call: 1-800-273-TALK (8255.) this is called the National Suicide Prevention Lifeline, and you can share all of your problems with them. A caring, non judgmental voice will be on the other end, listening.

Chapter 55

Substance Abuse Treatment

Adolescents in treatment report abusing different substances than adult patients do. For example, many more people aged 12–17 received treatment for marijuana use than for alcohol use in 2011 (65.5 percent versus 42.9 percent), whereas it was the reverse for adults (see figure). When adolescents do drink alcohol, they are more likely than adults to binge drink. Adolescents are less likely than adults to report withdrawal symptoms when not using a drug, being unable to stop using a drug, or continued use of a drug in spite of physical or mental health problems; but they are more likely than adults to report hiding their substance use, getting complaints from others about their substance use, and continuing to use in spite of fights or legal trouble.

Adolescents also may be less likely than adults to feel they need help or to seek treatment on their own. Given their shorter histories of using drugs (as well as parental protection), adolescents may have experienced relatively few adverse consequences from their drug use; their incentive to change or engage in treatment may correspond to the number of such consequences they have experienced. Also, adolescents may have more difficulty than adults seeing their own behavior patterns (including causes and consequences of their actions) with enough detachment to tell they need help.

Principles Of Adolescent Substance Use Disorder Treatment

- Adolescent substance use needs to be identified and addressed as soon as possible.

- Adolescents can benefit from a drug abuse intervention even if they are not addicted to a drug.

About This Chapter: Information in this chapter is excerpted from "Principles of Adolescent Substance Use Disorder Treatment: A Research-Based Guide," National Institute on Drug Abuse (NIDA), January 2014.

- Routine annual medical visits are an opportunity to ask adolescents about drug use.

- Legal interventions and sanctions or family pressure may play an important role in getting adolescents to enter, stay in, and complete treatment.

- Substance use disorder treatment should be tailored to the unique needs of the adolescent.

- Treatment should address the needs of the whole person, rather than just focusing on his or her drug use.

- Behavioral therapies are effective in addressing adolescent drug use.

- Families and the community are important aspects of treatment.

- Effectively treating substance use disorders in adolescents requires also identifying and treating any other mental health conditions they may have.

- Sensitive issues such as violence and child abuse or risk of suicide should be identified and addressed.

- It is important to monitor drug use during treatment.

- Staying in treatment for an adequate period of time and continuity of care afterward are important.

Evidence-Based Approaches To Treating Adolescent Substance Use Disorders

Research evidence supports the effectiveness of various substance abuse treatment approaches for adolescents. Examples of specific evidence-based approaches are described below, including behavioral and family-based interventions as well as medications. Each approach is designed to address specific aspects of adolescent drug use and its consequences for the individual, family, and society. In order for any intervention to be effective, the clinician providing it needs to be trained and well-supervised to ensure that he or she adheres to the instructions and guidance described in treatment manuals. Most of these treatments have been tested over short periods of 12–16 weeks, but for some adolescents, longer treatments may be warranted; such a decision is made on a case-by-case basis. The provider should use clinical judgment to select the evidence-based approach that seems best suited to the patient and his or her family.

Group Therapy For Adolescents

Adolescents can participate in group therapy and other peer support programs during and following treatment to help them achieve abstinence. When led by well-trained clinicians following well-validated Cognitive-Behavioral Therapy (CBT) protocols, groups can provide positive social reinforcement through peer discussion and help enforce incentives to staying off drugs and living a drug-free lifestyle.

However, group treatment for adolescents carries a risk of unintended adverse effects: Group members may steer conversation toward talk that glorifies or extols drug use, thereby undermining recovery goals. Trained counselors need to be aware of that possibility and direct group activities and discussions in a positive direction.

Behavioral Approaches

Behavioral interventions help adolescents to actively participate in their recovery from drug abuse and addiction and enhance their ability to resist drug use. In such approaches, therapists may provide incentives to remain abstinent, modify attitudes and behaviors related to drug abuse, assist families in improving their communication and overall interactions, and increase life skills to handle stressful circumstances and deal with environmental cues that may trigger intense craving for drugs. Below are some behavioral treatments shown to be effective in addressing substance abuse in adolescents (listed in alphabetical order).

Adolescent Community Reinforcement Approach (A-CRA)

A-CRA is an intervention that seeks to help adolescents achieve and maintain abstinence from drugs by replacing influences in their lives that had reinforced substance use with healthier family, social, and educational or vocational reinforcers. After assessing the adolescent's needs and levels of functioning, the therapist chooses from among 17 A-CRA procedures to address problem-solving, coping, and communication skills and to encourage active participation in constructive social and recreational activities.

Cognitive-Behavioral Therapy (CBT)

CBT strategies are based on the theory that learning processes play a critical role in the development of problem behaviors like drug abuse. A core element of CBT is teaching participants how to anticipate problems and helping them develop effective coping strategies. In CBT, adolescents explore the positive and negative consequences of using drugs. They learn to monitor their feelings and thoughts and recognize distorted thinking patterns and cues that trigger their substance abuse; identify and anticipate high-risk situations; and apply an array of self-control skills, including emotional regulation and anger management, practical problem solving, and substance refusal.

Contingency Management (CM)

Research has demonstrated the effectiveness of treatment using immediate and tangible reinforcements for positive behaviors to modify problem behaviors like substance abuse. This approach, known as Contingency Management (CM), provides adolescents an opportunity to earn low-cost incentives such as prizes or cash vouchers (for food items, movie passes, and other personal goods) in exchange for participating in drug treatment, achieving important goals of treatment, and not using drugs. The goal of CM is to weaken the influence of reinforcement derived from using drugs and to substitute it with reinforcement derived from healthier activities and drug abstinence.

Motivational Enhancement Therapy (MET)

MET is a counseling approach that helps adolescents resolve their ambivalence about engaging in treatment and quitting their drug use. This approach, which is based on a technique called motivational interviewing, typically includes an initial assessment of the adolescent's motivation to participate in treatment, followed by one to three individual sessions in which a therapist helps the patient develop a desire to participate in treatment by providing non-confrontational feedback.

Twelve-Step Facilitation Therapy

Twelve-Step Facilitation Therapy is designed to increase the likelihood that an adolescent with a drug abuse problem will become affiliated and actively involved in a 12-step program like Alcoholics Anonymous (AA) or Narcotics Anonymous (NA). Such programs stress the participant's acceptance that life has become unmanageable, that abstinence from drug use is needed, and that willpower alone cannot overcome the problem.

Behavioral Interventions

Behavioral interventions help adolescents to actively participate in their recovery from drug abuse and addiction and enhance their ability to resist drug use.

Family-Based Approaches

Family-based approaches to treating adolescent substance abuse highlight the need to engage the family, including parents, siblings, and sometimes peers, in the adolescent's treatment. Involving the family can be particularly important, as the adolescent will often be living with at least one parent and be subject to the parent's controls, rules, and/or supports. Family-based approaches generally address a wide array of problems in addition to the young person's substance problems, including family communication and conflict; other co-occurring behavioral, mental health, and learning disorders; problems with school or work attendance; and peer networks. Research shows that family-based treatments are highly efficacious; some studies even suggest they are superior to other individual and group treatment approaches.

Brief Strategic Family Therapy (BSFT)

BSFT is based on a family systems approach to treatment, in which one member's problem behaviors are seen to stem from unhealthy family interactions. Over the course of 12–16 sessions, the BSFT counselor establishes a relationship with each family member, observes how the members behave with one another, and assists the family in changing negative interaction patterns.

Family Behavior Therapy (FBT)

FBT, which has demonstrated positive results in both adults and adolescents, combines behavioral contracting with contingency management to address not only substance abuse but other behavioral problems as well. The adolescent and at least one parent participate in treatment planning and choose specific interventions from a menu of evidence-based treatment options. Therapists encourage family members to use behavioral strategies taught in sessions and apply their new skills to improve the home environment.

Functional Family Therapy (FFT)

FFT combines a family systems view of family functioning (which asserts that unhealthy family interactions underlie problem behaviors) with behavioral techniques to improve communication, problem-solving, conflict resolution, and parenting skills. Principal treatment strategies include (1) engaging families in the treatment process and enhancing their motivation for change and (2) modifying family members' behavior using CM techniques, communication and problem solving, behavioral contracts, and other methods.

Multidimensional Family Therapy (MDFT)

MDFT is a comprehensive family- and community-based treatment for substance-abusing adolescents and those at high risk for behavior problems such as conduct disorder and delinquency. The aim is to foster family competency and collaboration with other systems like school or juvenile justice. Sessions may take place in a variety of locations, including in the home, at a clinic, at school, at family court, or in other community locations. MDFT has been shown to be effective even with more severe substance use disorders and can facilitate the reintegration of substance abusing juvenile detainees into the community.

Multisystemic Therapy (MST)

MST is a comprehensive and intensive family- and community-based treatment that has been shown to be effective even with adolescents whose substance abuse problems are severe and with those who engage in delinquent and/or violent behavior. In MST, the adolescent's substance abuse is viewed in terms of characteristics of the adolescent (e.g., favorable attitudes toward drug use) and those of his or her family (e.g., poor discipline, conflict, parental drug abuse), peers (e.g., positive attitudes toward drug use), school (e.g., dropout, poor performance), and neighborhood (e.g., criminal subculture).

Addiction Medications

Several medications have been found to be effective in treating addiction to opioids, alcohol, or nicotine in adults, although none of these medications have been approved by the FDA to treat adolescents. In most cases, only preliminary evidence exists for the effectiveness and safety of these medications in people under 18, and there is no evidence on the neurobiological impact of these medications on the developing brain. However, despite the relative lack of evidence, some health care providers do use medications "off-label" when treating adolescents (especially older adolescents) who are addicted to opioids, nicotine, or (less commonly) alcohol.

Opioid Use Disorders

Buprenorphine reduces or eliminates opioid withdrawal symptoms, including drug cravings, without producing the "high" or dangerous side effects of heroin and other opioids. It does this by both activating and blocking opioid receptors in the brain (i.e., it is what is known as a partial opioid agonist). It is available for sublingual (under-the-tongue) administration both in a stand-alone formulation (called Subutex®) and in combination with another agent called naloxone. The naloxone in the combined formulation (marketed as Suboxone®) is included to deter diversion or abuse of the medication by causing a withdrawal reaction if it is intravenously injected.

Methadone also prevents withdrawal symptoms and reduces craving in opioid-addicted individuals by activating opioid receptors in the brain (i.e., a full opioid agonist). It has a long history of use in treatment of opioid dependence in adults, and is available in specially licensed methadone treatment programs.

Naltrexone is approved for the prevention of relapse in adult patients following complete detoxification from opioids. It acts by blocking the brain's opioid receptors (i.e., an opioid antagonist), preventing opioid drugs from acting on them and thus blocking the high the user would normally feel and/or causing withdrawal if recent opioid use has occurred.

Alcohol Use Disorders

Acamprosate (Campral®) reduces withdrawal symptoms by normalizing brain systems disrupted by chronic alcohol consumption in adults.

Disulfiram (Antabuse®) inhibits an enzyme involved in the metabolism of alcohol, causing an unpleasant reaction if alcohol is consumed after taking the medication.

Naltrexone decreases alcohol-induced euphoria and is available in both oral tablets and long-acting injectable preparations (as in its use for the treatment of opioid addiction, above).

Nicotine Use Disorders

Bupropion, commonly prescribed for depression, also reduces nicotine cravings and withdrawal symptoms in adult smokers.

Nicotine Replacement Therapies (NRTs) help smokers wean off cigarettes by activating nicotine receptors in the brain. They are available in the form of a patch, gum, lozenge, nasal spray, or inhaler.

Varenicline reduces nicotine cravings and withdrawal in adult smokers by mildly stimulating nicotine receptors in the brain.

Chapter 56

Helping A Friend With A Substance Abuse Problem

How Do I Know If My Adult Friend Or Loved One Has A Substance Use Problem?

This chapter is filled with resources and information to help someone you care about who might have a drug use (use of illicit drugs, prescription drugs, or alcohol) problem. First, try to answer the questions below as honestly as possible. If the person is willing, you can include him or her in the discussion.

- Does the person take the drug in larger amounts or for longer than they meant to?

- Do they want to cut down or stop using the drug but can't?

- Do they spend a lot of time getting, using, or recovering from the drug?

- Do they have cravings and urges to use the drug?

- Are they unable to manage their responsibilities at work, home, or school, because of drug use?

- Do they continue to use a drug, even when it causes problems in their relationships?

- Do they give up important social, recreational or work-related activities because of drug use?

- Do they use drugs again and again, even when it puts them in danger?

About This Chapter: Information in this chapter is excerpted from "What to Do If Your Adult Friend or Loved One Has a Problem with Drugs," National Institute on Drug Abuse (NIDA), October 2015; and information from "Real Teens Ask: How Can I Help? NIDA for Teens, National Institute on Drug Abuse (NIDA), November 5, 2013.

- Do they continue to use, even when they know they have a physical or psychological problem that could have been caused or made worse by the drug?

- Do they take more of the drug to get the effect they want?

- Have they developed withdrawal symptoms, which can be relieved by taking more of the drug? (Some withdrawal symptoms can be obvious, but others can be more subtle—like irritability or nervousness.)

If the answer to some or all of these questions is yes, your friend or loved one might have a substance use problem. In the most severe cases, it is called an addiction. It can happen to people from all backgrounds, rich or poor, and it can happen at any age.

Anyone Can Become Addicted To Drugs

Through scientific research, we now know more than ever about how drugs work in the brain, and we also know that drug addiction can be successfully treated to help people stop abusing drugs and lead productive lives.

Why Can't Addicts Stop Using Drugs On Their Own?

Repeated drug use changes the brain, including parts of the brain that give a person self-control. These and other changes can be seen clearly in brain-imaging studies of people with a drug addiction. These brain changes explain why quitting is so difficult, even when an addicted person feels ready.

If My Friend Or Loved One Asks For My Help, Where Do I Start?

If someone you care about has asked for help, he or she has taken an important first step. If they are resistant to help, see if you can at least convince them to get an evaluation from a doctor.

You can always take steps to locate an appropriate physician or health professional, and leave the information with your friend. You can call health professionals in advance to see if they are comfortable speaking with their patients about addiction. If not, ask for a referral to another doctor with more expertise in the area of addiction. There are 3,500 board certified physicians who specialize in addiction in the United States. The American Society of Addiction Medicine Web site (www.asam.org) has a *Find a Physician* feature on its home page. The American Academy of Addiction Psychiatry (www.aaap.org) also has a Patient Referral Program.

Emphasize to your friend or loved one that it takes a lot of courage to seek help for a drug problem, because there is a lot of hard work ahead. There is a great deal of scientific evidence that treatment works, and people recover every day. Like other chronic diseases, addiction can be managed successfully. Treatment enables people to counteract the powerfully disruptive effects of drugs on the brain and behavior and to regain control of their lives. Like many diseases, it can take several attempts at treatment to find the right approach. But assure them that you will support them in their courageous effort.

My Friend Has Considered Treatment, But Is Afraid Of What Others Will Think. What Can I Tell My Friend?

Many employers, friends, and family members will be compassionate if they see a person is making a sincere effort to recover from a substance use problem. But you can also reassure your friend that laws protect the privacy of a person seeking drug treatment—or in fact, any medical treatment. Healthcare providers may not share information with anyone else without a patient's permission. Some jobs may require a doctor's note saying an employee is being treated for a medical condition, but the nature of the condition need not be specified.

If My Friend Or Loved One Refuses To Cooperate, Should We Conduct An Intervention?

Many people are compelled to enter treatment by the pressure of their family, friends, or a court system. However, there is no evidence that confrontational "interventions" like those familiar from TV programs are effective at convincing people they have a problem or motivating them to change. It is even possible for such confrontational encounters to escalate into violence or backfire in other ways. Instead, you should focus on creating incentives to at least get the person to a doctor. Often people will listen to professionals rather than have conversations with friends and family members, as the latter encounters can sometimes be driven by fear, accusations, and emotions.

Can I Explore Treatment Centers Even If My Friend Is Not Willing To Go Into Treatment?

Yes. If you find centers that might appeal to your friend, either by their location or medical approach, it might encourage him or her to enter treatment.

You can call this helpline and get some advice on how to proceed: 1-800-662-HELP (4357) (This service is supported by the U.S. Department of Health and Human Services.). You can also look for a treatment center online (www.findtreatment.samhsa.gov), which will allow you to search for a treatment center in your area, and it will also give you information about the kind of addiction or patients it treats.

What Should I Look For In A Treatment Center?

Treatment approaches must be tailored to address each patient's drug abuse patterns and also their other medical, psychiatric, and social problems. Some treatment centers offer outpatient treatment programs, which allow patients to continue to perform some daily responsibilities. However, many people do better in inpatient (residential) treatment. An addiction specialist can advise your friend or loved one about the most promising options.

My Loved One Is Afraid Of Being Forced To Stop Using Drugs, And What Will Happen. Do Treatment Centers Force People To Stop Taking Drugs Immediately?

People of all ages with substance use disorders live in fear of what will happen if their drugs are taken away. You can ensure the person you care about that professional treatment centers will keep them safe and as comfortable as possible if a detoxification process is needed.

Treatment is always individualized based on the person's needs. However, if someone is using a drug upon admission to a treatment program, one of the first things needed is to help them safely remove the drugs from their system (often referred to as "detox"). This is important, because drugs impair the mental abilities needed to engage with and stay in treatment.

When patients first stop using drugs, they can experience a variety of physical and emotional withdrawal symptoms, including depression, anxiety, and other mood disorders; restlessness; and sleeplessness. Remind your loved one that treatment centers are very experienced in helping patients get through this process and keeping them safe during it. Depending on your loved one's situation, there may also be medications to reduce these symptoms, which make it easier to stop using.

Who Will Be Providing Treatment?

There are different kinds of specialists who are involved in addiction care, including doctors, nurses, therapists, social workers, and others. In some treatment programs, different specialists work as a team to help patients recover from addiction.

What Is Treatment Like?

Everyone entering treatment for a substance use disorder is unique. That is why the patient and the treatment staff work together to develop an individualized treatment planen. It may include some type of behavioral treatment ("talk therapy") designed to engage the patient in the treatment process, alter destructive attitudes and behaviors related to drug use, and increase healthy life skills. Behavioral treatment can also enhance the effectiveness of medications that might be available and help patients stay in treatment longer.

Treatment for substance use disorders can be delivered in many different settings using a variety of different approaches.

Do Most Treatment Centers Offer Medication?

Some do, and that is a good question to ask them. Medications are currently available to treat addictions to alcohol, nicotine, and opioids (heroin and prescription pain relievers), and your loved one's treatment team may recommend one of those medications. There are also medicines to treat mental health conditions (such as depression) that might be contributing to the addiction. In addition, medication is sometimes prescribed to help with the symptoms associated with drug withdrawal.

When medication is available, it can be combined with behavioral therapy to ensure success for most patients. Some treatment centers follow the philosophy that they should not treat a drug addiction with other drugs, but research shows that medication can help in many cases.

My Friend Was In Rehab Before But Relapsed Afterward. How Do We Know Treatment Will Work This Time?

This means your friend has already learned many of the skills needed to recover from addiction and should try it again. The fear of relapse should not get in the way of trying treatment potentialagain. People being treated or recovering from addiction relapse about as often as do people with other chronic diseases, such as hypertension, diabetes, and asthma. Treatment of any chronic disease involves changing deeply imbedded behaviors, and relapse sometimes goes with the territory—it doesn't mean treatment failed. A return to drug abuse indicates that treatment needs to be started again or adjusted, and your friend might benefit from a different treatment approach.

How Can People Find A Treatment Center They Can Afford?

If they have health insurance, it may cover substance abuse treatment services. Many insurance plans cover inpatient stays. When setting up appointments with treatment centers, you can ask about payment options and what insurance plans they take. They can also advise you on potential low-cost options.

To find treatment—and to learn about payment options—try the Mental Health Facility Treatment Locator provided by the Substance Abuse and Mental Health Services Administration. This free tool offers payment information for each of the treatment services listed, including information on sliding fee scales and payment assistance. Its "Frequently Asked Questions" section addresses cost of treatment.

You can also call the treatment helpline at 1-800-662-HELP (1-800-662-4357) or 1-800-487-4889 (TTY) to ask about treatment centers that offer low- or no-cost treatment. You can also contact your state substance abuse agency—because many states will help pay for substance abuse treatment.

Note that the new Mental Health Parity and Addiction Equity Act ensures that co-pays, deductibles, and visit limits are generally not more restrictive for mental health and substance abuse disorder benefits than they are for medical and surgical benefits. The Affordable Care Act builds on this law and requires coverage of mental health and substance use disorder services as one of ten essential health benefits categories. Under the essential health benefits rule, individual and small group health plans are required to comply with these parity regulations. For more information on the Affordable Care Act you can call 1-800-318-2596 or go to: www.healthcare.gov.

I Think My Loved One Takes Drugs Because He Feels Depressed—But He's Depressed Because Drugs Are Overtaking His Life. How Do We Know Which Problem Came First?

It is very possible your friend needs to find treatment for both depression and addiction. This is very common—it's called "comorbidity," "co-occurrence" or "dual diagnosis" when you have more than one health problem at the same time.

Encourage your friend to discuss all symptoms and behaviors with the doctor. There are many non-addictive drugs that can help with depression or other mental health issues. Sometimes health care providers do not communicate with each other as well as they should, so you can be your friend's advocate (with his permission) and make sure all of his health care providers know about all of the health issues that concern you. People who have co-occuring issues should be treated for all of them at the same time.

Hotline

If you know people who are so depressed that you think they will hurt themselves, there is a hotline that can help: The National Suicide Prevention Lifeline at 1-800-273-TALK (8255.) You are also welcome to call to discuss your friend's symptoms and get advice on how to best handle the situation.

I Am Worried That My Loved One Is Driving While Using Drugs. What Do I Do?

If you share a vehicle, you should demand that your loved one see a physician before using the car again. This can be very inconvenient for both of you, but it is imperative that drug users not drive. Their life, yours, and others' could be at risk.

In many cases, you may not be able to control your loved one's ability to drive. You must tell him or her that the single most responsible thing to do is not drive while using drugs (including abusing prescription medications). All drugs can impair skills necessary for the safe operation of a vehicle, including motor skills, balance and coordination, perception, attention, reaction time, and judgment. Even small amounts of some drugs can have a measurable effect on driving ability.

Drugs also affect a person's ability to tell if they are impaired—so you might have to make some difficult choices. If you believe your loved one is driving and impaired, you should consider calling law enforcement. This can be a difficult decision, but sometimes court intervention can actually help force a loved one to seek help.

If you are an employer and suspect an employee is using drugs, you should immediately suspend any driving privileges while you get it sorted out. You can contact this government helpline to find out more about workplace drug testing:

Drug-Free Workplace Helpline: 800-967-5752 (800-WORKPLACE) or helpline@samhsa.hhs.gov

How Can My Friend Talk To Others With Similar Problems?

Although they are not a substitute for treatment, self-help groups like 12-step programs can be a great source of support and encouragement while a person is engaged in treatment, and after. The most well-known self-help groups are those affiliated with Alcoholics Anonymous (AA), Narcotics Anonymous (NA), and Cocaine Anonymous (CA), all of which are based on the 12-step model.

Most drug addiction treatment programs encourage patients to participate in a self-help group during and after formal treatment. These groups can be particularly helpful during recovery, as they are a source of ongoing communal support and encouragement to stay drug free. Information on local meetings can be found on their Web sites. Support groups for family members of people with addictions, like Al-Anon and Alateen, can also be helpful.

There are other groups in the private sector that can provide a lot of support. To find meetings in your area, contact local hospitals, treatment centers, or faith-based organizations. These organizations often coordinate support groups for substance abuse.

I Am Not Sure What Drugs My Loved One Is Taking. Where Can I Find Information On Specific Drugs And Their Health Effects?

It is important to remember that people who struggle with addiction can have a lot of shame, fear and anger, and do not always tell the truth about their drug use. You can focus instead on encouraging your loved one to see a doctor, as a first step.

If My Friend Does Go Into Treatment, How Can I Offer Support?

This is a great conversation to have with your loved one's treatment provider. Different patients need different levels of support. If there are difficult dynamics in a family group or set of friends, the counselor may recommend little contact for a while. It is important to tell loved ones struggling with addiction that you admire their courage for tackling this medical problem directly through treatment and that as long as they stick with the treatment plan, you will offer encouragement and support. When residential treatment is over, your loved one will have to re-enter the community and it will be a difficult time.

Tips For Helping A Friend

It can be really upsetting and scary to have friends who are struggling with drug abuse and addiction. Here are some tips for helping them:

- Start by being a good friend, which you likely already are because you're concerned. As a good friend, you're someone who can be trusted to provide good advice and listen when your friend needs to talk.

- Educate yourself about drugs and alcohol and the problems they can cause. Then, you can give your friend the facts and refer your friend to resources to help him or her learn more. A good place to start is on the NIDA for Teens Web site. This site includes fact sheets about many different drugs and their effects.

- Next, encourage your friend to talk to an adult who he or she can trust—maybe a teacher, coach, or a parent of another friend. If your friend doesn't feel comfortable talking to a trusted adult but is ready to seek help, then you can check out treatment resources in your community (some are available just for teens). If your friend feels like he or she is in crisis, then he or she (or you) can call 1-800-273-TALK to talk confidentially to a professional who can help.

There will be triggers everywhere that could promote a relapse—such as driving by places where the person once took drugs, or seeing friends who provided those drugs. You can encourage your friend to avoid these triggers, and you can make an effort to ask him or her what those triggers are. However, people addicted to drugs have to fight much of this struggle on their own, without the help and advice of friends, using the knowledge and skills learned in treatment. Offer as much love and support you can as long as they continue to follow the treatment plan. If your loved one relapses, you should encourage additional treatment.

Part Nine
If You Need More Information

Chapter 57

National Organizations For Drug Information

Action on Smoking and Health (ASH)
2013 H St. N.W.
Washington, DC 20006
Phone: 202-659-4310
Website: http://www.ash.org

Alcoholics Anonymous (AA)
AA World Services, Inc.
P.O. Box 459
New York, NY 10163
Phone: 212-870-3400
Website: http://www.aa.org

Al-Anon
1600 Corporate Landing Pkwy.
Virginia Beach, VA 23454
Phone: 757-563-1600
Fax: 757-563-1655
Website: http://www.al-anon.alateen.org
E-mail: wso@al-anon.org

American Council for Drug Education (at Phoenix House)
50 Jay Street
Brooklyn, NY 11201
Phone: 718-222-6641
Website: http://www.acde.org
E-mail: acde@phoenixhouse.org

Campaign for Tobacco-Free Kids
1400 Eye Street, N.W.
Ste. 1200
Washington, DC 20005
Phone: 202-296-5469
Website: http://www.tobaccofreekids.org

Center of Alcohol Studies Rutgers, the State University of New Jersey
607 Allison Rd.
Piscataway, NJ 08854
Phone: 732-445-2190
Fax: 732-445-5300

About This Chapter: Information in this chapter was compiled from many sources deemed reliable. Inclusion does not constitute endorsement, and there is no implication associated with omission. All contact information was verified in November 2015.

Center for Substance Abuse Prevention (CSAP)

Substance Abuse and Mental Health
Services Administration
1 Choke Cherry Rd.
Rockville, MD 20857
Phone: 240-276-2420
Fax: 301-443-5447

Center for Substance Abuse Treatment (SAMHSA)

800-487-4889
Phone: 240-276-2750
Toll-Free: 800-662-HELP (4357)
Website: http://csat.samhsa.gov

Centers for Disease Control and Prevention (CDC)

1600 Clifton Rd.
Atlanta, GA 30333
Toll-Free: 800-CDC-INFO (232-4636)
Toll-Free TTY: 888-232-6348
Website: http://www.cdc.gov
E-mail: cdcinfo@cdc.gov

Co-Anon Family Groups World Services

P.O. Box 12722
Tucson, AZ 85732
Phone: 520-513-5028
Toll-Free: 800-898-9985
Website: http://www.co-anon.org
E-mail: info@co-anon.org

Cocaine Anonymous World Services

21720 S. Wilmington Ave.
Ste. 204
Long Beach, CA 90810
Phone: 310-559-5833
Fax: 310-559-2554
Website: http://www.ca.org
E-mail: cawso@ca.org

Do It Now Foundation (Drug Information)

P.O. Box 27568
Tempe, AZ 85285
Phone: 480-736-0599
Fax: 480-736-0771
Website: http://www.doitnow.org

Drug Enforcement Administration (DEA)

Office of Diversion Control
8701 Morrissette Dr.
Mailstop: AES
Springfield, VA 22152
Phone: 202-307-1000
Toll-Free: 800-882-9539
Website: http://www.justice.gov/dea
E-mail: ODE@usdoj.gov

Drug Policy Information Clearinghouse

Office of National Drug Control Policy
P.O. Box 6000
Rockville, MD 20849
Toll-Free: 800-666-3332
Fax: 301-519-5212
Website: http://www.whitehousedrugpolicy.
gov/about/clearingh.html

Families Anonymous, Inc.
P.O. Box 3475
Culver City, CA 90231-3475
Phone: 800-736-9805
Website: www.FamiliesAnonymous.org
E-mail: famanon@FamiliesAnonymous.org

Hazelden Foundation
P.O. Box 11
Center City, MN 55012-0011
Phone: 651-213-4200
Toll-Free: 800-257-7810
Website: http://www.hazelden.org
E-mail: info@hazelden.org

Health Information Network (SAMHSA)
P.O. Box 2345
Rockville, MD 20847
Toll-Free: 877-726-4727
Fax: 240-221-4292
Toll-Free TTY: 800-487-4889
Website: http://www.samhsa.gov/shin
E-mail: SHIN@samhsa.hhs.gov

Higher Education Center for Alcohol and Other Drug Abuse and Violence Prevention
Education Development Center, Inc.
55 Chapel St.
Newton, MA 02458
Toll-Free: 800-676-1730 (TDD Relay Friendly, Dial 711)
Fax: 617-928-1537
E-mail: HigherEdCtr@edc.org

Institute on Black Chemical Abuse
African American Family Services
2616 Nicollet Ave.
Minneapolis, MN 55408
Phone: 612-871-7878
Fax: 612-871-2567
E-mail: contact@aafs.net

Join Together
580 Harrison Ave., 3rd Fl.
Boston, MA 02118
Phone: 617-437-1500
Fax: 617-437-9394
E-mail: info@jointogether.org

Nar-Anon Family Group Headquarters, Inc.
22527 Crenshaw Blvd., #200B
Torrance, CA 90505
Phone: 310-534-8188
Toll-Free: 800-477-6291
Website: http://www.nar-anon.org

Narcotics Anonymous
P.O. Box 9999
Van Nuys, CA 91409
Phone: 818-773-9999
Fax: 818-700-0700
Website: http://www.na.org

National Asian Pacific American Families Against Drug Abuse
340 East 2nd Street, Ste. 409
Los Angeles, CA 90012
Phone: 213-625-5795
Fax: 213-625-5796
Website: http://www.napafasa.org
E-mail: napafasa@napafasa.org

National Association for Children of Alcoholics

11426 Rockville Pike, Ste. 301
Rockville, MD 20852
Phone: 301-468-0985
Toll-Free: 888-55-4COAS (2627)
Fax: 301-468-0987
Website: http://www.nacoa.net
E-mail: nacoa@nacoa.org

National Center on Addiction and Substance Abuse at Columbia University (CASA)

633 Third Ave., 19th Fl.
New York, NY 10017
Phone: 212-841-5200
Fax: 212-956-8020
Website: http://www.casacolumbia.org

National Council on Alcoholism and Drug Dependence

244 E. 58th St., 4th Fl.
New York, NY 10022
Phone: 212-269-7797
Toll-Free Hopeline: 800-NCA-CALL (622-2255)
Fax: 212-269-7510
Website: http://www.ncadd.org
E-mail: national@ncadd.org

National Criminal Justice Reference Service (NCJRS)

P.O. Box 6000
Rockville, MD 20849
Phone: 301-519-5500 (international callers)
Toll-Free: 800-851-3420
Fax: 301-519-5212
Toll-Free TTY: 877-712-9279
Website: http://www.ncjrs.gov

National Drug Intelligence Center

U.S. Department of Justice
Robert F. Kennedy Bldg., Rm. 3341
950 Pennsylvania Ave., N.W.
Washington, DC 20530
Phone: 202-532-4040
Website: http://www.justice.gov/ndic
E-mail: NDIC.Contacts@usdoj.gov

NIDA-Sponsored Websites

http://www.backtoschool.drugabuse.gov
http://www.clubdrugs.gov
http://www.hiv.drugabuse.gov
http://www.inhalants.drugabuse.gov
http://www.marijuana-info.org
http://www.researchstudies.drugabuse.gov
http://www.smoking.drugabuse.gov
http://www.steroidabuse.

National Institute on Alcohol Abuse and Alcoholism (NIAAA)

5635 Fishers Ln.
MSC 9304
Bethesda, MD 20892
Phone: 301-443-3860
Website: http://www.niaaa.nih.gov
E-mail: niaaaweb-r@exchange.nih.gov

National Institute on Drug Abuse (NIDA)

6001 Executive Blvd., Rm. 5213
Bethesda, MD 20892
Phone: 301-443-1124 (Public information and liaison in science and communications)
Fax: 301-443-7397
Websites: http://www.nida.nih.gov; and http://www.drugabuse.gov
E-mail: information@nida.nih.gov

National Institute of Justice

810 7th St. N.W.
7th Fl.
Washington, DC 20531
Phone: 202-307-2942
Toll-Free: 800-851-3420 (National
Criminal Justice Reference Service)
Fax: 202-307-6394
Website: http://www.ojp.usdoj.gov/nij

National Parents Resource Institute for Drug Education (PRIDE)

PRIDE Youth Programs
4 W. Oak St.
Fremont, MI 49412
Phone: 231-924-1662
Toll-Free: 800-668-9277
Fax: 231-924-5663
E-mail: info@pridyouthprograms.org

Nemours Foundation

1600 Rockland Rd.
Wilmington, DE 19803
Phone: 302-651-4000
Website: http://www.kidshealth.org
E-mail: info@kidshealth.org

Office of Applied Studies (OAS) (SAMHSA)

Phone: 240-276-1212
E-mail: oaspubs@samhsa.hhs.gov

Office of National Drug Control Policy (ONDCP)

Drug Policy Information Clearinghouse
P.O. Box 6000
Rockville, MD 20849
Toll-Free: 800-666-3332
Fax: 301-519-5212
Website: http://www.whitehousedrugpolicy.
gov
E-mail: ondcp@ncjrs.gov

ONDCP Sponsored Websites

http://www.abovetheinfluence.com
http://www.methresources.gov
http://www.whitehousedrugpolicy.gov/
mediacampaign
http://pushingback.com

Partnership for a Drug-Free America

352 Park Ave. South
9th Fl.
New York, NY 10174
Phone: 212-922-1560
Fax: 212-922-1570

Phoenix House

164 W. 74th Street
New York, NY 10023
Website: http://www.phoenixhouse.org

Safe and Drug-Free Schools
400 Maryland Ave. SW
Washington, DC 20202
Toll-Free: 800-872-5327 (Information
Resource Center at U.S. Department of
Education)
Toll-Free TTY: 800-437-0833
Website: http://www.ed.gov/offices/OESE/
SDFS
E-mail: safeschl@ed.gov

Students Against Destructive Decisions (SADD)
255 Main Street
Marlborough, MA 01752
Fax: 508-481-5759
Website: http://www.sadd.org
E-mail: info@sadd.org

Substance Abuse and Mental Health Services Administration (SAMHSA)
1 Choke Cherry Rd.
Rockville, MD 20857
Phone: 240-276-2130
Website: http://www.samhsa.gov

U.S. Bureau of Alcohol, Tobacco, Firearms, and Explosives
Office of Public and Governmental Affairs
99 New York Ave., N.E.
Rm. 5S 144
Washington, DC 20226
Toll Free: 800-800-3855
Website: http://www.atf.gov

U.S. Food and Drug Administration (FDA)
10903 New Hampshire Ave.
Silver Spring, MD 20993
Toll-Free: 888-INFO-FDA (463-6332)
Website: http://www.fda.gov

Chapter 58

Substance Abuse Hotlines And Helplines

Al-Anon/Alateen Information Line
800-344-2666
Monday–Friday, 8:00 a.m.–6:00 p.m. ET

Alcohol and Drug Help Line
WellPlace
800-821-4357

Alcohol Hotline
Adcare Hospital
800-ALCOHOL (800-252-6465)
7 days a week, 24 hours a day

American Council on Alcoholism
800-527-5344
10:00–6:00 p.m. MT

Center for Substance Abuse Treatment
800-662-HELP (800-662-4357) (English)
877-767-8432 (Spanish)
800-487-4889 (TDD)

Ecstasy Addiction
800-468-6933

Emergency Shelter for Battered Women (and Their Children)
888-291-6228

Girls and Boys Town National Hotline
800-448-3000

Marijuana Anonymous
800-766-6779
7 days a week, 24 hours a day

About This Chapter: Information in this chapter was compiled from many sources deemed reliable. Inclusion does not constitute endorsement, and there is no implication associated with omission. All contact information was verified in November 2015.

NAMI Information Helpline
Nation's Voice on Mental Illness
800-950-NAMI (6264)
Monday–Friday, 10:00 a.m.–6:00 p.m. ET

Narconon International Help Line
800-893-7060

National Child Abuse Hot Line
Childhelp USA
800-4-A-CHILD (800-422-4453)

National Clearinghouse for Alcohol and Drug Information
800-729-6686
Monday–Friday, 9:00 a.m.–7:00 p.m. ET

National Council on Alcoholism and Drug Dependence
800-622-2255
7 days a week, 24 hours a day

National Domestic Violence Hot Line
800-799-7233
800-787-3224 (TTY)

National Drug and Alcohol Treatment Referral Service
800-662-HELP (4357)
Monday–Friday, 9:00 a.m.–3:00 a.m.

National Organization for Victim Assistance
800-TRY-NOVA (800-879-6682)
Monday–Friday, 9:00 a.m.–5:00 p.m. ET

National Runaway Switchboard
800-RUNAWAY (800-786-2929)
TDD: 800-621-0394

National Sexual Assault Hotline
Rape, Abuse, and Incest National Network (RAINN)
800-656-HOPE (800-656-4673)

National Suicide Hopeline
800-SUICIDE (800-784-2433)
7 days a week, 24 hours a day

National Suicide Prevention Lifeline
800-273-TALK (800-273-8255)

Stop It Now!
888-PREVENT (888-773-8368)
Limited phone hours; also online at www.stopitnow.org

Victims of Crime Help Line
800-FYI-CALL (800-394-2255)
Monday–Friday, 8:30a.m.–8:30 p.m. ET

Chapter 59

State-By-State List Of Alcohol And Drug Referral Phone Numbers

Alabama

Substance Abuse Services Div.
Toll-Free: 800-367-0955
Phone: 334-242-3454
Fax: 334-242-0725
Website: http://www.mh.alabama.gov

Alaska

Div. of Behavioral Health
Dept. of Health and Social Services
Phone: 907-465-3370
Fax: 907-465-2668
Website: http://www.hss.state.ak.us

American Samoa

American Samoa Government
Dept. of Human and Social Services
Phone: 684-633-2609
Fax: 684-633-7449

Arizona

Div. of Behavioral Health Services
Dept. of Health Services
Toll-Free: 800-867-5808
Phone: 602-542-1025
Fax: 602-364-4558
Website: http://www.azdhs.gov

Arkansas

Office of Alcohol and Drug Abuse
Prevention
Div. of Behavioral Health Services
Phone: 501-686-9866
Website: http://www.arkansas.gov/dhs/
dmhs/alco_drug_abuse_ prevention.htm

California

Dept. of Alcohol and Drug Programs
Toll-Free: 800-879-2772
E-mail: ResourceCenter@adp.ca.gov

About This Chapter: Information in this chapter excerpted from "Facility Locator," Substance Abuse and Mental Health Services Administration (SAMHSA). All contact information was verified as current in November 2015.

Colorado
Div. of Behavioral Health
Dept. of Human Services
Phone: 303-866-7400
Fax: 303-866-7481

Connecticut
Toll-Free: 800-446-7348
Phone: 860-418-7000
TTY: 860-418-6707
Website: http://www.ct.gov/dmhas

Delaware
Alcohol and Drug Services
Div. of Substance Abuse and MH
Phone: 302-255-9399
Fax: 302-255-4427
Website: http://www.dhss.delaware.gov/
dsamh/index.html

District of Columbia
Addiction, Prevention, and Recovery
Administration
Phone: 202-727-8857
Fax: 202-777-0092
Website: http://www.dchealth.dc.gov/doh

Florida
Substance Abuse Program Office
Dept. of Children and Families
Phone: 850-487-1111
Fax: 850-922-4996

Georgia
Addictive Diseases Services
Toll-Free: 800-715-4225
Phone: 404-657-2331
Fax: 404-657-2256
Website: http://mhddad.dhr.georgia.gov

Guam
Drug and Alcohol Treatment Services
Dept. of Mental Health and Substance
Abuse
Phone: 671-647-5330
Fax: 671-649-6948

Hawaii
Alcohol and Drug Abuse Division
Dept. of Health
Phone: 808-692-7506
Fax: 808-692-7521
Website: http://hawaii.gov/health/
substance-abuse

Idaho
Div. of Behavioral Health
Dept. of Health and Welfare
Toll-Free: 800-926-2588
Phone: 208-334-5935
Fax: 208-332-7305
Website: http://healthandwelfare.idaho.gov

Illinois
Div. of Alcoholism and Substance Abuse
Dept. of Human Services
Toll-Free: 800-843-6154
Toll-Free TTY: 800-447-6404
Website: http://www.dhs.state.il.us/page.
aspx?item=29725

Indiana
Div. of Mental Health and Addiction
Family and Social Services Administration
Toll-Free: 800-457-8283
Phone: 317-232-7895
Fax: 317-233-3472
Website: http://www.in.gov/fssa/dmha/
index.htm

Iowa

Div. of Behavioral Health
Dept. of Public Health
Toll-Free: 866-227-9878
Phone: 515-281-7689
Website: http://www.idph.state.ia.us/bh/
substance_abuse.asp

Kansas

Addiction and Prevention Services
Dept. of Social and Rehab Services
Phone: 785-296-6807

Kentucky

Div. of Mental Health and Substance Abuse
Dept. for MH/MR Services
Phone: 502-564-4456
Fax: 502-564-9010

Louisiana

Office for Addictive Disorders
Toll-Free: 877-664-2248
Phone: 225-342-6717
Fax: 225-342-3875

Maine

Maine Office of Substance Abuse
Toll-Free (ME only): 800-499-0027
Phone: 207-287-2595
Fax: 207-287-8910
Toll-Free TTY: 800-606-0215
Website: http://www.maine.gov/dhhs/osa
E-mail: osa.ircosa@maine.gov

Maryland

Alcohol and Drug Abuse Administration
Dept. of Health and Mental Hygiene
Phone: 410-402-8600
Website: http://dhmh.maryland.gov/adaa

Massachusetts

Bureau of Substance Abuse Services
Dept. of Public Health
Toll-Free: 800-327-5050
Toll-Free TTY: 888-448-8321
Website: http://www.mass.gov/dph/bsas

Michigan

Bureau of Substance Abuse and Addiction
Services
Phone: 517-373-4700
Fax: 517-335-2121
TTY: 571-373-3573
Website: http://www.michigan.gov/mdch-
bsaas
E-mail: MDCH-BSAAS@michigan.gov

Minnesota

Alcohol and Drug Abuse Division
Dept. of Human Services
Phone: 651-431-2460
Fax: 651-431-7449
Toll-Free Disability Linkage Line: 866-
333-2466
Website: http://www.minnesotahelp.info/
public (online access to state resources)
http://www.dhs.state.mn.us (click
Disabilities, then Alcohol and Drug Abuse)
E-mail: dhs.adad@state.mn.us

Mississippi

Bureau of Alcohol and Drug Abuse
Dept. of Mental Health
Toll-Free: 877-210-8513
Phone: 601-359-1288
Fax: 601-359-6295
TDD: 601-359-6230
Website: http://www.dmh.state.ms.us/
substance_abuse.htm

Missouri

Div. of Alcohol and Drug Abuse
Missouri Dept. of Mental Health
Toll-Free: 800-364-9687
Phone: 573-751-4122
Fax: 573-751-8224
TTY: 573-526-1201
E-mail: dmhmail@dmh.mo.gov

Montana

Addictive and Mental Disorders Division
Dept. of PH and HS
Phone: 406-444-3964
Fax: 406-444-4435
Website: http://www.dphhs.mt.gov/amdd

Nebraska

DHHS Division of Behavioral Health
Substance Abuse Hotline: 402-473-3818
Phone: 402-471-7818
Fax: 402-471-7859
Website: http://www.dhhs.ne.gov/sua/
suaindex.htm
E-mail: BHDivision@dhhs.ne.gov

Nevada

DHHS Mental Health and Developmental
Services
Phone: 775-684-5943
Fax: 775-684-5964

New Hampshire

DHHS Bureau of Drug and Alcohol
Services
Phone: 603-271-6110
Website: http://www.dhhs.state.nh.us/dhhs/
atod/a1-treatment

New Jersey

Div. of Addiction Services
NJ Addictions Hotline: 800-238-2333
E-mail: contact@addictionshotlineofnj.org

New Mexico

Behavioral Health Services Div.
Dept. of Health
Toll-Free TTY Hotline: 800-855-2881
Toll-Free Consumer Hotline: 866-660-7185
Website: http://www.bhc.state.nm.us
Website for Consumer Assistance: http://
www.optumhealthnewmexico.com

New York

Office of Alcoholism and Substance Abuse
Services
Phone: 518-473-3460
E-mail: communications@oasas.state.ny.us

North Carolina

Community Policy Management
Div. of MH/DD/SA Services
Toll-Free: 800-662-7030
Phone: 919-733-4670
Fax: 919-733-4556
Website: http://www.dhhs.state.nc.us/
mhddsas
E-mail: contactdmh@ncmail.net

North Dakota

Div. of MH and SA Services
Dept. of Human Services
Toll-Free (ND only): 800-472-2622
Phone: 701-328-2310
Fax: 701-328-2359
Website: http://www.nd.gov/dhs/services/
mentalhealth
E-mail: dhseo@nd.gov

Ohio
Dept. of Alcohol and Drug Addiction
Services
Toll-Free: 800-788-7254
Phone: 614-466-3445
Fax: 614-752-8645
E-mail: info@ada.ohio.gov

Oklahoma
ODMHSAS
Toll-Free: 800-522-9054
Phone: 405-522-3908
Fax: 405-522-3650
TDD: 405-522-3851
Website: http://www.odmhsas.org

Oregon
Addictions and Mental Health Div.
Dept. of Human Services
Toll-Free: 800-544-7078
Phone: 503-945-5763
Fax: 503-378-8467
Toll-Free TTY: 800-375-2863
Website: http://www.oregon.gov/DHS/
addiction/index.shtml
E-mail: omhas.web@state.or.us

Pennsylvania
Bureau of Drug and Alcohol Programs
Pennsylvania Dept. of Health
Toll-Free: 877-724-3258
Phone: 717-783-8200
Fax: 717-787-6285
Website: http://www.portal.state.pa.us/
portal/server.pt/community/drug_
alcohol/14221

Puerto Rico
Mental Health and Anti-Addiction
Services Administration
Toll-Free 800-981-0023
Phone: 787-763-7575
Fax: 787-765-5888

Rhode Island
Div. of Behavioral Health
Phone: 401-462-4680
Fax: 401-462-6078

South Carolina
SC Dept. of Alcohol and Other Drug
Abuse Services
Phone: 803-896-5555
Fax: 803-896-5557
Website: http://www.daodas.state.sc.us

South Dakota
DHS Div. of Alcohol and Drug Abuse
Toll-Free: 800-265-9684
Phone: 605-773-3123
Fax: 605-773-7076
Website: http://dhs.sd.gov

Tennessee
Dept. of Mental Health and DD
TN Dept. of Health
Phone: 615-741-3111
Toll-Free Crisis: 800-809-9957
Website: http://health.state.tn.us/index.htm
E-mail: tn.health@tn.gov

Texas

DSHS Substance Abuse Services
Toll-Free: 866-378-8440
Phone: 512-206-5000
Fax: 512-206-5714
Toll-Free Hotline: 877-966-3784
Website: http://www.dshs.state.tx.us/sa/
default.shtm
E-mail: contact@dshs.state.tx.us

Utah

Div. of Substance Abuse and Mental Health
Utah Dept. of Human Services
Phone: 801-538-3939
Fax: 801-538-9892
Website: http://www.dsamh.utah.gov

Vermont

Alcohol and Drug Abuse Programs
Dept. of Health
Toll-Free (VT only): 800-464-4343
Phone: 802-863-7200
Fax: 802-865-7754
Website: http://healthvermont.gov/adap/
adap.aspx

Virginia

Office of Substance Abuse Services
Dept. of MH, MR, and SAS
Phone: 804-786-3921
Fax: 804-371-6638
TTY: 804-786-1587

Virgin Islands

Div. of MH, Alcoholism, and Drug
Dependency Services
Dept. of Health
Phone: 340-774-4888
Fax: 340-774-4701

Washington

Div. of Alcohol and Substance Abuse
Dept. of Social and Health Services
Toll-Free (WA only): 800-737-0617
Phone: 877-301-4557
Website: http://www.dshs.wa.gov/DASA
E-mail: DASAInformation@dshs.wa.gov

West Virginia

Bureau for Behavioral Health and Health
Facilities
Phone: 304-558-0627
Fax: 304-558-1008
E-mail: obhs@wvdhhr.org

Wisconsin

Bureau of Prevention, Treatment, and
Recovery
Phone: 608-266-1865
Fax: 608-266-1533
Toll-Free TTY: 888-701-1251
Website: http://dhs.wisconsin.gov/
substabuse/INDEX.HTM

Wyoming

Mental Health and Substance Abuse
Services Division
Toll-Free: 800-535-4006
Phone: 307-777-6494
Fax: 307-777-5849

Index

Index

Page numbers that appear in *Italics* refer to tables or illustrations. Page numbers that have a small 'n' after the page number refer to citation information shown as Notes. Page numbers that appear in **Bold** refer to information contained in boxes within the chapters.

E

M

N